"Packed with innovative, vibrantly flavored recipes that reflect Devi's gift for blending her Indian culinary background with ideas from some of America's best and brightest chefs."

— *Washington Post*

"Full of life, full of flavor, vibrant and healthy . . . a most alluring East-West blend, an intriguing approach that is both exotic and familiar."

— Deborah Madison

"A sure-fire hit . . . Devi's dishes are clever, robustly flavored and very satisfying."

— *San Diego Union Tribune*

"A mind-expanding book."

— *Minneapolis Star-Tribune*

"An enticing blend of Indian seasonings and methods with American health and cooking concerns . . . a book that could easily be consulted on a daily basis . . . a winner on all counts."

— *Portland Oregonian*

"The seasonings are always complex and the cooking is often so, yielding vivid platters that emphasize Devi's greatest gift — her imagination."

— *American Health*

YAMUNA DEVI is the author of the 1987 IACP Cookbook of the Year, *Lord Krishna's Cuisine* (Dutton), and of *The Best of Lord Krishna's Cuisine* (Plume). She has studied food and cooking in India, and was personal chef to Indira Gandhi. Based in Washington, D.C., she teaches throughout this country and the United Kingdom.

"Peppered with useful historical tidbits and hands-on techniques that transform everyday Western dishes into exotic, healthful entrées and give traditional Indian food new life."

—*St. Louis Post-Dispatch*

"Outstanding . . . an interesting cookbook . . . even if you're not a vegetarian, you'll want to try these appealing dishes."

— Jacques Pépin

"A new lighter style that's contemporary and ethnically eclectic."

—*Philadelphia Inquirer*

"Light, lively, meatless cooking. . . . Devi has a way of mixing Indian and Western foods for exciting, original flavors."

—*Christian Science Monitor*

"Daring and intense recipes . . . vegetarians will cheer."

—*Seattle Times*

YAMUNA'S TABLE

Healthful Vegetarian Cuisine

Inspired by the Flavors of India

Yamuna Devi

A PLUME BOOK

FOR SRILA PRABHUPADA

PLUME
Published by the Penguin Group
Penguin Books USA Inc., 375 Hudson Street, New York, New York 10014, U.S.A.
Penguin Books Ltd, 27 Wrights Lane, London W8 5TZ, England
Penguin Books Australia Ltd, Ringwood, Victoria, Australia
Penguin Books Canada Ltd, 10 Alcorn Avenue, Toronto, Ontario, Canada M4V 3B2
Penguin Books (N.Z.) Ltd, 182–190 Wairau Road, Auckland 10, New Zealand

Penguin Books Ltd, Registered Offices: Harmondsworth, Middlesex, England

Published by Plume, an imprint of Dutton Signet,
a division of Penguin Books USA Inc.
Previously published in a Dutton edition.

First Plume Printing, May, 1995
10 9 8 7 6 5 4 3 2 1

Ⓟ REGISTERED TRADEMARK—MARCA REGISTRADA

The Library of Congress has catalogued the Dutton edition as follows:
Yamuna Devi.
    Yamuna's table : healthful vegetarian cuisine inspired by the
flavors of India / Yamuna Devi.
        p.   cm.
    ISBN 0-525-93487-1 (hc.)
    ISBN 0-452-27238-6 (pbk.)
    1. Vegetarian cookery.   2. Cookery, Indic.   I. Title.
TX837.Y3626   1992
641.5'636—dc20   92–52862
                                                  CIP

Printed in the United States of America
Designed by Eve L. Kirch
Illustrated by Kim Waters-Murray

BOOKS ARE AVAILABLE AT QUANTITY DISCOUNTS WHEN USED TO PROMOTE PRODUCTS
OR SERVICES. FOR INFORMATION PLEASE WRITE TO PREMIUM MARKETING DIVISION,
PENGUIN BOOKS USA INC., 375 HUDSON STREET, NEW YORK, NEW YORK 10014.

ACKNOWLEDGMENTS

So many people have directly or indirectly affected the contents of this book. On a personal level, old and new friends have each been an inspiration for various reasons. Working on the book in Reston, Virginia, and Washington, D.C., was a community of friends that I am indebted to, including Kim Waters-Murray, Vesna Scharf, and Joe Gardiner. Henry Schoellkopf deserves special mention for assistance on my kitchen renovations. Dina Sugg, whose creative sensibilities have seen me through many aspects of this book, is a treasured friend. Sruti Sims has been a steady inspiration on all levels, and there is no one I enjoy cooking with more. From Atlanta, David and Nirmala Eldridge have shared much regarding nutrition and health. In Columbus, Malati's enthusiasm for life has been an inspiration from afar. To Graham Schweig and Andy Marks, special thanks.

Special thanks to Judith Weber, my agent, a friend I greatly value for insights and good judgment and to Carole DeSanti, my editor at Dutton, for all her support and enthusiasm.

A special acknowledgment of thanks to the late Bert Greene, whose words of encouragement were deeply appreciated. So many food writers, cooks, and teachers have been an inspiration: Deborah Madison, Jeanne Jones, Brother Ron Pikarski, Patience Gray, Dr. Vasant Lad, Marcel Lavabre, and Paula Wolfert.

Thanks are also due to several people for offering me outstanding products for my test kitchen: Philip Teverow at Dean & DeLuca who supplied me

with a line of exceptional old-world legumes to experiment with; Polly Murray at McCormick/Schilling, who offered a full set of spices, herbs, and seasonings; and Linda Field at Chantal Cookware, who provided me with stunning black enamel cookware for recipe testing and cooking demonstrations. Ellen Klempner-Beguin at Nutra Cane International shared samples of Sucanat — organic natural cane sugar; Nancy Kramer of Tryson House supplied me with numerous oil sprays; and Caryn Yarnell, NSRD at the USDA, provided invaluable nutrition information.

CONTENTS

Introduction
1

Appetizers

Salads

LEAFY SALADS

LITTLE SALADS

COMPOSED SALADS

BEAN, GRAIN, AND PASTA SALADS

Soups

Entrees

NEW WAYS WITH CRÊPES

LEGUME MAINSTAYS

SAVORY PASTRIES

CONTENTS

BOILED, BAKED, AND GRILLED VEGETABLES

Desserts

SORBETS, GRANITÉS, AND OTHER FROZEN DESSERTS

MOUSSES

FRESH FRUIT CONCLUSIONS

Appendix

THE BASICS

Index

INTRODUCTION

As you cook with this book, you will begin a flavor journey. If you experiment with these dishes on a daily basis, and use them as inspiration for your own creations, you may enjoy a diet transformation, one that enlivens the quality of your life. Your palate may never be the same. For me, the style of cooking and eating that has evolved over several years of study and experimenting in the kitchen, and that is reflected in these pages, has been a pleasure and a joy.

Simply stated, this is a book in which flavor meets well-being on the palate; a personal cuisine inspired by many traditions, best characterized by ease of preparation and lightness; simple, elegant food with its own unique esprit. To experience the tastes in this book, nibble on Wheat-Berry Caviar or Gingered Chickpeas; feast on a crunchy Bengali Chef Salad topped with creamy Cashew Dressing and Bitter-Melon Chips; when temperatures fall, dig into a bowl of earthy Black Bean Chili served with flame-toasted wheat tortillas; or relish lemon pasta enveloped in a coconut-peppercorn glaze on a more temperate evening. Cheesy Artichoke Croustade makes a wonderful centerpiece for a feast, especially accompanied with Three-Grain Vegetable Salad with Cilantro Cream.

My approach to cooking is constantly evolving, influenced by people, travel, and working in many kitchens. The study of nutrition and spa cuisine has affected this book, but without doubt the strongest influence on my

cooking style has been a love for the vegetarian cuisines of India, explored in depth in my first book, *Lord Krishna's Cuisine: The Art of Indian Vegetarian Cooking.*

FLAVORS AND INGREDIENTS

Indian food is often characterized as spicy and hot, though regional cuisines vary enormously. West coast Marawadi food is mild and refined compared to the torrid, robust flavors of the Rajastani desert. In both cases, though, the purpose of spices and flavor combinations goes well beyond the palate. The preventative and curative properties of hundreds of herbs and spices are explained in the texts of India's ancient medical science, Ayurveda or the "yoga of herbs." Though yoga means many things, in this context it refers to "right usage" or "right combination" of flavors in the kitchen for the purpose of promoting well-being and good health. In this book, I have developed dishes that bridge East and West, largely through the application of Ayurvedic prinicples to ingredients that are readily available to the American home cook.

Using herbs and spices common to most kitchens, vegetables, fruits, legumes, and grains take on new vibrancy. Ayurvedic teachings explain that aside from lending warmth and a nutty taste, toasted cumin, mustard, and fennel seeds help to "lighten" foods and allow them to be digested more easily. Turmeric is a blood purifier that helps to digest proteins — a pinch added to the bean or legume pot will help to prevent flatulence. When used with coriander and cumin, it helps in the digestion of complex carbohydrates. Black pepper not only improves the taste of food, it is an effective digestive stimulant, especially for raw foods. A few grindings of pepper on sliced tomatoes or cucumbers does wonders for digestion and taste. Ginger root lends warmth and flavor to food. It is especially welcome in cold weather, and is a good respiratory tonic. Ayurveda suggests that cinnamon aids in the absorption of nutrients; and fragrant cardamom, when added to milk, helps to neutralize its mucus-forming properties. Cilantro, the most widely used herb in the world, is rich in minerals and vitamins.

In a few recipes I recommend using a specific type of hot chili or peppercorn. Not only do chilies enliven a dish with heat, they stimulate digestion, and

add layers of subtle flavor and color. Two of the world's finest peppercorns, Malabar and Tellicherry, come from India's West Coast, and along with white Muntok and Sarawak, are available at specialty food stores or by mail order (see the Appendix for sources). Richly flavored dried New Mexico and ancho chilies lend robust distinction to sauces, chutneys, and pilafs. Moderate to hot jalapeño and serrano chilies make more of a flavor statement, but used in moderation enliven a dish rather than overwhelm it with heat.

The products at supermarkets and natural-food stores reflects food trends and shopper demands. As ethnic diversity increases, so does the variety on grocers' shelves. Some of the ingredients in this book once considered gourmet or exotic — cilantro, baby vegetables, basmati rice, red oak lettuce, bitter melon, blood oranges, millet, or even organic foods — are now commonplace in many stores. The spices used in this book are widely available; in fact, the McCormick/Schilling company supplied me with all of the spices used in recipe testing. Fresh jalapeño chilies, herbs, cilantro, ginger root, sprouts, and many types of dried chilies are now available in supermarkets and natural-food stores. No matter where you shop, keep in mind that quality ingredients are the single most important element in the preparation of fine food and maintaining good health.

THE USE OF COOKING OILS

The less refined a cooking oil is, the more each calorie in it reflects the rich flavor of its source. In this book, I use very small amounts of high-quality, unrefined cooking oils to very favorable effect. A whiff of unrefined walnut oil is redolent of a bowl of freshly shelled nuts, and amber corn oil bursts with the aroma of sweet roasted corn. If you haven't sampled unrefined (or expeller-pressed) oils, experiment with small bottles of aromatic peanut, walnut, sesame, corn, pumpkin seed, or extra-virgin olive oil and note the body and character they possess and impart to foods, even in trace amounts.

The most effective way I've found to cut down on fat content from oil is to use it in spray form. For example, when steamed vegetables or cooked pasta are sprayed with a mist of virgin olive oil just before serving, each bite is bathed with exquisite perfume and rich flavor. The same is true for many of the soup, entree, and vegetable dishes here that include little or no oil in their

preparation. For outstanding flavor in any green salad bowl, generously mist the leaves with a fragrant nut oil and finish with splashes of freshly squeezed lemon juice and grindings of cracked pepper and salt.

In many recipes I recommend using a virgin olive oil spray. When choosing a commercial spray, look for an extra-virgin oil, preferably one without additives, in an environment-friendly container. For quality and variety, homemade sprays may be your best option, even if the mist is not consistently fine. Full instructions for making oil sprays are in the Appendix, as are some suggestions for commercial brands. Olive, corn, pecan, walnut, and almond oil are all good choices for sprays.

SHOPPING AND MENU PLANNING

In this book, entrees range from no-fuss, one-pot meals to more elaborate presentations that include sauces and side dishes. Depending on your proximity to good shopping sources, you can spend more time buying food than cooking a meal. If you live in a city of any size, I recommend two sources for most of the ingredients in the book: a large natural-food store and a supermarket or farmer's market. I shop at the natural-food store first to stock up on organic produce and dry goods, and then hit the supermarket for anything else left on the shopping list. If your situation warrants it, order hard-to-find items from the mail-order suppliers in the Appendix. For convenience, I've also listed pantry items in the Appendix — items like roasted peppers, wheat chapatis, or frozen vegetables for those days when time is short and you need a quick soul-satisfying meal.

Though this book is organized by course, virtually any dish in these pages can take center stage in a meal if you adjust ingredient amounts for the number of servings desired. On busy days, a memorable meal might consist of a simple soup or salad served with flame-toasted chapatis. As you cook with this book and find your own top-ten favorites, your own special menus will fall into place. To help you get started on marrying dishes and flavors for multi-course meals, I've provided a number of menus for seasonal meals, entertaining, and weekday fare. Suggestions for combination also appear in the recipe introductions throughout the book.

❊ ❊ ❊

What does the next decade hold for your kitchen? In 1990, *Cook's* magazine publisher Christopher Kimball wrote, "Cooking and eating is more profound than a matter of taste — food will become an issue of health, safety, philosophy, and ethics." Food is so much more than nourishment, as we are all in the process of discovering. It can lift, energize, and enliven you, or bind and restrict, depending on its nature. The ancient philosophers of India understood this, and I have tried here to render their knowledge in a usable and contemporary form. I hope that you, like me, will find in this book simple pleasures that create tremendous well-being. So I invite you to take a few deep breaths, kick off your shoes, sip some cool water, and enjoy in the kitchen.

Appetizers

Nothing in Indian cuisine translates directly into an appetizer or first course — primarily because courses, as we know them, don't exist. An entire meal, including dessert, is served at once on a large platter. The light finger foods that most resemble appetizers are included, invariably placed next to a complementary fresh or cooked chutney. Depending on the region, diners sample foods in an order, juxtaposing tastes and textures. Aside from balancing all of the flavors in a meal, six tastes are represented — sour, sweet, salty, pungent, bitter, and astringent. The sequence of sampling food not only affects taste on the tongue, it affects digestion.

The appetizer selection that follows defines a new tradition. Though the flavors are Indian-inspired, the dishes are easier to make and stand on their own, as simple finger foods. And breaking from traditional Indian appetizers, there is not one deep-fried dish in the lot. Oven-toasted, roasted, water bath–cooked, and baked dishes replace their fried counterparts, with mouth-watering results. I have proposed healthful adaptations of fat-laden classics, using health-food store and supermarket ingredients. Other recipes have no Indian counterparts yet may reflect techniques or seasonings traditionally used in regional cuisines. These dishes are pleasantly spicy, infused with warmth from aromatics such as fresh ginger and jalapeño chilies.

Generally, appetizers are served in small quantities, as palate teasers to

stimulate the appetite. Precede soup or salad with an appetizer or work it into an entree presentation. As an alternative, serve entree portions of appetizers. The recipes best suited to this approach are accompanied by condiments: Potato Tikki with Almond-Cilantro Chutney (page 16), Spicy Mung Bean Pâté with Cilantro-Mint Cream (page 30), and Avocado Pâté with Pistachio Chutney (page 34). A salad, soup, or vegetable would round out a meal perfectly.

For an appetizer party, include nibblers such as Gingered Chickpeas (page 27), Malabar Pepper–Lemon Crackers (page 19), or Bombay Cashews (page 20), as well as more substantial selections. Allow larger servings and include several dishes so that guests feel they have eaten a meal. Try the crackers and biscuits in this chapter with soups, salads, pâtés, or fruit.

CANAPÉS

Baby Potatoes Coated with Almonds

These potatoes are great as part of a party buffet or served as a side-dish vegetable. I first tasted them on a lunch plate in a West Bengal village — marble-sized potatoes coated with powdered cashews and minced fresh fenugreek leaves. Though I pair almonds with cilantro in this recipe, other nut-herb combinations are equally delicious.   MAKES 30 TO 36 POTATOES

> 3 pounds baby new potatoes (1 to 1½ inches in diameter)
> 2 tablespoons almond oil
> 1 to 2 jalapeño chilies, seeded and minced
> 1 to 2 tablespoons grated fresh ginger
> ½ cup powdered almonds (see Note)
> 2 tablespoons minced cilantro
> Salt
> Freshly ground pepper
> Fresh lemon juice

Steam the potatoes until they are just tender, about 15 minutes. Set them aside.

Combine the oil, chilies, ginger, almonds, and cilantro in a large bowl. Add the potatoes and toss until well coated. Season with salt and pepper and sprinkle with lemon juice.

Spear the potatoes with cocktail sticks; arrange them on a platter. Serve hot or keep warm in a 250°F oven for up to ½ hour.

Note: To powder almonds, place blanched almonds in a food processor and "pulse" until they are reduced to a powder.

Pear Tomatoes with Sarawak Pepper Cheese

If you have never tried Sarawak pepper, this is a good way to sample it. This pepper, which comes from the northwestern coast of Borneo, Malaysia, is relatively mild and is particularly pleasant with bland cheeses (see Note). Alternately, try ground Pepper Medley (page 282), or coarsely ground black pepper. The cheese spread will keep well for several days in the refrigerator. If tomatoes are not in season, try it as a dip with any seasonal raw or blanched crudités.   6 TO 8 SERVINGS

⅓ **cup mixed fresh herbs: minced cilantro, parsley, chervil**
½ **cup blanched almonds or pine nuts, finely chopped**
½ **pound Yogurt Cheese (page 289) or light cream cheese, at room temperature**
1 **cup shredded Monterey Jack cheese (4 ounces)**
½ **teaspoon freshly ground pepper, preferably Sarawak**
  Salt to taste
2 **pints yellow pear or cherry tomatoes**

Combine all of the ingredients, except the tomatoes, in a bowl, and mix well. Halve the tomatoes and place them, cut sides down, on paper towels to drain. Spread half of the tomatoes with small spoonfuls of cheese, and top with the remaining halves. Serve at room temperature or slightly chilled.

Note: Sarawak and six other exciting pepper varieties are available through mail-order sources (see Appendix) and at speciality food stores.

Green Pea Phyllo Purses

Indian deep-fried pea *kachoris* are rich and irresistible. They are also time-consuming and somewhat difficult to make. This lighter baked version, seasoned Gujarati-style, is quick and easy to assemble and tastes heavenly. If you have flavor-infused Ginger-Pineapple or Cilantro Oil (pages 292 and 293), use it instead of olive oil for added flavor.   MAKES 2 DOZEN PURSES

3¾ cups frozen petite peas, defrosted (1 pound)
1 tablespoon extra-virgin olive oil
1 to 2 jalapeño chilies, seeded and minced
1 tablespoon grated fresh ginger
½ tablespoon fresh lemon juice
1 teaspoon honey
1 tablespoon minced cilantro
1 tablespoon minced fresh mint
10 phyllo sheets
Olive-oil spray or olive oil

Place the peas between several thicknesses of kitchen towels to absorb excess liquid. Place in a food processor and pulse until reduced to a coarse pulp (about 2½ cups). Combine the peas, oil, chilies, ginger, lemon juice, and honey in a large skillet; sauté over moderate heat for 2 to 3 minutes. Stir in the herbs; let cool and divide into twenty-four portions in the pan or on a tray.

Preheat the oven to 350°F. Cut the phyllo sheets in half lengthwise and into fourths crosswise, forming eighty 4 × 6-inch squares. Cover the phyllo with a slightly damp towel. Lay one square on a sheet of waxed paper. Spray it with olive-oil spray or brush it lightly with oil. Repeat with two more squares. Place a portion (about 1½ tablespoons) of the filling in the center. Bring up the opposite corners of the phyllo, crimp firmly, and twist the ends to form purses, each with a pointed top. Repeat with the remaining phyllo.

Spray or brush nonstick baking sheets with olive oil. Transfer the pastries to the sheets and bake until golden brown, 20 to 25 minutes. Transfer to a platter and serve at once.

Quick Squash Samosas

Samosas — deep-fried pastries stuffed with zesty vegetables — are a culinary passion in India and a favorite in Indian restaurants everywhere. The filling is usually textured, featuring diced potatoes or cauliflower and mashed peas.

In this instance, a few traditions are broken. The pastries are baked, not fried, using a food-processor dough that is quick to assemble and effortless to handle (see Note). These *samosas* freeze well, either uncooked or baked, and can be ready at a moment's notice for appetizers or dinner savories.
MAKES 24 TO 28 SAMOSAS

Pastry

1	cup unbleached all-purpose flour
1 to 2	jalapeño chilies, seeded and coarsely chopped
¼	teaspoon salt
¼	teaspoon sugar
½	cup (1 stick) chilled butter, cut into ½-inch dice
4	ounces chilled light cream cheese, cut into ½-inch dice

Filling

two	14-ounce packages frozen squash puree (winter type squash) or 2½ cups cooked winter squash puree
2	teaspoons unsalted butter
½	teaspoon freshly ground nutmeg
½	teaspoon freshly ground white pepper, preferably Muntok
1½	jalapeño chilies, seeded and minced or pureed with a Japanese ginger grater
½	teaspoon salt
⅓	cup freshly grated coconut or grated frozen coconut, defrosted
3	tablespoons chopped pecans

To prepare the pastry, combine all of the pastry ingredients in a food processor work bowl fitted with a metal blade and process until the dough forms a ball (usually less than a minute). Shape into 3 smooth patties, cover with plastic wrap, and refrigerate. (Can be made 1 to 2 days ahead of use.)

To prepare the filling, defrost the frozen squash in a strainer to allow the excess liquid to drain off. Place the defrosted or fresh squash puree and 1 teaspoon of butter in a large nonstick frying pan over moderate heat. Cook for 15 minutes, stirring frequently, until the squash has reduced to a thick paste (1⅔ cups) that sticks onto an upside-down spoon. Remove from the heat and stir in the remaining butter, seasonings, coconut, and nuts; cool. Cover and refrigerate for up to 2 days.

To assemble the *samosas*, preheat the oven to 375°F. On a lightly floured surface, roll out one portion of the pastry into an oblong approximately 9 × 16 inches in length. Using a fluted or plain 3½-inch cutter, cut out eight rounds from the dough. Gather the scraps and set aside. Place 1 tablespoon of filling on each round; dampen the edges and fold the dough over the filling. Press the edges firmly with your fingertips to seal. Place the *samosas* on ungreased baking sheets. Repeat the process with the other two portions of dough to assemble 24 pastries. Reroll scraps to make 3 or 4 additional *samosas*. Bake until puffed and lightly browned, about 20 minutes. Alternately, bake 15 minutes, cool, wrap, and freeze for up to 1 month. Brown and warm for 5 minutes at 375°F. Serve hot or at room temperature.

Note: The filling is smooth, barely textured with coconut and pecan bits. It is made with frozen squash puree, though you could steam a seasonal winter squash and puree it in a food processor. You may want to keep a partially cooked batch on hand in the freezer for entertaining appetizers or a workday dinner.

Tropical Fruit Brochettes

Chat masala is the unique seasoning blend that transforms cut fruits into an Indian appetizer. Packaged *chat masala* is a complex blend of up to fifteen exotic ingredients, such as black salt, asafetida, and mango powder. The gingery, homemade *chat* seasoning in this dish is uncomplicated, focusing on "warm" elements such as fresh ginger, pepper, and nutmeg, offset with the flavor of fresh orange and lime juice. Feel free to substitute other fruits to suit the menu or occasion.   MAKES 12 TO 15 BROCHETTES

Chat Seasoning

¼ cup fresh lime juice

3 tablespoons fresh orange juice

½ tablespoon grated fresh ginger

1 tablespoon olive oil

⅛ teaspoon freshly ground nutmeg

Herb salt

Cracked black pepper

1 fresh pineapple, peeled, cored, and cut into 1-inch cubes

2 fresh papayas, peeled, seeded, and cut into ¾-inch cubes

3 firm, ripe bananas

3 firm, ripe kiwis

12 to 15 bamboo skewers

1 small cantaloupe

Place all of the ingredients for the chat seasoning in a large casserole dish; whisk to mix. Peel the bananas, cut them into 1-inch rounds, and place in the dressing. Toss gently, drain (reserving the dressing), and set aside. Peel the kiwis and cut each into quarters.

Spear the fruit on skewers, leaving 2 inches on one end. Dip the brochettes in the seasoning to coat the fruit on all sides, then set aside to marinate. Cover with plastic wrap and refrigerate. (Can be made ½ to 3 hours ahead.)

To serve, cut a 1-inch slice off the cantaloupe; peel and seed the melon. Place it cut side down on a serving tray and stick the skewers in the cantaloupe.

Wheat-Berry Caviar

At my first meeting with the inestimable Bert Greene, I expressed my appreci-
ation for his recipe bearing the same name. In my favorite adaptation of his
classic, gingery olive puree envelops toothsome wheat berries. Of my tasters,
many prefer the flavor of mild California olives over any other variety. If you
have a fondness for bold Greek Kalamatas, refined French Niçoise, or tart
Sicilian greens, give them a try, alone or in any combination. If the olives are
salty, rinse them well before use. As an appetizer, serve the caviar with Melba
toast, toasted baguette rounds, chapati chips, or apple slices. Also welcome as
part of an hors d'oeuvres buffet.   4 TO 6 SERVINGS

  1   teaspoon coarsely chopped fresh ginger
  ½   tablespoon coarsely chopped jalapeño chili, seeded
  ¼   teaspoon mustard seeds
  ¼   teaspoon fennel seeds
1¼   cups pitted black olives
  2   tablespoons extra-virgin olive oil
  2   tablespoons water or tomato-vegetable juice
  ½   teaspoon salt
1½   cups cooked wheat berries (see Note)
      Chopped cilantro or fresh parsley for garnish

With the food processor running, drop the ginger, chili, and mustard and
fennel seeds through the feed tube. When minced, add the olives, oil, water,
and salt. Process until the olives are nearly pureed, scraping down the sides of
the work bowl as necessary.

Combine the cooked wheat berries and olive mixture and toss to mix.
Garnish with Cilantro.

Note: To cook wheat berries, combine ¾ cup of wheat berries in a saucepan with
5 cups of water. Bring to a boil and cook for 2 minutes. Remove from the heat,
cover, and set aside for 1 hour. Return to the heat and simmer rapidly for 1
hour, or until the berries are tender but still crunchy. (Check the pot occasionally to see if there is enough water; add more if necessary.) Drain and cool.

Potato Tikki with Almond-Cilantro Chutney

Pronounced "tee-kee," this is a very popular griddle-fried item in Delhi cafés and snack houses. These seasoned mashed potatoes with a delicate crisp crust are irresistible as a snack or light meal.   8 APPETIZER SERVINGS; 4 FIRST-COURSE SERVINGS

        4   large boiling potatoes (about 1½ pounds)
       ¼   cup chopped almonds, slightly toasted
       ¼   cup minced red bell pepper
   1 to 2   jalapeño chilies, seeded and minced
       ½   tablespoon fresh lime juice
        2   tablespoons minced cilantro
      1½   tablespoons arrowroot
            Salt
            Freshly ground pepper
            Olive oil for pan-frying
        1   cup finely shredded romaine or lettuce leaves (optional)
            Almond-Cilantro Chutney (recipe follows)

Boil the potatoes in their skins until fork-tender. Cool slightly, peel, and force through a potato ricer or coarse sieve to produce smooth mashed potatoes. Add the almonds, pepper, chili, lime juice, cilantro, and arrowroot; season with salt and pepper and mix well. Rub a film of oil on your hands. Divide the mixture into eight portions and flatten into smooth patties ½ inch thick.

Brush a seasoned cast-iron or nonstick griddle with a film of oil. Place over low heat, and when hot, slip on the patties. Pan-fry slowly for 10 to 15 minutes per side, or until a crisp crust forms.

For a first course, distribute lettuce on four small plates. Top with two patties and pour a little chutney over both *tikki* and greens. For an appetizer, place a bowl of chutney on a serving dish and surround with *tikki*.

Almond-Cilantro Chutney

MAKES ABOUT 1 CUP

  ¼ **cup chopped almonds**
  3 **tablespoons chopped cilantro**
  ¾ **cup plain nonfat yogurt**
     Salt
     Hot paprika

In a food processor, pulse the nuts until they are reduced to a powder. Add the cilantro and yogurt and process until smooth and pale green. Season with salt and paprika.

Vegetable Antipasto in Cilantro Marinade

For this dish, select the freshest seasonal vegetables you can find — preferably organic. Use 2 pounds of trimmed vegetables in all. Serve as an hors d'oeuvre, an accompaniment for a green salad, or an in-between-meal nibbler.
12 SERVINGS

> **Spring and summer vegetables: yellow, green, and red bell-pepper strips; zucchini sticks; whole sugar snap peas or snow peas; whole yellow or red pear tomatoes. Fall and winter vegetables: cauliflower and broccoli florets; baby carrots cut into 2½-inch lengths; celery sticks; fennel bulb, cored and cut into ½-inch-wide strips.**

Marinade
- ¼ **cup fresh lime juice**
- 2 **tablespoons fresh orange juice**
- 1 **cup hot vegetable stock**
- ⅓ **cup extra-virgin olive oil**
- 2 **tablespoons maple syrup**
- ¼ **teaspoon cayenne**
- ¼ **teaspoon curry powder**
- ¼ **cup chopped cilantro**
- **Salt**
- **Freshly ground pepper**

Half fill a large bowl with ice cubes and cold water. Individually parboil the vegetables (except tomatoes and celery) for 30 seconds to 3 minutes, depending on variety and size. Plunge the vegetables in ice water to cool, and drain them in a colander; pat dry.

Place the marinade ingredients in a large ceramic or glass dish, using only half of the cilantro, and whisk well. Add the vegetables and toss well. Cover and refrigerate overnight, stirring once at night and again in the morning. Before serving, drain, and sprinkle with the remaining cilantro. (This will keep well for up to 3 days. The marinade also makes an excellent salad dressing.)

NIBBLERS

Malabar Pepper–Lemon Crackers

Malabar pepper, from India's northern Malabar coast, is slightly milder than its famed relative, Tellicherry pepper. Both selections are available in gourmet stores; generic bottled peppercorns or pepper blends are a convenient alternative. These nibblers are good with anything from soup and cheese to salad or fruit.   MAKES ABOUT 50 CRACKERS

> ½ teaspoon black peppercorns, preferably Malabar
> 2 cups unbleached all-purpose flour
> 3 tablespoons Familia or toasted wheat germ
> 1 teaspoon salt
> 1 teaspoon baking powder
>   Grated zest of 1 lemon
> ¼ cup (½ stick) chilled unsalted butter
> 4 tablespoons fresh lemon juice
> ⅔ cup skim milk or buttermilk

Coarsely crush the pepper in a mortar with a pestle, or with a rolling pin. Mix with the flour, Familia, salt, baking powder, and lemon zest in a medium bowl. Blend in the butter until the mixture resembles coarse meal. Add the lemon juice and milk, and mix until a rough dough forms. (Add more water or flour if necessary.) Knead on a lightly floured surface for 30 seconds; avoid overworking the dough.

Preheat the oven to 425°F. Divide the dough in half. On a lightly floured board, roll the dough out very thin (about ⅛ inch thick). Prick the dough with a fork. Using a 3-inch biscuit cutter, cut out rounds and transfer them to nonstick baking sheets. Reknead and reroll the trimmings and cut out more rounds in the same manner. Continue until the dough is used up.

Bake in the oven for 10 to 15 minutes, or until crisp and pale gold. Cool on wire racks. The crackers will keep in an airtight container for up to 2 weeks.

Bombay Cashews

These oven-roasted nuts are irresistible and are a snap to make. They come out of the oven soft but crisp up as they cool. Try them in place of croutons on a green salad.   MAKES 4 CUPS

> 2 tablespoons coriander seeds
> 2 tablespoons cumin seeds
> 3 tablespoons avocado or almond oil
> 1 tablespoon hot paprika
> ½ tablespoon freshly ground pepper, preferably Tellicherry
> ½ teaspoon freshly ground nutmeg
> ½ teaspoon ground cinnamon
> 1 teaspoon salt or herb salt
> 4 cups raw cashew halves or assorted raw nuts

Preheat the oven to 325°F. Grind the spice seeds in a grinder and place the mixture in a large pan. Add the oil and the remaining seasonings and stir to mix. Pour in the nuts and coat with the seasoned mix.

Divide the nuts into two batches and spread on greased baking pans. Bake for about 20 minutes, stirring every 5 minutes, until golden. Serve warm or at room temperature. (Cool completely before storing. These will keep well for 2 weeks in an airtight container.)

Bengali-Style Oven-Fried Potatoes

These baked potato "fries," cooked with hot air instead of hot oil, are virtually fat free and definitely delicious. Crisp on the outside and moist on the inside, they are infused with traces of aromatic cumin, turmeric, and cayenne. These are classic seasonings for a deep-fried potato dish called *aloo bhaji*, but the potatoes are equally receptive to a number of other seasonings. Try them with a sprinkle of salt and pepper, or a dusting of curry powder, crushed dried rosemary, or marjoram.

These "fries" make ideal party fare and are also terrific as a snack or vegetable dish. Top with a splash of lemon juice, a drizzle of catsup, or a dollop of cilantro chutney.   8 APPETIZER SERVINGS (¼ POUND PER PERSON)

2 pounds russet (Idaho) potatoes
   Olive- or vegetable-oil spray
¼ teaspoon ground turmeric
½ teaspoon ground cumin
¼ teaspoon cayenne or paprika
   Herb salt
   Freshly ground pepper

Preheat the oven to 450°F. Remove the oven racks and spray them with olive or vegetable oil. Wash the potatoes and slice them lengthwise, into sticks ½ inch thick, or crosswise, into rounds ⅓ inch thick. Transfer them to a baking pan and spray well with oil. Add the seasonings and toss to coat. Place the rounds in a single layer on the oven racks. Place the racks in the center of the oven. Bake until the potatoes are tender, with a deep, golden-brown crust, about 20 to 25 minutes. Serve piping hot.

Notes: If you have one on hand, try an infused oil such as Curry-Infused Walnut Oil (page 293). Reduce the cooking time if using a convection oven — the hot air circulating around the potatoes cooks them faster. There are no hard-and-fast rules.

Poppy Seed Wafers

Like Bengali *neemki,* these wafers are made with flour, poppy seeds, and oil, but instead of being deep-fried in mustard oil, they are baked. The resulting crisp wafers are something in between the Indian original and a cracker served at the Sonoma Mission Inn and Spa. You'll find them pleasant as appetizers or accompaniments to soups or salads.   MAKES 20 WAFERS

> 1½ cups whole-wheat pastry flour
> 2½ teaspoons baking powder
> ½ teaspoon salt or herb salt
> ¼ teaspoon baking soda
> 4 tablespoons mustard oil or 4 tablespoons (½ stick) cold butter, diced
> ⅔ cup buttermilk
> ½ cup black or white poppy seeds

Preheat the oven to 400°F. Combine the dry ingredients in a food processor and pulse to mix. Add the oil and pulse until the mixture resembles cornmeal. With the machine running, pour the buttermilk through the feed tube. Process until a soft ball of dough forms on the sides of the work bowl. (You may have to add additional flour or milk to make a medium-soft dough.)

On a work surface, knead the dough briefly and divide it into two equal portions. Roll one portion into a 1-inch-wide log and cut it into ten equal pieces. Repeat with the remaining dough and set aside.

Using your fingertips, pat each piece of dough into a 1½-inch disk. Sprinkle ½ tablespoon poppy seeds on the work surface. Coat both sides of one disk and roll it into a circle about 3 inches in diameter. Place it on a nonstick baking sheet. Shape the remaining pieces of dough until you have twenty crackers. Bake in the oven until golden-brown (12 to 15 minutes). Cool on racks. (Can be stored in a tightly covered tin for up to 5 days.)

Chili-Roasted Peanuts

America loves peanuts — from fried and salted to sweet honey-roasted. These spicy nuts are baked. The heat intensity depends on the amount and type of chili used. Crushed red-pepper flakes give you an occasional burst of heat; cayenne provides steady, strong heat; while ground ancho chilies or a chili blend offer warm, mellow heat. Use peanuts with or without skins, whole almonds, or assorted mixed nuts — all classic Indian nut nibblers. Try these at parties, give them as holiday gifts, or use them instead of salad croutons. MAKES 4 CUPS

1½ tablespoons peanut oil
½ tablespoon crushed red-pepper flakes, cayenne, ground ancho chilies, or a blend
1 tablespoon ground cumin
¼ teaspoon ground turmeric
1 tablespoon sugar, preferably date sugar (optional)
4 cups raw peanuts or other nuts

Preheat the oven to 325°F. Combine all of the ingredients except the nuts in a baking pan and mix well. Add the nuts and toss to mix. Spread the nuts in an even layer and bake for about 20 minutes, or until golden, stirring two or three times during cooking. Serve barely warm or at room temperature.

Oat Bran Wafers

When catering for people on wheat-free diets, I often rely on a variation of this wafer, adapted from a recipe found in Edward J. Safdie's *Spa Food*—the dough is made entirely of oats. The wafers are crisp when they come out of the oven but soften during storage. Delicious with soup or salad.
MAKES 36 CRACKERS

2½ cups old-fashioned rolled oats
2 teaspoons dried dill
2 teaspoons sesame or caraway seeds
1½ tablespoons safflower oil
½ cup water
Coarsely ground sea salt

In a food processor fitted with a metal blade, grind 1 cup of the oats into a coarse powder. Transfer to a bowl and add the dill, sesame seeds, oil, remaining oats, and water. Stir the mixture until it forms a dough. (Add additional sprinkles of water or oats as needed.)

Preheat the oven to 325°F. Halve the dough and shape it into two smooth patties. Place one patty on a 14-inch sheet of plastic wrap and top with a few grindings of salt. Top with a second piece of plastic wrap and roll out until thin. Remove the top piece of plastic wrap. Using a 2-inch biscuit cutter, cut out rounds and place them on a nonstick baking sheet. Reknead and reroll the trimmings and repeat until you have used all of the dough and have about thirty-six crackers.

Bake them in the center of the oven until pale gold (40 to 45 minutes). Cool on racks before serving or storing in airtight containers. These will keep well for 2 weeks.

Lime Biscuit Thins

A little tart from both citrus juice and zest, these flaky biscuits are spectacular. You can vary the flavors with the choice of citrus. My favorite variation is made with Key limes. At other times I have used Meyer lemons, blood oranges, Mercot tangerines, and plain old supermarket limes.

MAKES ABOUT 24 THINS

- ⅓ cup skim milk
- 2 teaspoons fresh lime juice
- 1 cup unbleached all-purpose flour
- 1 teaspoon baking powder
- ¼ teaspoon baking soda
- ¼ teaspoon salt
- ⅛ teaspoon cayenne
- ½ tablespoon freshly grated lime zest
- ¼ cup (½ stick) cold butter, cut into bits

Stir the milk and lime juice in a small bowl and set aside for 15 minutes. Combine the flour, baking powder, soda, salt, cayenne, and lime zest in a bowl and mix well. Add the butter and blend until the mixture resembles coarse meal. Pour in the milk mixture and blend with a fork just until a soft dough forms. Divide into two balls.

Preheat the oven to 400°F. Roll one portion of dough between two sheets of plastic wrap, lightly dusted with flour, until ⅛ inch thick. Using a 2-inch biscuit cutter, cut out rounds and arrange them on greased baking sheets. Gather the scraps, reroll, and cut into rounds. Repeat with the second portion of dough.

Bake in the center of the oven until pale gold, about 10 minutes. Cool on racks. Keeps well for two weeks.

Puffed Rice Nibbler

In many an Indian back-alley bazaar, you'll find shops that specialize in making freshly puffed rice, which is often eaten in a nut–and–dried fruit snack mixture. It is regarded much like our Chex cereal–pretzel nibbler. This takes just minutes to make and is a good traveling companion — for anything from a car trip to a backyard sleep-out.   2 SERVINGS

> 2 **cups puffed rice, wheat, corn, or Kashi (a seven-grain puffed cereal)**
> ⅛ **teaspoon ground turmeric**
> ⅛ **teaspoon ground cumin**
> ⅛ **teaspoon ground coriander**
> 2 **tablespoons grated fresh or dried coconut**
> 2 **tablespoons currants or raisins**
> 2 **tablespoons slivered almonds or pumpkin seeds, pan-toasted until golden**
> 2 **teaspoons date- or maple-sugar granules**
>   **Pinch salt**
>   **Olive- or vegetable-oil spray**

Preheat the oven to 400°F. Combine all of the ingredients except the oil spray on a nonstick baking sheet and mix well. Spray the mixture with a mist of olive or vegetable oil and toss again. Bake in the oven for 5 minutes. Serve warm or at room temperature. (Alternately, combine the ingredients in a 1-quart microwave-proof bowl. Microwave, uncovered, on medium-high for 2 minutes. Toss to mix and serve.)

Gingered Chickpeas

These make good party fare, a pleasant change from the nut bowl. In India, the chickpeas would be deep-fried. Here, they are baked until crispy and light. A good unrefined, cold-pressed oil really shines here. Instead of olive oil, you might infuse the snack with the flavor of walnut or almond oil. Look for ground ancho chilies and chili blends in gourmet stores; you can also use chili powder or cayenne.   TWELVE ⅓-CUP SERVINGS

1 **pound chickpeas (garbanzo beans), soaked overnight and drained, or two 16-ounce cans cooked chickpeas (preferably Eden) Extra-virgin olive-oil spray**
2 **tablespoons grated fresh ginger**
½ **teaspoon salt**
½ **tablespoon ground ancho chilies or 1½ tablespoons ground chili blend**

In a covered pan, simmer the chickpeas in fresh water until tender but not breaking down (anywhere from 1 to 2½ hours). Drain cooked or canned chickpeas in a colander and rinse under running water. Drain, then dry the chickpeas on paper towels.

Preheat the oven to 325°F. Place the chickpeas on one or two baking trays and spray them liberally with oil. Sprinkle with ginger and salt. Using your hands, rub the chickpeas between your palms to coat them evenly with oil and seasonings. Spread them out in a single layer and spray them again with oil.

Bake in the oven for 1 to 1¼ hours, stirring every 15 minutes and spraying with oil, until they are toasted and crispy. While they are still hot, add the ground chilies and toss to mix. Serve warm or at room temperature. Can be made 2 to 3 days ahead. Store in a paper towel–lined jar, well sealed.

Crunchy Nut-and-Cereal Mix

There is a broad range of Indian snack mixtures, based around deep-fried rice cakes, called *chidwa*. This takeoff on the *chidwa* theme is baked and features two cold cereals instead of rice flakes — corn flakes and crispy brown-rice cereal. It is a light mixture, perfect when you want something easy for a party or a snack. All of the ingredients are available at natural-food stores.

TEN ½-CUP SERVINGS

½	tablespoon ground coriander
½	teaspoon cayenne or 1½ tablespoons ground ancho chilies
2	tablespoons date sugar or raw (Sucanat) cane sugar
¼	teaspoon salt
2	cups crispy brown-rice cereal
1½	cups juice-sweetened corn flakes
	Virgin olive-oil spray
1	cup sliced almonds, pan-toasted until golden
½	cup pumpkin seeds, pan-toasted until golden
⅔	cup raisins

Preheat the oven to 325°F. Mix the coriander, cayenne, sugar, and salt in a small bowl. Spread the cereals out on a baking pan and spray liberally with oil. Sprinkle half of the spice mix over the cereals and toss to mix. Bake for 8 to 10 minutes; transfer to a large bowl to cool.

Mix the almonds, pumpkin seeds, and raisins on the baking pan. Spray well with olive oil, sprinkle with the remaining spice mix, and toss to coat. Bake for 4 to 5 minutes, until flavors merge, then remove and cool to room temperature. Add to the cereal mixture and mix well. Serve at room temperature. Store in a tightly covered container for up to 1 week.

PÂTÉS, DIPS, AND SPREADS

Light Tahini Dip with Crudités

Dips are popular with people of all ages. This one features tahini, also called sesame butter. I recommend organic, toasted sesame butter for the dip. Raw sesame butter tends to go rancid quickly and often leaves a bitter taste in the back of the mouth. Many good brands are available in natural-food stores.

The dip takes only minutes to assemble and stores well for between-meal snacks. Thinned down with water or fruit juice, it can be drizzled over steamed, baked, or broiled vegetables.   MAKES ABOUT 1⅓ CUPS

Dip

1	teaspoon cumin seeds
¾	cup tahini
¼	cup fresh lime juice
¼	cup fresh orange juice
¼ to ½	cup water
⅛	teaspoon hot paprika or cayenne
	Crudités such as carrot sticks, bell pepper slices, celery sticks, cherry tomatoes, and pear tomatoes

Place the cumin seeds in a small pan and toast them lightly over moderate heat. Transfer to a food processor, add the remaining dip ingredients, and process until the cumin is crushed and the texture is light and creamy. Serve with crudités.

Spicy Mung Bean Pâté with Cilantro-Mint Cream

In India, rich and spicy legume purees are deep-fried into savories called *baḍa*. Nearly oil-free, this baked version of *baḍa* is high in protein, low in fat, and quite unforgettable.

The pâté can be served as an appetizer, first course, entree, or sandwich loaf. When baked into a loaf, cut cubes are good as appetizers. Thick slices are perfect for a first course, and thin slices are good for sandwiches. For an entree, bake the pâté in individual buttered ramekins or tart tins and serve in a pool of Cilantro-Mint Cream.   12 SERVINGS

1	pound trimmed cauliflower florets (to make 4 cups finely shredded cauliflower)
One	1-inch piece peeled fresh ginger, chopped
1 to 2	jalapeño chilies, seeded and chopped
¾	cup water, or as needed
1	cup skinned split mung beans or whole mung beans, soaked overnight and well drained
3	tablespoons chopped cilantro or fresh parsley
½	teaspoon ground coriander
1	teaspoon ground cumin
¼	teaspoon ground turmeric
¼	teaspoon baking powder
3	tablespoons arrowroot
1	teaspoon salt
	Freshly ground pepper
1½	tablespoons virgin olive oil
	Non stick olive- or vegetable-oil spray
	Cilantro-Mint Cream (recipe follows)

Preheat the oven to 350°F. Fit a food processor with a fine shredding disk and shred the cauliflower; transfer to a mixing bowl. Fit the processor with the

metal blade, and with the machine running, add the ginger and chilies; mince. Add the water and the drained mung beans and process until smooth, 3 to 5 minutes. Scrape the puree into the bowl with the cauliflower and remaining ingredients, except for the olive-oil spray and Cilantro-Mint Cream. Mix well.

Generously mist a nonstick twelve-cup muffin pan, twelve individual tart tins, or a 9 × 5 × 3-inch loaf pan with nonstick vegetable spray. (Use the loaf pan for appetizers and lunch salad; use the muffin or tart pans for first course or entree. If you do not have nonstick cookware, butter the pans.)

Spoon the mixture into the muffin or loaf pan, smoothing the surface. Bake muffins or tarts for 45 minutes and the loaf for 1 to 1¼ hours, or until a wooden skewer inserted in the center comes out clean. Cool for 5 minutes on a rack; unmold.

For appetizers, cut the room-temperature loaf into ¾-inch cubes and spear them with toothpicks. Arrange the cut pâté on a platter, spray with olive oil, and drizzle with Cilantro-Mint Cream. For a lunch salad or entree, cut the loaf into ½-inch slices. For a first course or light entree, place nearly-room-temperature muffin- or tart-size ramekins on individual dinner plates and surround with barely warm Cilantro-Mint Cream.

Cilantro-Mint Cream

This room-temperature sauce can dress up anything from soup to salad. MAKES 1 CUP

> 1 cup nonfat plain yogurt
> 2 tablespoons minced cilantro
> 1 tablespoon minced fresh mint
> ¼ teaspoon freshly ground Pepper Medley (page 282) or commercially prepared pepper blend

Combine all of the ingredients in a food processor or blender and blend until pale green. Serve at room temperature.

Yogurt Cheese Balls

Here, a homemade yogurt cheese is seasoned, rolled into balls, and coated with finely chopped nuts, seeds, or fresh herbs, such as toasted almonds, pecans, white or black poppy seeds, sesame seeds, ground ancho chilies, paprika, medium-grind peppercorns, or finely chopped fresh chervil, parsley, dill, or mint. Serve with crackers or fruit slices.   12 SERVINGS (3 PER PERSON)

3	cups plain nonfat yogurt
1	teaspoon cumin seeds
½	tablespoon coriander seeds
	Several grinds of fresh pepper
3 to 4	tablespoons finely chopped toasted nuts
1½	tablespoons seeds or spices
⅓	cup finely chopped fresh herbs

To make the yogurt cheese, line a colander with a triple layer of cheesecloth, letting it fall over the sides. Place the colander over a bowl and spoon the yogurt into the colander. Fold the excess cheesecloth over the top and cover with plastic wrap.

Place the colander in a large bowl, allowing space for the drained-off whey to collect beneath it. Drain the yogurt in the refrigerator for 24 to 36 hours, or until a thick-curd cheese forms. (Can be made 2 to 3 days in advance. Keep covered and refrigerated.)

Place the cumin and coriander seeds in a pan and cook over moderate heat until they darken a few shades. Crush in a mortar with a pestle. Place the spice mixture in a bowl; add the yogurt cheese, salt, and pepper. Mix well.

Place a nut, seed, and herb selection on three different plates. Divide the yogurt into three portions. Using a measuring spoon, scoop up about ½ tablespoon of yogurt and drop twelve measured portions on each of the coatings (for a total of thirty-six balls). Carefully roll the balls in the coatings until round and well coated. Arrange on a serving platter and refrigerate until needed.

New Delhi–Style Chickpea Hummus

This mint, jalapeño, and lime–infused dip is a takeoff on Middle Eastern hummus. Instead of the traditional accompaniment of pita wedges, try it with toasted chapati wedges. It's also a delicious sandwich spread. Instead of almond butter, try pistachio, cashew, or hazelnut butter, all available at natural-food stores. Thinned down with fresh orange or tomato juice, this hummus makes a terrific salad dressing.   MAKES ABOUT 2½ CUPS

1	cup dried chickpeas (garbanzo beans), soaked overnight, or 2 cups cooked chickpeas (rinse commercial cooked chickpeas well)
1	¼-inch-thick slice peeled fresh ginger
1 to 2	small jalapeño chilies, seeded
3	tablespoons fresh lime juice
¼	cup roasted almond butter
1½	tablespoons almond oil
2	tablespoons chopped cilantro
8 to 10	fresh mint leaves, torn
	Salt
	Freshly ground pepper
½	tablespoon cumin seeds, pan-toasted and crushed
	Crudités such as bell peppers, carrots, snow peas, and celery

If you are using uncooked chickpeas, drain and rinse them. Place them in a large heavy saucepan. Add enough water to cover by 3 inches. Bring to a boil, reduce the heat, and slowly boil until the beans are very tender, 1½ to 3 hours. Cool to room temperature.

Drain the cooked chickpeas. Transfer them to a food processor; add the ginger, chilies, lime juice, almond butter, almond oil, and herbs, and process until smooth. (If desired, thin with additional water or olive oil.) Season with salt and pepper.

Place in a shallow serving dish, smoothing the top with a spatula. Sprinkle with cumin and serve with crudités. This dip can be prepared 3 days ahead, covered and stored in the refrigerator.

Avocado Pâté with Pistachio Chutney

This treasure of a recipe is a slightly amended version of one created by gifted author and teacher Betty Rosbottom. When shaped into a loaf, the pale green pâté, accompanied by the deep green chutney, is striking looking and is ideal for entertaining. Right out of the food processor, without chutney, it works well for anything from a dip to a sandwich spread. Serve with vegetable crudités and Lime Biscuit Thins (page 25).   12 SERVINGS

Chutney

- 1 ⅛-inch-thick slice peeled fresh ginger
- ½ serrano chili, seeded and chopped
- ⅓ cup pistachio nuts
- ¼ cup trimmed fresh parsley
- 2 tablespoons trimmed cilantro

Pâté

- Avocado oil or olive oil
- 3 smallish, ripe avocados, peeled and pitted
- 1 pound light cream cheese, kefir, or Yogurt Cheese (page 289), or extra-firm tofu, drained, pressed, and patted dry
- 1 tablespoon fresh lime juice
- ¼ teaspoon cayenne
- ½ teaspoon salt

With a food processor running, drop the ginger and chili through the feed tube and mince. Add the nuts and pulse to chop coarsely. Add the herbs and continue to pulse until the chutney is reduced to a powder. Transfer to a bowl.

Line a 6-cup glass loaf pan with three layers of waxed paper extending over the sides slightly. Brush the paper with olive oil. Puree the avocados in the food processor; add the remaining pâté ingredients and process until velvety smooth. Transfer half of the mixture to the prepared pan and sprinkle with half of the pistachio chutney. Add the remaining mixture and smooth the top. Cover with plastic wrap, pressing out all air bubbles so that the container

is airtight. (Air will cause the avocado to turn brown.) Refrigerate for at least 12 hours or up to 24 hours, along with the remaining pistachio chutney.

Uncover the pâté and unmold onto a rectangular serving dish. Remove the waxed paper and smooth the loaf with an oiled spatula. Sprinkle with the remaining chutney before serving.

Broccoli-Spinach Spread

Though typically served as a side-dish vegetable called *sak*, here this slow-cooked vegetable mixture serves as a dark, rich topping for crackers or croutons. This spread is so delicious, I've seen adaptations on the menus of fine restaurants, including Alice Waters's famous Chez Panisse in Berkeley.
MAKES 24 CANAPÉS

¼ cup extra-virgin olive oil
1 teaspoon cumin seeds
½ teaspoon crushed red-pepper flakes
2 tablespoons fresh lime juice
½ teaspoon salt
¼ teaspoon freshly ground pepper
1 pound broccoli (including stems and leaves), cut into ¼-inch pieces
¼ pound fresh spinach, trimmed, washed, and chopped
½ cup water
24 Poppy Seed Wafers (page 22) or oven-toasted French-bread rounds
2 tablespoons grated fresh or dry coconut

Heat the oil in a nonstick frying pan over medium-low heat. Add the cumin seeds and pepper flakes and fry for ½ minute. Stir in the lime juice, salt, pepper, vegetables, and water. Cover and simmer until the vegetables are reduced to a chunky puree (45 to 60 minutes), stirring occasionally.

Immediately before serving (to avoid soggy crusts), spread about 1 table-spoon of the mixture on each cracker or bread round. Sprinkle with coconut.

Roasted Eggplant and Vegetable Pâté

In India, ash-baked eggplant puree is the featured element in a dish called *baigun bharta*. Here, eggplant marries with tomatoes, peppers, and zucchini, yielding a versatile and nutritious spread. For a more intense, smoky-flavored pâté, grill the bell peppers, sliced zucchini, and halved tomatoes on a stovetop grill before using them. (Remove the pepper and tomato skins before use.)

As an appetizer, serve the pâté with toasted pita triangles or baguette rounds, spread on grilled zucchini rounds, or spooned into hollowed-out cherry tomatoes. Or, spread on bread, add cheese and grill.   MAKES 2 CUPS

    1 medium eggplant (about 1 pound)
    2 tablespoons extra-virgin olive oil
One ¾-inch piece peeled fresh ginger, cut into fine julienne
    1 jalapeño chili, seeded and slivered
    1 teaspoon cumin seeds
    2 yellow bell peppers, deribbed, seeded, and chopped
    1 medium zucchini, coarsely shredded
    2 tomatoes, peeled, seeded, and chopped
    2 tablespoons fresh lime juice
       Salt
       Freshly ground pepper
       Olive-oil spray
       Minced cilantro for garnish

Preheat the oven to 450°F. Char the eggplant over a moderate gas flame, turning it frequently, until all the skin blackens. Transfer to a baking sheet and bake until butter-soft, 15 to 20 minutes. Cool slightly, carefully scrape off most of the charred skin, and coarsely chop.

Heat the oil in a skillet over moderate heat. Add the ginger, chili, and cumin seeds and fry for 30 seconds. Stir in the bell peppers and sauté until softened, 6 to 8 minutes. Add the zucchini and tomato, and continue cooking for 2 minutes. Cool slightly.

Place the eggplant in a food processor and pulse briefly to puree coarsely. Add the pepper mixture and process until the vegetables are coarsely chopped. Add the lime juice and season with salt and pepper. Pack into a crock and spray with olive oil. At serving time, garnish with cilantro.

The pâté may be covered and stored in the refrigerator for 1 week.

Toasted Pecan-Mushroom Pâté

I created this pâté, on request, for a party that I catered. Though I am not a mushroom aficionado, the crowd gave it raves. Try it as an hors d'oeuvre or a light first course accompanied by sesame crackers or wheat Melba toast.
12 SERVINGS

One ¾-inch piece peeled fresh ginger, sliced
1 to 2 jalapeño chilies, seeded and sliced
2 slices whole-grain bread, quartered
8 ounces mushroom caps, cleaned and sliced (about 2 cups)
1 cup toasted pecans (see Note)
½ cup part-skim ricotta cheese or extra-firm silken tofu
1 teaspoon salt
1 tablespoon fresh lemon juice
3 tablespoons chopped cilantro
1 roasted red bell pepper (page 288), coarsely chopped

Preheat the oven to 350°F. With the food processor running, drop the ginger and chilies through the feed tube and mince. Add the bread and pulse until it is reduced to crumbs. Add the mushrooms and pecans and puree. Add the ricotta, salt, and lemon juice and blend well. Add the cilantro and red pepper and pulse until the pepper is finely chopped.

Place in a buttered 4-cup loaf pan and bake for 1 hour, or until golden-brown. Serve warm or at room temperature.

Note: To toast pecans, spread them in a single layer on a baking tray. Bake them in a preheated 300°F oven for 10 minutes.

Dried Fruit Pâté on Fruit Slices

This fruit-sweetened pâté is excellent on fruit slices as an hors d'oeuvre, or shaped into balls, rolled in chopped nuts, and served as an after-dinner confection.

The pâté has a long history in my kitchen, and I rarely make it the same way twice. Here, I used organic sweet Mission almonds, Flora Gold dried apricots, and pure bitter almond oil. Use fruit juice — orange, tangerine, apple, or pear juice are all good choices — to thin the pâté to a workable consistency.   MAKES ABOUT 1⅔ CUPS PÂTÉ (ENOUGH FOR 24 CANAPÉS)

¾	**cup blanched whole or sliced almonds**
1	**teaspoon fennel seeds**
3	**tablespoons maple syrup**
2 to 3	**drops almond oil or 1 tablespoon orange flower water**
1	**teaspoon grated fresh orange zest**
¼	**cup fresh orange, apple, or pear juice**
	Cayenne
½	**pound dried apricots (about ⅔ cup)**
3 to 4	**Granny Smith apples or Asian pears**

Preheat the oven to 325°F. Bake the almonds and fennel seeds on a cookie sheet until barely toasted, 6 to 7 minutes. Cool slightly.

Combine the maple syrup, almond oil, zest, juice, and a bare sprinkle of cayenne in a bowl and whisk. Grind the almonds to a medium-fine consistency in a food processor. Steam or microwave tough apricots and add the apricots and process until the mixture is reduced to a fluffy powder. With the machine running, pour the liquid mixture through the feed tube and process until smooth. Scrape down the sides of the work bowl with a spatula as necessary.

Just before serving, core the apples and cut them into ¼-inch-thick rounds. Brush the apple slices with lemon juice and spread the top surface of each with a generous tablespoon of pâté. Alternately, spray the inside of a disposable pastry bag with vegetable spray. Fit it with a large star nozzle, add the pâté, and pipe onto the fruit slices. Arrange on a serving platter and serve immediately. May be stored for up to 1 week, refrigerated and well covered.

Salads

The recipes in this chapter are influenced by past and present and inspired by Indian, European, and American traditions. I've divided the salads into categories based on the types of ingredients used and the way they are assembled: Leafy Salads, Little Salads, Composed Salads, and Bean, Grain, and Pasta Salads.

LEAFY SALADS

These salads rely on few ingredients, are unpretentious, and are quick to make. In India, lettuces are virtually unknown, largely because a hot tropical climate is not conducive to growing, shipping, and storing delicate salad plants. But Indian flavors marvelously complement the large array of leafy salad plants available in temperate climates. Specific lettuce varieties are often suggested in the recipes, but feel free to use other greens and salad ingredients.

There are no rules as to when to serve a green salad. The French often serve salad after the main course. For decades, most Americans have served salads as a separate course before the entree. Indians serve an entire meal at once, from salad to dessert, on one plate. I often serve salads in between courses in the middle of the meal. No matter what your choice, use high-quality, fresh ingredients, preferably organic. An appealing presentation,

neatly arranged and garnished, showcases the colors and textures of the ingredients. Herbs, edible flowers, croutons, and toasted spice garnishes add both flavor and visual appeal.

LITTLE SALADS

This salad collection is derived from Indian *kachambers*. Traditionally, these are zesty, palate-stimulating shredded salads served in small quantity, like a relish or salsa, directly on the entree plate. Dressed in hot, chili-laced citrus vinaigrettes, they consist of vegetables or fruits, raw, blanched, or wilted. These salads needn't be "hot," but they should be snappy and sassy from the hot-chili content. Several recipes are Gujarati-inspired, reflecting regional seasonings such as toasted nuts, mustard seeds, cilantro, and lime juice.

COMPOSED SALADS

These salads feature vegetables, in some cases paired with a grain or legume. These dishes can easily serve as the center of the meal. For example, Orange-Glazed Winter Vegetable Salad (page 56) or Swiss Chard Rolls Stuffed with Quinoa and Mango (page 61) are terrific as a main course. The salad vegetables are cooked by both wet and dry cooking methods, from steaming and stir-frying to baking and grilling. Let the recipes stimulate your imagination. Bengali Chef Salad, for example, is irresistible as is, but you can take it in many directions according to available seasonal produce.

BEAN, GRAIN, AND PASTA SALADS

Complex carbohydrates—legumes, grains, and pasta—take center stage in these salads. Dressed or marinated in vinaigrettes, pestos, or fresh herb chutneys, they acquire deep and vivid flavors. These ingredients are combined with seasonal vegetables, sometimes raw and crisp, at other times cooked until butter-soft. These salads are good one-dish meals, ideal for entertaining and for brown-bag lunches.

Many bean salads feature old-world legumes with evocative names such as Scarlet Runners, Appaloosas, Jacob's Cattle, China Yellows, and Rattle-snakes. Their names often reflect unusual patterns or colors, which make the

salads particularly interesting. (See Appendix for sources.) All recipes featuring these beans include alternative supermarket and health-food-store ingredients.

VINAIGRETTES

A traditional French vinaigrette consists of one part acid (lemon juice, lime juice, or vinegar) to two or three parts oil. To make light vinaigrettes for this salad collection, I use a variety of oils and citrus juices, keep the oil content low, and use hot water to help emulsify the dressings.

In India, virtually all salad vinaigrettes are made with a citrus fruit called *nimbu,* quite similar to Key lime. Vinegar is rarely if ever used as a sour acid element, for like wine and ale, it is the product of fermentation. Citrus fruits, however, are native to the tropics and warm temperate regions.

I prefer citrus juices as the acid elements in vinaigrettes for their fresh, sweet, and sour dimensions. Because of the balance between the sugars and fruit acids in citrus juice, and the essential oils released from the citrus zest, sparkling flavors are possible. Some vinaigrettes feature a single citrus fruit, such as lemon or lime, but a few combine several selections — for example, lime and orange or tangerine and lemon juice.

Most of these vinaigrette recipes call for extra-virgin olive oil. In addition, some recipes call for walnut, almond, and avocado oil. These oils have a wonderful flavor, body, and aroma that work very well in vinaigrettes. Indian-inspired salads may also rely on peanut or sesame oil. No matter what your selection, use cold-pressed, unrefined oils and keep them refrigerated or in a cool, dark place.

In some recipes, I recommend a homemade flavor-infused oil such as Tomato, Saffron, Curry, or Cardamom-Cinnamon Oil for added aroma and flavor dimensions. Recipes for these are found in the Appendix. Try one or two that intrigue you. I keep three or four on hand year-round.

If you want to explore salads in depth, I highly recommend *The Salad Garden* by Joy Larkcom. Even if you can't have your own garden, you can always request a local farmer or greengrocer to supply some of the varieties of salad vegetables mentioned in the book. Everyone will benefit. Salads are colorful, nutritious, and satisfying. Work one into your life on a daily basis.

LEAFY SALADS

Butterhead Lettuce with Pomegranate and Pine Nuts

Vermicelli-like shreds of dark green spinach contrast beautifully with pale green, loosely folded leaves of butterhead lettuce in this salad. It is dressed only in olive oil and lemon juice; the flavor is heightened by a sprinkle of toasted pine nuts and ruby-red pomegranate seeds. This salad makes a dynamic visual presentation.   4 SERVINGS

  2 tablespoons pine nuts
10 spinach leaves, rinsed and trimmed
  5 cups butterhead or leafy green lettuce, rinsed, dried, and torn for salad
  2 tablespoons extra-virgin olive oil
    Salt
    Freshly ground pepper, preferably Malabar
¼ cup pomegranate seeds
  2 tablespoons fresh lemon juice

Place the pine nuts in a frying pan and toast them over moderate heat until golden-brown, stirring constantly; set aside. Roll the spinach leaves into a tight cigar shape and cut crosswise into ⅛-inch chiffonade or shreds. Combine the lettuce and spinach in a salad bowl. Drizzle with oil, season with salt and pepper, and toss to mix. Sprinkle with pomegranate seeds, pine nuts, and lemon juice.

Spring Lettuce and Papaya

Golden julienned papaya and toasted almonds top off this mixture of delicate spring salad greens. When I lived in South Cornwall, where I had a large walled kitchen garden filled with Victorian edible flowers, I often finished this salad off with a sprinkle of tiny anise hyssop blossoms. The deep lilac-colored flowers have a delicate fragrance and sweet licorice flavor that beautifully complement the salad flavors. Many greengrocers and supermarkets carry edible flowers year-round. Give anise hyssop or another selection a try for a touch of this Victorian-era tradition. If papayas are not in season, try mangoes or pears.   4 SERVINGS

1 firm, ripe papaya (about ¾ pound)
2 tablespoons fresh orange juice
2 tablespoons fresh lime juice
3 tablespoons extra-virgin olive oil
  Salt
  Freshly cracked pepper, preferably Malabar
6 cups torn mixed lettuce, such as Bibb, looseleaf, romaine, red oakleaf, or buttercrunch
2 tablespoons minced cilantro
2 tablespoons sliced almonds, pan-toasted until golden

Halve, seed, and peel the papaya. Cut two-thirds of it into fine julienne strips 2 inches long. Sprinkle with the orange juice; set aside. Roughly chop the remaining papaya and transfer it to a blender along with the lime juice and olive oil. Process until smooth; season with salt and pepper.

Place the lettuce and cilantro in a large salad bowl. Add the papaya dressing and toss gently. Sprinkle with julienned papaya and nuts.

Romaine with Avocado, Radish, and Orange

If you like avocado-and-grapefruit salad, you'll love this variation. Though supermarket romaine may be your only option at times, if you can find it, combine half Rouge d'Hiver red romaine with its famous soft-green cousin. For color contrast, give Mercot tangerines or blood oranges a try when they are available.   4 SERVINGS

> 3 tablespoons fresh lime juice
> 2 tablespoons fruit-sweetened orange marmalade
> 3 tablespoons avocado oil
>   Salt
>   Freshly ground pepper, preferably Tellicherry
> 3 tablespoons hot water
> 2 smallish heads romaine lettuce, trimmed and shredded
> 12 red radishes, thinly sliced
> 2 seedless oranges, peeled and thinly sliced
> 1 small avocado

Combine the lime juice, marmalade, oil, salt, and pepper in a blender and process until creamy. With the machine running, slowly add the water and process until creamy. Set aside.

Line a shallow bowl with lettuce. Alternate circles of radish and orange slices over the top. Cover and refrigerate. (Can be prepared 3 hours ahead.)

At serving time, peel, pit, and cut the avocado into ½-inch dice. Add to the top of the salad and drizzle with dressing. Serve immediately, as is or tossed.

Warm Savoy Cabbage with Mustard Butter

Prepared in the Gujarati style, this crinkly-leaf savoy cabbage salad is at its brightest and best in winter months. You might even toss in a little of a beautiful crimson pink–and–purple or gray green–and–white cabbage along with the savoy. The few ingredients in the salad marry well, though you could easily add strips of grilled red pepper and toasted pumpkin seeds for flavor and color. In the spring, use a loose-headed spring cabbage; in the summer, select a round-headed, compact type. Any leftovers are wonderful folded into buttermilk, sprinkled with toasted cumin and served as a chilled soup.   4 SERVINGS

1	teaspoon mustard seeds
One	1-inch piece peeled fresh ginger, slivered
6 to 8	cups finely sliced savoy cabbage
¼	cup water or vegetable broth
½	cup frozen petite peas, defrosted
1½	tablespoons unsalted butter
2	tablespoons minced cilantro
	Salt
	Freshly ground pepper

Preheat a nonstick wok over moderately high heat. Add the mustard seeds; cover and cook until they pop and turn gray. Stir in the ginger, cabbage, and water. Stirring frequently, cook until the green color intensifies and the texture is tender-crisp, about 5 minutes. Remove the pan from the heat, stir in the remaining ingredients, and season with salt and pepper. Serve warm.

Bibb Salad with Honey-Mustard Vinaigrette

A salad with simple elements showcases the freshness, quality, and flavor of its ingredients. This blend is near-perfect, though you can easily change directions by adding a touch of seasonal salad greens or minced fresh herbs to the Bibb lettuce base. If the menu warrants the change, experiment with flavor in the vinaigrette by featuring a single tart citrus juice or a combination of several juices.   4 SERVINGS

    4 small heads Bibb lettuce, trimmed and torn
    ½ cup finely shredded jícama
    ½ cup finely shredded carrot
    3 tablespoons currants or yellow raisins
    2 tablespoons chopped almonds, pan-toasted until golden

Vinaigrette
    2 tablespoons fresh tangerine juice
    2 tablespoons fresh lime juice
    2½ tablespoons almond oil
    1½ tablespoons honey
    ½ teaspoon mustard seeds
    ⅛ teaspoon salt
    ⅛ teaspoon cayenne

Arrange the lettuce on individual serving plates; sprinkle with the shredded vegetables, dried fruit, and almonds. Combine the vinaigrette ingredients in a blender and process for 30 seconds. Pour the vinaigrette over the salads and serve at once.

Banaras-Style Wilted Kale with Yams

The inspiration for this salad is a hot, spicy vegetable dish I was served in Banaras — a volcanic mélange of mustard greens and the root vegetable colocassia. With my first bite, I could imagine its potential using American produce — a warm and inviting fall salad of autumn kale and yams, these tastes offset by shredded jalapeño chilies. The resultant green-and-orange wilted salad is great for newcomers to kale and much loved by its aficionados.

6 SERVINGS

1¾   pounds tender young kale, washed, stems removed, and torn
1   pound (2 medium) yams or sweet potatoes, peeled and cut into
      ½-inch dice
1¾   cups Winter Vegetable Stock (page 78) or commercially prepared
      vegetable stock
½   teaspoon curry powder
⅛   teaspoon ground cloves
⅛   teaspoon ground cinnamon
⅛   teaspoon cayenne
⅛   teaspoon ground cardamom
     Salt
     Freshly ground pepper
2   tablespoons fresh lime juice
1   tablespoon olive oil
1   jalapeño chili, seeded and cut lengthwise into fine julienne

Combine the vegetables, stock, and ground spices in a large nonstick casserole and toss to mix. Place over moderately high heat and bring to a boil. Partially cover, reduce heat slightly, and cook, stirring occasionally, until the liquid has nearly evaporated (15 to 20 minutes) and the root vegetables are fork-tender. Season with salt and pepper; toss well and transfer to a serving dish. Drizzle with lime juice and olive oil. Serve warm or at room temperature, sprinkled with jalapeño chili.

Four-Greens Salad with Yellow Tomato Vinaigrette

The vinaigrette is the star of this salad. It's my version of a superb cumin-tomato creation served at the famed Dakota's restaurant in Dallas. When low-acid yellow tomatoes are unavailable, use red or orange. The vinaigrette is also good on vegetable, grain, pasta, and bean salads.   4 SERVINGS

Vinaigrette
 2 medium yellow tomatoes, peeled, seeded, and quartered
 2 tablespoons fresh lemon juice
 1 tablespoon almond butter
 ½ teaspoon salt
 ¼ teaspoon paprika
 ½ teaspoon cumin seeds, pan-toasted
 2 tablespoons walnut oil
 2 tablespoons chopped cilantro

Salad
 1 Granny Smith apple
 6 cups torn mixed greens, including Boston, Bibb, oakleaf, and endive
 2 tablespoons chopped walnuts, pan-toasted until golden

To make the vinaigrette, puree the tomato, lemon juice, almond butter, salt, and spices in a food processor or blender. With the machine running, slowly add the oil, then the cilantro. Refrigerate until chilled.

Peel and core the apple and cut it into fine julienne. Add a few tablespoons of vinaigrette and toss to coat. Divide the greens among four plates; sprinkle with apple and nuts. Serve, passing the remaining vinaigrette separately.

LITTLE SALADS

Indian Summer Tomatoes

Vegetable-patch tomatoes, scarlet and heavy to the hand, dressed with a little salt, pepper, olive oil, and basil, were a staple in my Italian grandmother's kitchen. This North Indian–style variation, which derives its warmth from aromatic toasted cumin and fennel seeds, lime juice, and cilantro, runs a close second.   4 TO 6 SERVINGS

> 4 large vine-ripened tomatoes, sliced
> 1 tablespoon fresh lime juice
> 2 tablespoons extra-virgin olive oil
> ¼ teaspoon cumin seeds
> ¼ teaspoon fennel seeds
> 1 dried hot chili pod (or more or less, according to taste)
> 2 tablespoons chopped cilantro
>   Salt
>   Freshly ground pepper, preferably Tellicherry

Arrange the tomato slices on a serving platter or shallow dish. Sprinkle them with lime juice. Warm the oil in a small pot over moderate heat. Add the cumin, fennel, and chili pod and cook for about 30 seconds. Remove from the heat, discard the chili pod, and cool. Whisk in the cilantro; spoon the seasoned oil over the tomatoes. Serve immediately or set aside for about 30 minutes to intensify the flavor. Season with salt and pepper before serving.

Shredded Beets with Fresh Coconut

For those who have yet to relish a good raw beet salad, this is your introduction. You can use any type of beet, from supermarket red crimsons to specialty white, golden yellow, or candy cane–striped Chioggia beets. White and yellow varieties don't tend to "bleed" the way red beets do, though all are attractive and delicious in this simple salad. If you use red beets, assemble the salad just before serving — or your snowy white coconut will be shocking pink!

4 SERVINGS

    2 cups very finely shredded, peeled beets
1½ tablespoons virgin olive oil
    1 teaspoon mustard seeds
    1 tablespoon honey or maple syrup
    2 navel oranges
    3 tablespoons grated fresh or frozen coconut
    1 tablespoon chopped cilantro or fresh mint

Place the beets in a mixing bowl. Heat the oil in a saucepan over moderate heat. Add the mustard seeds, partially cover, and fry until the seeds turn gray and pop. Remove the pan from the heat; stir in the honey and pour over the beets. Toss to mix.

Using a sharp paring knife, cut the peel from the oranges, removing all of the white pith. Slice the oranges crosswise into ¼-inch slices. Arrange the orange slices on individual serving plates and top with a mound of beets. Garnish with coconut and fresh herbs. (A good alternate garnish is one apple, finely shredded, tossed with a splash of lime juice.)

Wilted Cabbage with Dill Yogurt

Use any type of locally grown seasonal cabbage, from tight- to loose-headed varieties. I make this salad year-round using selections such as pale-green spring cabbage, curly-leaf savoy, ornamental red winter cabbage, kale, and crinkled bok choy. The barely wilted cabbage is folded into yogurt seasoned with toasted caraway and coriander seeds, serrano chili, and fresh dill. Though this salad takes just minutes to assemble, the flavors are rich and deep.

6 SERVINGS

½ teaspoon caraway seeds
½ tablespoon coriander seeds
2½ cups finely shredded cabbage
1 fresh serrano chili, seeded and minced
1 tablespoon fresh dill
1 cup plain nonfat yogurt, whisked until smooth
Herb salt
Freshly ground pepper

Heat a nonstick wok over moderately high heat. Add the spice seeds and stir-fry until darkened a few shades. Set aside and coarsely crush with a stone mortar and pestle.

Place the cabbage and a few tablespoons of water in the wok; cook for 1 to 2 minutes. Set aside and allow to cool. Place the cabbage in a bowl and add the toasted seeds, chili pepper, dill, and yogurt. Season with salt and pepper and mix well. Serve at room temperature or chilled.

Carrot Slaw with Cashews

This salad is popular along much of India's west coast, where it is known as *gajar kachamber*. Regional cuisines in this area often feature the seasoning quartet of jalapeño chili, cilantro, lime juice, and unrefined sugar, as illustrated in this brilliant orange slaw. Though cashews are the preferred nut for this salad in Indian kitchens, I find slivered almonds or chopped peanuts equally delicious. Any leftovers are great in tossed salads or sandwiches.   6 SERVINGS

> 3 cups finely shredded carrots
> 1 quart boiling water
> ½ serrano chili, seeded and minced
> 2 tablespoons fresh lime juice
> ½ tablespoon maple syrup
> 2 tablespoons chopped cashews, pan-toasted until golden
> 1 tablespoon finely chopped cilantro

Place the carrots in a colander and pour the boiling water over them; drain well. Combine the chili, lime juice, and maple syrup in a bowl and whisk with a fork. Add the carrots, cashews, and cilantro and toss to mix. Serve at room temperature or chilled.

Cucumber and Fennel with Orange-Mint Dressing

I use raw fennel in several salads, but this is probably my favorite. Also known as *finocchio* or sweet fennel, this vegetable has a crisp anise flavor that blends well with fruits, particularly apples and pears, and with cucumber. The walnut-oil vinaigrette and a final sprinkle of toasted walnuts make a perfect finale. If you like, substitute hazelnut oil and toasted hazelnuts, or an almond combination. 6 SERVINGS

Salad
1 cucumber, peeled, halved, seeded, and diced
1 small fennel bulb, trimmed and finely slivered
1 Granny Smith apple, cored, quartered, and thinly sliced
2 teaspoons fresh lemon juice
2 tablespoons chopped walnuts, pan-toasted until golden

Vinaigrette
2 tablespoons fresh orange juice
2 tablespoons walnut oil
1 tablespoon chopped fresh mint
1 tablespoon chopped cilantro
⅛ teaspoon mild or hot paprika
Salt
Freshly ground pepper

Combine the cucumber, fennel, apple, and lemon juice in a serving bowl and gently mix.

In a small bowl, whisk the vinaigrette ingredients until emulsified. Season with salt and pepper and pour over the salad. Serve immediately or marinate, covered, in the refrigerator for 1 to 2 hours. Toss before serving and garnish with toasted nuts.

Jícama and Snow Peas with Grapes

With its vivid white, green, and purple colors, this salad is as beautiful as it is refreshing. Mexican jícama has a crisp alabaster flesh with mild radish and pear flavor overtones. Dressed in an orange, lime, and hazelnut-oil vinaigrette, it is an excellent light starter salad or in-between-course palate refresher.

In India, I make this salad with a nippy white *mooli* radish, sweet peas, and red grapes. In America, I've experimented with several varieties of radishes—early spring Cherry Belle, winter Japanese and Chinese, and maroon-brown–skinned French Long Noir de Paris, usually just picked from the garden. Use any radish in season, either alone or combined with shredded apple for a sweet twist.   6 SERVINGS

Vinaigrette
- 1½ tablespoons fresh orange juice
- 1½ tablespoons fresh lime juice
- 2 tablespoons hazelnut oil
- ½ teaspoon minced jalapeño chili
- 1 tablespoon minced fresh chervil or cilantro
- ½ tablespoon hot water
- Salt

Salad
- 1½ cups finely julienned jícama
- 15 snow peas, tailed and slivered diagonally
- 1 cup seedless grapes
- 6 radicchio or Bibb lettuce leaves
- 2 tablespoons chopped hazelnuts, pan-toasted until golden

In a mixing bowl, whisk the vinaigrette ingredients until blended. Stir in the jícama and snow peas, tossing to coat. Cover and marinate for at least 1 hour or overnight. Add the grapes and gently mix. Mound the salad in radicchio or Bibb leaf cups. Garnish with a sprinkle of nuts.

Endive, Apple, and Almond Salad

A member of the chicory family, Belgian or witloof ("white leaf") endive is the whitened shoot of chicory root, blanched in a dark environment. Its flavor is faintly bitter, similar to that of its leafy cousin, curly endive. If you haven't acquired a taste for endive, you may want to temper its flavor with shredded leaf lettuce. Offset with winter apples or pears in the cold season, and peaches or berries in the warmer season, this salad is delicate and elegant.
6 SERVINGS

    2 tablespoons fresh orange juice
    2 tablespoons fresh lime juice
  2½ tablespoons almond oil
   ⅛ teaspoon paprika
    2 tablespoons chopped cilantro
    2 heads Belgian endive, cored
  1½ cups thinly sliced tart apples
    3 tablespoons sliced almonds, pan-toasted until golden

Whisk the juices, oil, paprika, and cilantro in a small bowl. Separate the endive heads into leaves. Arrange the endive and apple slices on plates; drizzle with dressing and sprinkle with almonds.

COMPOSED SALADS

Orange-Glazed Winter Vegetable Salad

With a blaze of orange, green, and alabaster hues, this warm vegetable mélange is just the thing to serve on a cold winter's day. The vegetables are dressed in a gingered, juice-sweetened glaze and topped with toasted sesame seeds for added flavor. Try it with Basmati Rice Pilaf (page 109) or Almond-Crusted Cheese Sticks with Lime-Horseradish Mayonnaise (page 192).
6 SERVINGS

    3 medium carrots
    2 medium parsnips
    2 broccoli stalks, florets removed
    2 cups cauliflower florets
    ½ cup fresh orange juice
    2 tablespoons fresh lemon juice
    3 tablespoons maple syrup
    1 tablespoon corn oil, preferably unrefined
    ½ tablespoon grated fresh ginger
       Salt
       Freshly ground pepper
    1 tablespoon sesame seeds, pan-toasted until golden

Peel the carrots, parsnips, and broccoli stalks, then halve the vegetables lengthwise. Roll-cut these vegetables: a ½-inch diagonal slice off an end, rotate a quarter turn, cut off another diagonal slice, and so forth. Steam the roll-cut vegetables and cauliflower florets until tender-crisp, 5 to 8 minutes.

In a large nonstick skillet, cook the remaining ingredients, except the salt, pepper, and sesame seeds, over moderately high heat until thick and syrupy, about 5 minutes. Add the vegetables, season with salt and pepper, and gently toss to mix. Serve hot or at room temperature, sprinkled with sesame seeds.

Gujarati-Style Roasted Potato Salad

I came up with this devilishly good salad for a book-signing picnic hosted by the Washington D. C. Vegetarian Society. Of the four dishes I brought for this gathering of nearly fifty, this lightly dressed salad was the first to disappear—long before the more traditional potato salad! I've presented the same offerings at other gatherings with similar results. I suggest you give this potato salad a try, for anything from a backyard picnic to a brown-bag lunch. Serve with Green Pea Phyllo Purses (page 11).   8 SERVINGS

    Virgin olive-oil spray
2 **pounds new potatoes, scrubbed and cut into ½-inch dice**
1 **teaspoon paprika or chili powder**
3 **carrots, finely julienned or shredded**
¼ **cup chopped cilantro or fresh parsley**
½ **tablespoon mustard seeds**
1 **teaspoon cumin seeds**
2 **tablespoons virgin olive oil**
½ **cup vegetable broth**
2 **tablespoons fresh lemon juice**
    Salt
    Freshly ground pepper
3 **tablespoons chopped pistachio nuts for garnish**

Preheat the oven to 375°F. Spray a baking pan with olive oil and spread the potatoes in a single layer. Spray the potatoes with olive oil and sprinkle with paprika. Bake until pale gold and just cooked, 35 to 40 minutes. Scrape into a mixing bowl; fold in the carrots and cilantro.

Preheat a pan over moderately high heat. Add the mustard seeds, cover, and while gently shaking the pan, cook until they begin to sputter. Add the cumin seeds, cover, and continue to cook until the mustard seeds have popped and turned gray. Remove the pan from the heat, add the olive oil, broth, and lemon juice, and whisk to mix. Pour the vinaigrette over the salad, season with salt and pepper, and toss to mix. Garnish with pistachios.

Bengali Chef Salad with Cashew Dressing and Bitter-Melon Chips

In the spring use stir-fried asparagus slivers, julienned snow peas, or cooked, diced artichoke bottoms for this salad. In the fall and winter, try fennel slices or steamed cauliflower or broccoli florets. Bitter-melon chips, a crouton-like final garnish, make the dish typically Bengali. Green, bumpy-skinned bitter melon looks like a small zucchini with pointed ends. It has a salubrious bitter taste and is available in some supermarket produce departments and at most Asian or Indian greengrocers. Alternately, garnish the salad with Bombay Cashews (page 20).   6 MAIN-DISH SERVINGS; 8 SIDE-DISH SERVINGS

Cashew Dressing

½ cup chopped cashews, pan toasted until golden
1 tablespoon chopped fresh ginger
¼ teaspoon crushed red-pepper flakes
1 cup vegetable broth or water
⅓ cup nonfat yogurt or tomato juice
1 tablespoon light sesame oil
2 tablespoons maple syrup
3 tablespoons chopped cilantro

Salad

1 head romaine lettuce, torn into bite-size pieces
1 head Bibb lettuce, torn into bite-size pieces
2 medium carrots, finely shredded
3 small yellow or ruby beets, peeled and finely shredded
12 icicle radishes, trimmed and finely shredded
2 small zucchini, finely shredded
2 medium cucumbers, peeled, halved lengthwise, seeded, and cut into fine julienne
1 large avocado, cut into ½-inch dice
Bitter-Melon Chips (recipe follows) or Bombay Cashews (page 20) for garnish

Place the cashews in a blender or food processor; cover and pulse until powdered. Add the remaining dressing ingredients and process until smooth. Season with salt and pepper.

Distribute lettuce greens on each of six serving plates. Top each salad with even-sized mounds of each salad ingredient, moving in a clockwise circle.

Just before serving, shake the dressing and pour over each salad. Top wtih Bitter-Melon Chips.

Bitter-Melon Chips

Use these crispy chips like croutons.

> **Olive-oil spray**
> 3 **small bitter melons (about 10 ounces total), cut into ⅛-inch-thick slices and sprayed with oil**
> **Paprika or cayenne**
> **Vegetable salt**

Preheat the oven to 375°F. Spray a baking tray with olive oil. Place the bitter melon slices in a dish. Sprinkle them with paprika and salt; toss to mix. Lay the slices on the baking tray in a single layer and bake until reddish-brown and crisp, about 20 minutes.

Sautéed Spinach and Eggplant Salad

In Bengal, spinach and eggplant are most often served together as a succulent side dish called *baigan-sak*. Here the combination is transformed into one of my favorite summer salads. For a light summer lunch, add flame-toasted chapatis and fresh limeade.   4 SERVINGS

     1 **pound spinach, washed, stems removed**
  1¼ **pounds eggplant, peeled and cut lengthwise into ½-inch cubes**
     1 **teaspoon mustard seeds**
    ¼ **teaspoon yellow asafetida powder (optional)**
        Olive-oil spray or 1½ tablespoons virgin olive oil
    ½ **teaspoon ground turmeric**
    ⅛ **teaspoon cayenne**
        Salt
        Freshly ground pepper
    ½ **cup plain nonfat yogurt**
     2 **tablespoons chopped cilantro**
    ½ **tablespoon fresh lemon juice**
     2 **tablespoons slivered almonds or pine nuts, pan-toasted until golden**

Place the spinach in a large nonstick pot; cover and steam over moderately high heat until wilted, 3 to 4 minutes. Coarsely chop and set aside.

Place the eggplant cubes in a steaming basket and steam until they are three-fourths cooked, 6 to 8 minutes. Drain on paper towels.

Preheat a large nonstick sauté pan over moderately high heat. Add the mustard seeds; cover and cook until the seeds pop and turn gray. Remove the pan from the heat and add the asafetida if you are using it. Within seconds, generously spray the pan with olive oil or add plain olive oil. Stir in the eggplant. Sprinkle with turmeric and cayenne and fry, flipping the pan to turn the vegetables, until lightly browned. Add the spinach; season with salt and pepper, gently mix, and cook for about 1 minute. Again spray with olive oil.

Cool slightly or to room temperature. Before serving, fold the ingredients into the yogurt and cilantro. Transfer to a serving plate and sprinkle with lemon juice and toasted nuts.

Swiss Chard Rolls Stuffed with Quinoa and Mango

This is a terrific salad for a hot summer's eve. Serve with Bengali-Style Oven-Fried Potatoes (page 21) and Summer Berry Gratin (page 275).
4 MAIN-DISH SERVINGS; 6 SIDE-DISH SERVINGS

16 large Swiss chard leaves, stemmed

Filling

2 cups cooked quinoa
1 large mango or papaya, halved, seeded, and coarsely chopped (about 1½ cups)
1 to 2 jalapeño chilies, seeded and minced
½ tablespoon grated fresh ginger
3 tablespoons chopped cilantro
½ teaspoon salt
3 tablespoons fresh lime juice

1 teaspoon peanut oil
1 teaspoon mustard seeds
1 bay leaf
¼ teaspoon medium-grind black pepper
⅔ cup vegetable stock

Preheat the oven to 350°F. Cut off the thick center rib from each chard leaf down to the stem. Steam the leaves until bright green and flexible enough to roll. Plunge the leaves in cold water, drain, and dry on paper towels.

Place all of the filling ingredients on a large platter. Mix well and divide into sixteen portions. Place one portion of filling (scant ¼ cup) at the base of a chard leaf. Fold the base and sides over the stuffing, then roll. Place it seam side down in an ovenproof casserole. Repeat for the remaining rolls.

Heat the oil in a small pan and add the mustard seeds. Cover and cook until the seeds turn gray and pop. Remove from the heat, add the remaining ingredients, and pour over the chard rolls. Cover with foil and bake for 30 minutes. Baste twice during baking. Serve with strained pan juices.

Tropical Fruit Salad with Papaya Cream

When temperatures climb and you want a light fruit dish for late breakfast or brunch, try this salad. To round off the meal, precede with Icehouse Pear Soup with Raspberry Sorbet (page 88) and finish off with strawberry dolmas. To make the fruit dolmas, simply wrap a large strawberry and a mint leaf in a barely blanched lettuce leaf and wrap into a parcel. Easy, light, and refreshing. Unsweetened papaya concentrate is available at natural-food stores. You could also use frozen pineapple-banana concentrate.

Try this salad as a warm-weather starter with guava; in the fall, use Asian or Bosc pears.   6 SERVINGS

Papaya Cream
    1 cup plain nonfat yogurt
    3 tablespoons unsweetened papaya concentrate
    3 tablespoons fruit-sweetened apricot jam
    ½ teaspoon grated fresh ginger

Salad
    1 small pineapple, peeled, cored, and cut into ¾-inch dice
    1 papaya, peeled, seeded, and cut into ¾-inch dice
    2 guavas, peeled and cut into ½-inch dice
    1 banana, peeled and cut into 1-inch slices
       Freshly grated nutmeg
    2 tablespoons fresh lime juice
    1 tablespoon finely chopped pistachio nuts

Combine the yogurt, sweetener, and ginger in a bowl and mix well.

In a serving bowl, gently mix the fruit and sprinkle with nutmeg and lime juice. To serve, spoon into 6 individual stemmed glasses or plates. Top with dressing and chopped pistachio nuts.

BEAN, GRAIN, AND PASTA SALADS

Lemon Pasta Salad with Peppercorn-Coconut Glaze

In India this salad would be made with white rice noodles, similar to Oriental rice sticks. In this instance, brown rice Udon noodles take center stage, both for flavor and nutritional value. Several types of Udon noodles are available at natural-food stores, and any type can be used here. You can also use herb-laced wheat fettuccine or Italian angel-hair pasta. If you don't have Tellicherry pepper on hand, use seasoned or lemon pepper. If you don't have grated frozen coconut on hand, use dry coconut and increase the stock slightly. Serve with steamed broccoli or green beans.   6 TO 8 SERVINGS

Two 7-ounce packages brown rice Udon noodles or 1 pound wheat-based pasta
2 tablespoons extra-virgin olive oil
¼ cup fresh lemon juice
2 tablespoons grated lemon zest
1 teaspoon coarse grind black pepper, preferably Tellicherry
½ cup vegetable stock
½ cup grated fresh or defrosted frozen coconut
2 cups slivered snow peas
1 teaspoon salt
¼ cup chopped cilantro
¼ cup chopped fresh basil

Cook the Udon noodles or pasta in a large amount of boiling salted water according to package directions until tender but still firm to the bite. Drain. Heat 1 tablespoon of oil in a large nonstick wok or skillet. Add the lemon juice, zest, pepper, vegetable stock, and coconut and bring to a boil. Cook over

moderately high heat for 2 minutes. Add the snow peas and continue to cook for about 1 minute. Remove the pan from the heat, add the drained noodles and stir to blend ingredients. Season with salt. When the salad has cooled to room temperature, add the herbs and stir to mix. (Can be covered and refrigerated up to 4 hours before serving.) Drizzle with the remaining oil and serve garnished with cilantro sprigs.

Madras Rice-Noodle Primavera with Green Pea–Cashew Chutney

This dish is loosely based on one I was served in the household of K. Vira Swami, Chief Justice of Madras, in the early seventies. It was my first taste of rice noodles, an event that launched me into an exploration of wheat-pasta alternatives from around the world. Although the dish parallels some elements of pasta primavera, the seasonings and accompanying creamy chutney are decidedly Indian. White rice noodles have a silky texture and are slightly slippery on the palate. Both thin rice sticks and flat rice noodles are sold with Oriental foods in supermarkets.

This salad is a visual delight — a bed of snowy white noodles topped with a colorful stir-fried vegetable mélange and drizzled with a pale green chutney.   6 TO 8 SERVINGS

      8 ounces dried flat rice noodles or rice sticks
      2 tablespoons peanut oil
      1 teaspoon mustard seeds
      ½ teaspoon crushed red-pepper flakes
      ½ cup vegetable broth
      ½ cup chopped cilantro
   1½ cups diced plum tomatoes
 One 1-inch piece peeled fresh ginger, finely chopped
      1 jalapeño chili, seeded and finely chopped
      3 large bell peppers — red, orange, and yellow, seeded, deribbed,
         and cut lengthwise into thin julienne

   2 **medium zucchini, cut lengthwise into julienne**
      Salt
      Freshly ground pepper
      Green Pea–Cashew Chutney (recipe follows)

Soak the noodles in a pot of boiling water for 15 minutes; drain. Heat 1 tablespoon of oil in a nonstick wok or large skillet. Add the mustard seeds; cover and fry until the seeds turn gray and pop. Add the crushed red-pepper flakes, broth, noodles, and half of the cilantro; season with salt and pepper. Add the tomatoes. Toss to mix, cover, and keep warm over very low heat.

Heat the remaining 1 tablespoon oil in a nonstick wok over medium-high heat. Add the ginger and chili and fry for 30 seconds. Add the vegetables and stir-fry until slightly wilted, 3 to 5 minutes. Stir in the remaining cilantro and season with salt and pepper.

Place a bed of noodles on individual plates or a platter; top with vegetables and drizzle with chutney. Serve warm or at room temperature.

Green Pea–Cashew Chutney

MAKES ABOUT 1¼ CUPS

  ½ to 1 **jalapeño chili**
     One **½-inch piece peeled fresh ginger**
       1 **cup frozen petite peas, defrosted**
      ⅓ **cup raw cashews or cashew bits, pan-toasted until golden**
      ½ **cup water, or as needed**
      2 **tablespoons chopped cilantro**
        Salt
        Freshly ground pepper

With the food processor running, drop the chili and ginger through the feed tube and mince. Add the peas and nuts and process until pulverized. Add the water and cilantro and process until smooth. Season with salt and pepper; if desired, thin with additional water.

Three-Grain Vegetable Salad with Cilantro Cream

Imagine the tastes of nutty brown rice, creamy barley, and earthy wild rice together. Here, the trio of chewy grains is combined with crisp cucumber and butter-soft zucchini and folded into a sassy serrano chili–cilantro dressing. Try this easy main-course salad for a summer lunch or dinner, accompanied by a cool fruit-juice spritzer.   8 SERVINGS

Salad
1   cup long-grain brown rice
⅓   cup pearled barley
¼   cup wild rice
2½ cups vegetable stock or water
1   tablespoon virgin olive oil
2   small yellow zucchini, cut into ¼-inch dice
2   small green zucchini, cut into ¼-inch dice
2   cucumbers, peeled, seeded, and cut into ¼-inch dice
2   tablespoons fresh lemon juice

Cilantro Cream
⅓   cup tahini
¾   cup water
3   tablespoons chopped cilantro or fresh dill
1   small serrano chili, seeded and chopped
½   tablespoon light sesame oil or French olive oil
Salt
Cayenne

Place the rice, barley, and wild rice in a saucepan and rinse under running water until the water runs clear. Drain, cover with stock, and set aside for 10 minutes. Bring to a boil, cover, and reduce the heat to low. Cook until the liquid has been absorbed, about 30 minutes. Remove from the heat and let stand for 10 minutes. Fluff with a fork and cool to room temperature. (May be prepared 1 day ahead, covered, and refrigerated.)

Blanch the zucchini in boiling water for 1 to 2 minutes. Transfer to a strainer, rinse under cold water, and drain. Add the zucchini, cucumber, and lemon juice to the grains and toss to mix.

Combine the dressing ingredients in a blender or food processor and process until creamy. Just before serving, add the dressing to the salad and gently toss to mix.

Radiatore with Almond-Cream Pesto

This light pesto is really a cross between a fresh Indian chutney and an Italian pesto. It is based on a recipe passed down by my Italian grandmother. The original, a Renaissance sauce, originated in Sicily's coastal city of Trapani. With pesto, you need pasta shapes that trap the sauce, like these small "radiators" or others such as rotelle, shells, or fusilli.   6 MAIN-DISH SERVINGS

Salad
- 1   **pound radiatore pasta**
- 4   **cups small broccoli florets**
- 1   **cup ¼-inch-dice carrots**
- 1   **red bell pepper, seeded, deribbed, and cut in long slivers**
- 1   **cup fresh or frozen corn kernels**
- 1   **cup slivered snow peas or frozen peas, defrosted**
      Olive-oil spray

Pesto
- ⅔   **cup chopped almonds, pan-toasted until golden**
- ½   **cup fresh basil leaves**
- ½   **cup cilantro leaves**
- 1   **jalapeño chili, seeded and chopped**
- 1   **cup skim milk**
- ⅓   **cup part-skim ricotta cheese or 3 large tomatoes, peeled, seeded, and chopped**
      Salt
      Freshly ground pepper

Cook the pasta in a large pot of boiling water until just tender, 10 to 12 minutes. After 5 minutes of cooking time, add the broccoli and carrot. After 8 minutes, add the bell pepper and corn. Add the snow peas in the last 30 seconds of cooking. Ladle out ½ cup cooking liquid; set aside. Remove the pan from the heat. Add the defrosted peas if you're using them, and drain the pasta and vegetables. Transfer to a bowl, and, while warm, spray with olive oil.

To make the pesto, grind the almonds in a food processor. Add the remaining ingredients and the reserved cooking liquid and process until smooth. Pour the pesto over the hot pasta and toss to mix. Season with salt and pepper, and spray again with olive oil. Serve warm or at room temperature.

Sweet White Runner Bean Salad with Peanuts

Sweet White Runners are big, old-world lima beans that fell out of popularity in this country about seventy years ago. They have been resurrected recently and are available at gourmet and natural-food stores and through the mail-order sources listed in the Appendix. The beans have a creamy texture with chestnut flavor overtones. You can substitute supermarket or health-food store limas, but you'll have to increase the cooking time slightly.

In this recipe the beans are treated with Gujarati flair, mixed into a creamy peanut–and–mustard seed dressing. For a fall or winter main-course salad, I serve the beans with an assortment of steamed winter vegetables such as cubed beets, broccoli and cauliflower florets, and yams or sweet potatoes. It's as colorful as it is delicious.   6 SERVINGS

Salad
½ pound Sweet White Runners or baby lima beans, soaked overnight and drained
4 cups water
3 tomatoes, seeded and chopped
⅔ cup diced celery
¼ cup pitted black olives, preferably oil-cured or Kalamata

Dressing

    1 teaspoon mustard seeds
   ¼ teaspoon crushed red-pepper flakes
    3 tablespoons dry-roasted chopped peanuts
    3 tablespoons fresh lemon juice
    3 tablespoons creamy peanut butter
   ⅔ cup water or vegetable stock
       Salt
       Freshly ground pepper
    2 tablespoons chopped cilantro for garnish
    2 tablespoons chopped fresh basil for garnish

Place the drained, soaked beans and water in a saucepan and bring to a boil. Cover, reduce heat to low, and gently boil until the beans are tender, 45 to 75 minutes. Drain and cool slightly. Combine the beans with the tomato, celery, and olives in a large bowl.

To make the dressing, heat a saucepan over moderate heat. When hot, add the mustard seeds. Cover and cook until they sputter and pop. Remove the pan from the heat. After it has cooled slightly, sprinkle in the pepper flakes. Add the peanuts, lemon juice, peanut butter, and water and whisk until the ingredients are well blended. Pour half of the dressing over the salad and toss to mix. (May be prepared up to 1 day ahead.)

At serving time, season the salad with salt and pepper. Mound the beans on individual serving plates, and if desired, surround with seasonal steamed vegetables. Drizzle the salad and vegetables with the remaining dressing and garnish with herbs.

Black Bean Salad with Three Roasted Peppers

In India, I would use whole *urad* beans and bonnet-shaped green bell peppers for this dish. Here, I use black beans (also known as turtle beans) and four different colors (representing varying degrees of ripening) of bell peppers — green, red, orange, and yellow. You can use supermarket Cuban black beans or natural-food store organic black beans, Swedish brown beans, or Anazaki beans. The finished salad is a brilliant mélange of flavors and colors.

6 SERVINGS

Salad

1	pound black (turtle) beans, soaked overnight and drained
two	¼-inch-thick slices peeled fresh ginger
1	bay leaf
5	cups water
	Olive-oil spray
2 *each*:	large green, red, orange, and yellow bell pepper
1	small avocado
½	tablespoon fresh lime juice
2	ripe salad tomatoes, peeled, seeded, and chopped
1	pound green beans, trimmed and steamed until tender

Dressing

1	teaspoon cumin seeds
1	teaspoon coriander seeds, crushed
2	tablespoons fresh lime juice
1	teaspoon grated lime zest
3	tablespoons chopped cilantro
¼	teaspoon herb salt
¾	cup tomato-vegetable juice or water
1	roasted pepper from Salad ingredients
1 to 2	tablespoons virgin olive oil

Place the drained beans, ginger, bay leaf, and water in a saucepan and bring to a boil. Cover, reduce the heat to low, and gently boil until the beans are tender, 45 to 75 minutes. Drain the beans and cool them in clear water. Drain again, transfer to a bowl, and spray the beans with olive oil. Gently mix with your hands and set aside, covered. (May be prepared 1 or 2 days in advance, covered, and refrigerated.)

Individually roast the peppers over open heat until they are evenly charred. Place them in a covered bowl to steam for 10 minutes, then scrape off the charred skins with a knife. Slit the peppers open; seed and devein them, and cut them into long slivers.

To make the dressing, roast the cumin and coriander seeds in a small pan over moderate heat until they darken a few shades. Place the seeds, the remaining dressing ingredients, and one color of roasted pepper in a blender and process until creamy.

Just before serving, peel, seed, and dice the avocado; sprinkle with lime juice. Pour one-third of the dressing over the beans and gently mix. On individual serving plates or a platter, arrange the black beans, peppers, tomatoes, green beans, and avocado. Top with the remaining dressing and drizzle with olive oil.

Scarlet Runner Bean and Potato Salad

Scarlet Runners, about the size of smallish, plump lima beans, might have been a favorite in an old-fashioned Victorian garden. They are striking in appearance—a scarlet purple-brown base color with streaks of black jetting out from the stem ends. This old-world bean is named for the vividly hued flower that grows on its ground-hugging "runner" vine. It is available at gourmet and natural-food stores and through the mail-order sources listed in the Appendix. If you don't have some on hand, use supermarket dried fava or Roman beans. An entirely different summer option is to skip the dried beans entirely and use just-picked green beans or broad, flat Romano beans.

For a summer meal, accompany the salad with warm whole-wheat tortillas and a tossed green salad. In colder months, try it with Gingered Tomato Broth with Pappadam Noodles (page 82) or Peanut Soup with Okra Croutons (page 90). 6 MAIN-DISH SERVINGS

Salad

- ½ pound Scarlet Runner or fava beans, soaked overnight and drained, or 1 pound fresh green beans, cut into ½-inch pieces and steamed
- 4 cups water
- 1 pound new potatoes (12 to 14 small), quartered
  Olive-oil spray
- 1 tablespoon fresh lemon juice
- 8 plum tomatoes, peeled, seeded and diced
- 1 firm ripe avocado

Vinaigrette

- 1 teaspoon cumin seeds
- 1 teaspoon coriander seeds
- 1 jalapeño chili, seeded and chopped
- ¼ teaspoon paprika
- 2 tablespoons chopped fresh mint
- ¼ cup chopped cilantro
- ½ teaspoon salt
- 2 tablespoons fresh orange juice
- 2 tablespoons fresh lime juice
- ½ teaspoon grated orange zest
- ½ teaspoon grated lime zest
- 2 tablespoons light olive oil

Place the beans and water in a saucepan and bring to a boil. Cover, reduce the heat to low, and gently boil until tender, 45 to 90 minutes. Cool in the cooking water, then drain.

Preheat the oven to 375°F. Spray a baking tray with olive oil; spread the potatoes out in a single layer and spray again. Roast until browned. Combine the potatoes, tomatoes, and beans in a bowl and sprinkle with half of the lemon juice. Peel, pit and dice the avocado; sprinkle with the remaining lemon juice.

Dry-roast the cumin and coriander seeds in a heavy pan over moderate heat. When darkened a few shades, transfer to a blender and add the remaining vinaigrette ingredients. Process until the seeds are crushed and the vinaigrette has emulsified. Add to the salad and toss to mix. Serve on a plate garnished with the avocado.

Appaloosa Bean Salad

Appaloosas are one of those treasures of days gone by—high-quality beans with a deep flavor and art deco appearance. The smallish, pinto-shaped beans are speckled white and purple-brown and are grown in the Palouse area of the American Northwest that also gave the similarly speckled horse its name. They can be used in any dish that calls for pinto or red beans and are available at gourmet and natural-food stores and through the mail-order sources listed in the Appendix.

Here, cooked Appaloosas, corn, and broccoli are dressed in a smoky roasted-pepper dressing, topping a bed of red and green leaf lettuce. Serve with one or two seasonal steamed vegetables. 6 SERVINGS

⅔	cup Appaloosa beans or black-eyed peas, soaked overnight and drained
1	jalapeño chili, seeded
One	¼-inch-thick slice peeled fresh ginger
4	cups water
2	roasted red bell peppers (see page 288)
1⅓	cups plain nonfat yogurt
1	tablespoon peanut oil
1	teaspoon mustard seeds
2	tablespoons fresh lime juice
2	tablespoons chopped cilantro
	Salt
	Freshly ground pepper
1	small head red leaf lettuce
1	small head green leaf lettuce
5	cups small broccoli florets, steamed
1½	cups corn kernels, steamed

Place the soaked beans, chili, ginger, and water in a saucepan and bring to a boil. Cover, reduce the heat to low, and gently boil until the beans are tender, 45 to 90 minutes. Cool the beans in the cooking liquid; drain. (May be prepared up to 2 days before use.)

Combine the roasted pepper and yogurt in a blender and process until smooth. Set the dressing aside.

Heat the oil in a saucepan. When hot, drop in the mustard seeds; cover and fry until the seeds pop and turn gray. Remove from the heat and stir in the beans, lime juice, and cilantro. Season with salt and pepper. Wash the lettuce leaves, trim the bases, and pat dry.

To assemble, fan alternately colored whole lettuce leaves from the center of each serving plate. Spoon the bean salad into the center of the lettuce. Arrange the broccoli and corn around the beans. Pour about ⅓ cup of dressing over each salad.

Soups

Soups, like salads, are everyday foods. In India, *dal*, or legume soup, represents the main body of daily lunch fare, and the variations are endless. *Dal* can be an herb-infused legume broth, a creamy bisque, a vegetable-thickened pureed soup, or a chunky bean-and-vegetable soup. Homemade soups are versatile and suggest a wealth of variations. Served hot, they help us to tolerate the biting cold of winter. Served chilled, there's nothing quite so refreshing on a summer scorcher. The techniques that follow will help you come up with fuller, more aromatic soups that easily rival their richer originals.

This soup collection focuses on "quick-and-easy" and low-fat recipes. Though often Indian-inspired, the recipes also borrow ingredients and seasonings from other classic cuisines. The soups are divided into sections focusing on Stocks and Broths, Pureed Soups, and Light Soups.

INGREDIENTS

To make an outstanding soup, one needs high-quality ingredients. As far as possible, all vegetables and fruits should be used close to harvesting time. This is especially true of tomatoes, corn, berries, and peaches. Avocados, on the other hand, are best picked and purchased slightly underripe, because ripe ones tend to bruise easily. I find that dark green California Haas avocados are

consistently of better quality than large Florida avocados, which are often flawed beneath a flawless skin. If you have access to organic produce, I strongly recommend it for purity and quality. You will marvel at its rich flavor.

A gourmet or natural-food store will generally stock a good variety of unrefined, cold-pressed oils. Their flavors are much more vibrant, alive, and intense than their processed counterparts. This means a little oil goes a long way in the flavor department. Don't take my word for it. Buy a small bottle of a few varieties mentioned in the soup recipes and taste the difference in flavor for yourself. Keep opened bottles refrigerated or store them in a cool, dark place. For those times when you don't have homemade vegetable stock on hand, or need small quantities, I recommend Vogue Very Veggie Soup base. It's a convenient, organic powder, available in natural-food stores.

TECHNIQUES

Since the creamy and pureed soups in this book are thickened with vegetables instead of cream or *roux,* you'll frequently need to pass ingredients through a fine-mesh sieve to remove roughage. If you're cooking in quantity, a large cone-shaped *chinois* is the best tool for the job. In home kitchens, all you need is a fine-mesh steel or plastic sieve.

When making a soup in quantity, the food processor is a great time saver for preparing sliced, julienned, shredded, or chopped vegetables.

CHILLED SOUPS

If you've never made cold soups, or have tried them only in restaurants as a first course, surprise yourself and make one for lunch or dinner. Like frozen *granités,* they are pleasant palate cleansers between courses of a formal meal. I have yet to experience a group of guests that has not raved about Icehouse Pear Soup with Raspberry Sorbet (page 88). Keep in mind that chilling mutes the taste of salt and seasonings. After chilling, just before serving, readjust the seasonings to balance the flavors.

STOCKS AND BROTHS

Summer Vegetable Stock

The presence of fresh curry leaves will give this stock a distinctively Indian flavor. Although virtually unknown in Europe and America, curry leaf is one of the most important flavorings in Indian cuisine. Its passionate lemon-pepper vibrancy adds character to a host of soups, vegetable dishes, and legume stews. I am hopeful that curry leaf will gain recognition in the nineties, much as lemon grass and cilantro did in the eighties. At present, it is sporadically available at Indian and Asian grocery stores. Fresh sprigs keep well for up to 6 weeks in a refrigerator. But even without them, this is a distinctive and delicious stock for all of your soup needs.   MAKES ABOUT 2 QUARTS

2   yellow squash
2   green squash
3   tomatoes
2   celery stalks
1   boiling-type potato
    Handful of string beans

1   tablespoon virgin olive oil
10 peppercorns, preferably Malabar
4   whole cloves
2   bay leaves
2   small bunches parsley, chopped
10 sprigs cilantro, chopped
5   sprigs curry leaves, if available
1   teaspoon salt
3   quarts cold water

Trim the vegetables and cut them into roughly ½-inch pieces. Heat the oil in a large stockpot over moderate heat. Stir in the spices and herbs and cook

for 2 to 3 minutes. Add the vegetables, salt, and water; bring to a boil and skim off any impurities on the surface. Reduce the heat and simmer, partially covered, for 1 hour. Strain through a fine-mesh sieve, pressing on the solids to extract as much liquid as possible. Use as is, or reduce over heat to 4 to 5 cups.

Cool, and store in the refrigerator for up to 1 week. Pour concentrated stock into ice-cube trays and freeze into cubes; use for up to 3 months.

Winter Vegetable Stock

In many Indian regional cuisines, dried legumes are added to stocks, both for nutritive value and flavor. You can use almost any legume, but bear in mind its flavor contrast with the vegetables used in the stock. For a root vegetable–based stock, one of my favorite selections is China Yellow beans, available from mail-order suppliers (see Appendix). You could also use lima beans, navy beans, or broad (fava) beans.   MAKES ABOUT 2 QUARTS

    4   celery stalks and chopped leaves
    3   medium carrots
    1   medium potato
    1   small parsnip or turnip
 1½   cups winter squash, peeled

    1   tablespoon mustard or olive oil
  ½   tablespoon coriander seeds
    1   teaspoon mustard seeds
One ¼-inch slice peeled fresh ginger
    1   bay leaf
  ¼   teaspoon dried thyme
    1   small bunch fresh parsley, chopped
  10   sprigs cilantro, chopped
  ½   cup dried China Yellow beans, navy beans, or broad beans,
        soaked overnight and drained
    1   teaspoon salt
    3   quarts cold water

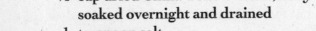

Trim the vegetables and cut them into roughly ½-inch pieces. Heat the oil in a large stockpot over moderate heat. Stir in the spices and herbs and cook for 2 to 3 minutes. Add the vegetables, beans, salt, and water. Bring to a boil and skim off any impurities on the surface. Reduce heat, and simmer, partially covered, for 1 hour. Strain through a fine-mesh sieve, pressing on the solids to extract as much liquid as possible. Use as is, or reduce over heat to 4 to 5 cups.

Cool, and store in the refrigerator for up to 1 week. Pour concentrated stock into ice-cube trays and freeze into cubes; use for up to 3 months.

Salt-Free Vegetable Stock

This is a good all-purpose salt-free stock. Use it in bean dishes and rice or grain pilafs, or as the basis of a cup of quick vegetable soup for lunch.
MAKES ABOUT 2 QUARTS

- 4 carrots, thinly sliced
- 2 celery stalks and tops, sliced
- 2 tomatoes, chopped
- 1 head butterhead lettuce, cored and sliced
- 1 small potato, peeled and diced
- 2 zucchini or yellow squash, sliced
- 6 sprigs fresh parsley
- 6 sprigs cilantro
- 1 bay leaf
- 2 sprigs fresh rosemary
- 2 sprigs fresh thyme
- ½ teaspoon black peppercorns
- 3 quarts cold water

Combine all of the ingredients in a large pot and bring to a boil. Reduce the heat and simmer for about an hour. Strain through a fine-mesh sieve, pressing on the solids to extract as much liquid as possible. Use as is, or reduce over heat to 4 to 5 cups. Cool, and store in a refrigerator, covered, for up to 1 week. Pour concentrated stock into ice-cube trays and freeze into cubes; use for up to 3 months.

Yellow Pea Broth with Tomatoes

In South India, this golden broth would be made with one of two legumes — *toovar* or *moong dal*. If you have either on hand, by all means use them to explore their flavors. This version, made with familiar and readily available yellow split peas, will surprise you with its rich flavor and aroma. Though the broth takes up to 2 hours from start to finish, it requires only a few minutes of hands-on preparation time. Delicious either hot or cold, accompanied with oven-toasted whole-wheat chapati wedges.   8 SERVINGS

⅔ cup yellow split peas
½ teaspoon ground turmeric
½ tablespoon ground coriander
8 cups water
½ tablespoon peanut oil
1 teaspoon mustard seeds
1½ pounds (3 large) ripe tomatoes, peeled, seeded, and chopped
1 tablespoon unsalted butter or corn oil
Salt
Freshly ground pepper
2 tablespoons chopped cilantro

Combine the split peas, turmeric, coriander, water, and oil in a large heavy saucepan. Bring to a boil, stirring occasionally. Reduce the heat to medium-low, partially cover, and gently boil until the split peas are soft and break down when crushed (1 to 1½ hours). Puree the mixture in a blender or food processor, in batches if necessary, until smooth and creamy.

Rinse the saucepan and heat over moderately high heat. Add the mustard seeds; cover and fry until the seeds turn gray and pop. Add the tomato and cook until it softens slightly, 2 to 3 minutes. Place a fine-mesh sieve above the pan and pour the soup through it, pressing to extract all of the broth; discard the split-pea roughage. Stir in the butter and season with salt and pepper. Serve hot or chilled, garnished with cilantro. (Can be made 2 days ahead and kept, covered, in the refrigerator. Reheat over a low flame.)

Dill-Mung Broth with Wide Zucchini Noodles

Indian mung broth is the restorative counterpart to American chicken soup, providing liquid comfort and nutrition. In India, the broth is made with dried *chilke moong dal*—split mung beans with the skins removed. For convenience, this recipe calls for whole or sprouted mung beans. Both are available in natural-food stores.   6 SERVINGS

1	cup small-tailed mung-bean sprouts or ½ cup whole mung beans
One	¼-inch slice peeled fresh ginger
1 to 2	jalapeño chilies, halved and seeded
½	tablespoon ground coriander
6	cups Summer Vegetable Stock (page 77) or water
1½	cups finely julienned carrot
1	cup diced sweet red bell pepper
2	medium zucchini, cut lengthwise into ⅛-inch slices
1	tablespoon chopped fresh dill or 1 teaspoon dried dill
½	tablespoon virgin olive oil
	Salt
	Freshly ground pepper

In a large pot, combine the sprouts or beans, ginger, chili, coriander, and stock. Bring to a boil, reduce the heat to low, and simmer, covered. (Cook the sprouts for 30 minutes and the beans for 1 hour.) Strain the broth through a fine-mesh sieve, pressing on the solids to extract as much liquid as possible.

Bring the mung broth to a gentle boil over moderate heat and add the carrot. Cover and cook for 3 minutes. Add the pepper and zucchini; cover and cook until tender, 2 to 3 minutes. Stir in the dill and oil; season with salt and pepper. Serve hot or chilled.

Gingered Tomato Broth with Pappadam Noodles

This is a cousin to Italian *risi e bisi*—rice and peas in broth. In this instance, the rice is replaced by ribbons of cut plain *pappadams* (see Glossary), available in specialty food stores and some supermarkets. You'll occasionally find other varieties of *pappadams*. If you like hot and spicy food, try black pepper–*moong pappadams* in this soup.   4 TO 6 SERVINGS

Five	5-inch plain *pappadams*
12	large spinach leaves (see Note)
1	tablespoon unsalted butter or peanut oil
1	teaspoon cumin seeds
1½	tablespoons grated fresh ginger
1	teaspoon minced jalapeño chili
¼	teaspoon ground turmeric
3	ripe tomatoes, peeled, seeded, and diced
5	cups stock, preferably Summer Vegetable Stock (page 77)
	Salt
	Freshly ground pepper
2	tablespoons chopped cilantro

Using scissors, cut the *pappadams* into 1-inch-wide noodles. Stack the spinach leaves, roll them into a tight log, and cut into ⅛-inch chiffonade.

Heat the butter in a saucepan over moderate heat. Add the cumin seeds, ginger, and chili and fry until the seeds darken slightly. Stir in the turmeric and tomato, and cook until the tomato is soft and pulpy, about 4 to 5 minutes. Add the stock and bring to a boil. Reduce the heat to low, cover, and simmer for 15 minutes. Season with salt and pepper.

Just before serving, add the noodles and spinach and simmer for no more than 1 minute. Ladle into warm soup bowls and garnish with cilantro.

Note: You can substitute 1 cup of blanched peas, snow peas, zucchini, or asparagus slivers for the spinach.

Eggplant Won Ton Soup

Inspired by New York chef Seppi Renggli's mushroom won ton soup, I came up with this earthy Indian-Asian variation. The eggplant-caviar stuffing for the won ton is richly flavored with coriander, roasted red peppers, and saffron. This soup easily forms the basis of a light meal accompanied by Pine Nut and Orange Wild Rice (page 113) and Carrot Slaw with Cashews (page 52).
8 SERVINGS

Eggplant-Caviar Filling

1	red bell pepper
1	pound eggplant
	Olive-oil spray
2	jalapeño chilies, seeded and minced
¼	cup chopped mixed fresh herbs: coriander, basil, chervil, and parsley
4 to 5	saffron threads, crushed
6	ounces extra-firm tofu, plain or herb-flavored, well drained and cut into ¼-inch dice
	Salt
	Freshly ground pepper
48	round won ton wrappers

Broth

5	cups Winter Vegetable Stock (page 78)
2	carrots, cut on the diagonal into thin slices
24	snow peas
2	yellow or red tomatoes, peeled, seeded, and diced
one	½-inch piece peeled fresh ginger, sliced into paper-thin julienne
24	large cilantro leaves for garnish
1	tablespoon extra-virgin olive oil or Curry Oil (page 293)

Place a portable stovetop grill on an electric or gas burner over moderate heat and preheat, or prepare a wood or charcoal fire in an open grill. Place the

pepper on the grill and char on all sides. Transfer to a bowl, cover, and set aside while grilling the eggplant (at least 15 minutes). Rub off the burned skins of the pepper and eggplant; seed, devein, and mince the pepper.

Cut the eggplant lengthwise into ⅜ inch-thick slices. Spray olive oil on both sides. Grill the slices over moderate to moderately low heat until golden-brown but not black. Cut into ¼-inch dice.

In a bowl, combine the pepper, eggplant, chilies, herbs, saffron, and tofu. Season lightly with salt and pepper. Place about ½ tablespoon of filling in the center of each won ton wrapper. Brush the edges of the wrapper with water and press one edge over the other, forming a semicircle. Press tightly to seal the entire edge. Repeat with the remaining wrappers.

Lay a round of parchment paper in a steamer basket. Cover it with a single layer of filled won tons and spray with olive oil. Top with a parchment round and continue to layer and spray won tons in between rounds of parchment paper. Cover the pot and steam over boiling water for 4 to 5 minuts. Set the entire pot aside, covered.

Place a soup pot over high heat. Add the vegetable stock and reduce it to 3½ cups. Reduce the heat to moderate, drop in the carrot slices, and cook for 2 to 3 minutes. Add the snow peas and tomato and cook for 1 to 2 minutes. Remove the pan from the heat; add the won ton, ginger, and cilantro. Serve in shallow bowls, allowing six won tons per person. Drizzle each serving with a few drops of oil.

PUREED SOUPS

Beet Vichyssoise

I came up with this soup for a menu featured at Philadelphia's Govinda's restaurant. It was served hot, paired with Fresh Pea Soup (see page 92), both ladled simultaneously into shallow soup bowls. This shocking pink soup, mildly seasoned with aromatic cumin and coriander, is served chilled with a swirl of yogurt. It is one of those soups that tastes best a day after it is made, by which time the flavors have had a chance to mingle and merge. Serve it chilled or hot, immediately or a day later.   6 SERVINGS

    1 **tablespoon extra-virgin olive oil**
    2 **medium baking potatoes, peeled and coarsely chopped**
    2 **medium beets, peeled and thinly sliced**
    6 **cups Winter Vegetable Stock (page 78)**
    1 **teaspoon ground coriander**
  ½ **teaspoon ground cumin**
  ½ **cup skim milk or evaporated skim milk**
      Salt
      Freshly ground pepper

  ⅓ **cup plain low-fat yogurt**
    1 **tablespoon grated lime zest**
    2 **tablespoons chopped fresh cilantro**

Heat the oil in a heavy saucepan over low heat. Add the potatoes and beets. Cover and cook slowly for 5 minutes; do not allow the vegetables to brown. Add the broth, coriander, and cumin and bring to a boil. Reduce the heat, cover, and simmer until the vegetables are very tender, 30 to 40 minutes.

Puree the ingredients with an immersion hand-blender or transfer to a food processor and blend until smooth. Strain through a fine-mesh sieve.

When cooled to room temperature, refrigerate the soup for at least 3 hours to allow the flavors to develop.

If serving chilled, whisk in the cold milk and season with salt and pepper. (If desired, reheat with milk over low heat.) In a small bowl, whisk the yogurt and zest until smooth.

Ladle into shallow soup bowls. Swirl in 1 tablespoon of lime yogurt and sprinkle with cilantro.

Chilled Avocado Bisque with Tangerine Cream

This soup was inspired by two chefs—Dean Fearing of The Mansion on Turtle Creek restaurant in Dallas and a housewife in South India. Both chefs keep their ingredients simple, focusing on crisp, fresh flavors. South Indians invariably use hot chilies, coconut oil, and fresh grated coconut in the soup. In this version I use coconut in the delicate Tangerine Cream garnish rather than the soup. Perfect for summer entertaining, this pistachio-green soup, garnished with a swirl of pale orange Tangerine Cream, is a visual feast.
6 SERVINGS

½ tablespoon avocado oil or unsalted butter
½ teaspoon coriander seeds
1 jalapeño chili, seeded and chopped
6 trimmed spinach leaves, washed and patted dry
4 cups Summer Vegetable Stock (page 77)
2 medium-size avocados, peeled, seeded, and coarsely chopped
1½ tablespoons fresh lemon juice
Salt
Freshly ground white pepper, preferably Muntok
Tangerine Cream (recipe follows)

Warm the oil or butter in a large saucepan over moderate heat. Add the coriander, jalapeño, and spinach and cook for 2 to 3 minutes. Pour in the stock

and bring to a boil. Remove from the heat and add the avocados.

Puree the mixture in a food processor or blender until it is smooth and the coriander seeds are crushed. Strain through a fine-mesh sieve. Add the lemon juice and season with salt and pepper. Cover and chill for several hours.

To serve, ladle the soup into shallow soup bowls and swirl about 2 tablespoons of Tangerine Cream into each bowl.

Tangerine Cream

MAKES ABOUT 1⅔ CUP

1¼ cups plain nonfat yogurt
¼ cup unsweetened shredded coconut
3 tablespoons fresh tangerine juice
1 teaspoon grated tangerine zest
2 tablespoons fruit-sweetened apricot jam

Drain the yogurt in a fine-mesh sieve for several hours or until reduced to ⅔ cup. Combine all of the ingredients and mix until creamy. (Can be made up to 1 day before use, covered, and refrigerated.)

Icehouse Pear Soup with Raspberry Sorbet

The North Indian spice combination of ginger, nutmeg, and cardamom lends subtle distinction to this light pear soup. It is equally delicious made with peaches or nectarines.   8 SERVINGS

  4 **large Bosc pears, peeled, cored, and sliced**
     Juice from 1 tangerine
 ½ **teaspoon grated tangerine zest**
 ½ **teaspoon chopped fresh ginger**
 ¼ **teaspoon freshly ground nutmeg**
 ⅛ **teaspoon ground cardamom**
  3 **tablespoons maple syrup**
2½ **cups buttermilk**
  8 **mint sprigs for garnish**
     Raspberry Sorbet (recipe follows)

Place the pears, tangerine juice, zest, and ginger in a food processor or blender and process until smooth. Pass through a fine-mesh sieve. Whisk into the remaining ingredients, except the mint and sorbet, and chill for at least 3 hours or overnight. Serve in shallow chilled bowls or goblets garnished with a small scoop of sorbet and a sprig of mint.

Raspberry Sorbet

8 SMALL SCOOPS

1¼ **cups frozen raspberries**
  2 **tablespoons white grape juice**
1½ **tablespoons fruit-sweetened raspberry preserves**

Combine all of the ingredients in a food processor. Pulse a few times, then process into a stiff slush. Use immediately or scoop into balls and refreeze.

Gingered Pumpkin Soup with Cranberry Chutney

Though made without cream or butter, this soup is rich and smooth. It pairs pumpkin with both cranberry juice and berries, an idea inspired by a soup recipe from gifted New York chef Michael Romano. If cranberries appear elsewhere in the menu, substitute apple juice and diced apples in the soup and chutney.   8 SERVINGS

> 1 tablespoon virgin olive oil
> 1½ pounds pumpkin (or winter squash), peeled, seeded, and cubed
> 1 baking potato, peeled and cubed
> 1 carrot, coarsely chopped
> 1 Granny Smith apple, peeled, cored, and sliced
> ¾ cup cranberries
> ½ tablespoon ground coriander
> 1 tablespoon grated fresh ginger
> 5 cups Winter Vegetable Stock (page 78) or water
> 1½ cups unsweetened cranberry-apple juice
> 1½ teaspoons salt
> Freshly ground pepper
> Freshly ground nutmeg
> Cranberry Chutney (recipe follows)

Heat the oil in a large heavy saucepan over low heat. Add the vegetables, fruits, and spices, and cook, stirring occasionally, for 15 minutes. Pour in the stock and juice. Bring to a boil, reduce the heat, and simmer until tender, 20 to 25 minutes. Remove from the heat and cool for 10 minutes.

Puree half of the vegetable mixture in a food processor. With the machine running, gradually add half of the liquid and process until smooth. Strain through a fine-mesh sieve set over another saucepan. Repeat the procedure with the remaining vegetable mixture and liquid. Stir and add more juice if a thinner consistency is desired. Reheat gently and season with salt, pepper, and nutmeg. Ladle into bowls and garnish with a spoonful of Cranberry Chutney.

Cranberry Chutney

MAKES ABOUT 1 CUP

    1 cup cranberries
    ⅔ cup diced apple
        Juice and grated zest from 1 tangerine or orange
¼ to ⅓ cup maple syrup, to taste
    2 teaspoons chopped cilantro

Cook the cranberries, zest, juice, and maple syrup in a small saucepan over moderate heat until the cranberries pop, about 5 minutes. Cool and stir in the cilantro. (For an all-apple chutney, use 1⅔ cups diced apple and simmer just until soft and chunky.)

Peanut Soup with Okra Croutons

I first tasted peanut soup in Indore, where peanuts are a staple crop. The moment I tasted it, I envisioned my own version, laced with lemon juice and cilantro. Here it is, creamy and inviting, garnished with crisp Okra Croutons. The croutons are also delicious on salads.　6 SERVINGS

    ½ tablespoon peanut oil
⅛ to ¼ teaspoon crushed red-pepper flakes
    ½ tablespoon coriander seeds
    ½ cup diced celery
    ½ cup diced carrot
    ⅔ cup diced butternut squash
    ⅔ cup diced potato
    1 cup roasted, shelled, unsalted peanuts
    6 cups vegetable stock
    1 tablespoon fresh lemon juice

Salt
Freshly ground pepper
Okra Croutons (recipe follows)

Place the oil, pepper flakes, and coriander seeds in a large nonstick saucepan and fry over moderate heat until the seeds begin to darken. Add the vegetables and peanuts, and cook for 2 to 3 minutes.

Pour in the stock and bring to a boil. Cover, reduce the heat, and simmer until the peanuts are tender, about 30 minutes. Cool slightly and puree in a food processor or blender. Pass through a fine-mesh sieve, pressing to extract as much liquid as possible.

If necessary, gently reheat. Add the lemon juice and season with salt and pepper. Serve in shallow soup bowls or a mug, garnished with crisp Okra Croutons or a sprinkle of dry-roasted chopped peanuts.

Okra Croutons

ABOUT ¾ CUP

1½	**cups thinly sliced okra**
3 to 4	**tablespoons fine cornmeal**
¼	**teaspoon ground cumin**
¼	**teaspoon cayenne**
¼	**teaspoon herb salt**
	Olive-oil spray

Preheat the oven to 375°F. Rinse the okra under running water, drain, and pat dry with paper towels. Combine the cornmeal, seasonings, salt, and okra in a bag. Seal and shake well to coat the slices with seasoned crumbs. Add sprinkles of water if necessary.

Spray a baking sheet with olive oil. Spread the okra slices in a single layer and spray them with olive oil. Bake until crisp and richly browned, spraying and stirring twice during cooking, about 30 minutes.

Fresh Pea Soup with Pistachio-Mint Cream

This soup is a snap to make, yet it always meets with raves. Rich and creamy, the pale green soup is light, low-fat, and luscious. If fresh curry leaves are available, a sprig will add a burst of lemon-pepper flavor to the soup. Without the Pistachio-Mint Cream, a cup makes an excellent light lunch. For entertaining, serve as part of a two-soup bowl, ladled simultaneously with Beet Vichyssoise (see Note).   6 SERVINGS

1½ tablespoons corn oil or virgin olive oil
1 small jalapeño chili, seeded
1 cup diced zucchini
2½ cups fresh shelled peas, chopped sugar snap peas, or frozen petite peas
1 baking potato, peeled and coarsely chopped
6 cups Summer Vegetable Stock (page 77)
½ teaspoon curry powder
   Sprig of fresh curry leaves, if available
   Salt
   Freshly ground pepper
   Pistachio-Mint Cream (optional; recipe follows)

In a large saucepan, warm the oil over low heat. Stir in the jalapeño, zucchini, peas, and potato, and without browning, slowly cook for 5 to 7 minutes. Add the stock and curry powder (and the fresh curry leaves if you are using them). Bring to a boil. Reduce the heat, cover, and simmer until the vegetables are tender.

Puree in a blender or food processor, in batches if necessary, until smooth. Strain through a fine-mesh sieve to remove roughage, and return to the saucepan.

Reheat gently over low heat and season with salt and pepper. Serve in a mug or shallow soup bowl, with or without a dollop of Pistachio-Mint Cream.

Note: If you want to serve this along with Beet Vichyssoise (page 85), fill a cup three-quarters full of vichyssoise and another cup three-quarters full with pea soup. Pour both soups into a bowl at the same time from opposite sides, and garnish with a sprig of mint.

Pistachio-Mint Cream

MAKES ABOUT ⅔ CUP

> 3 tablespoons chopped fresh mint leaves
> 3 tablespoons chopped pistachios
> 3 trimmed spinach leaves, chopped
> ½ cup plain nonfat yogurt or Neufchâtel cheese, whisked until creamy
> Sprig of mint for garnish

Combine the mint, pistachios, and spinach in a blender or food processor. Add enough cold water (2 to 4 tablespoons) to moisten the ingredients and make a smooth puree. Force through a fine-mesh sieve, pressing on the solids to extract as much liquid as possible. Just before serving, stir the mint puree into the yogurt or Neufchâtel cheese.

Gujarati-Style Corn Soup with Yellow Tomato Chutney

Made from nothing more than water, corn kernels, a bit of potato, and a Gujarati seasoning combination, this soup is the next best thing to just-picked corn on the cob. For best results, make this soup during corn season. Cold-pressed corn oil heightens the intensity of the soup, with its rich, buttery flavor overtones. It is available in gourmet and natural-food stores, and a little goes a long way. If yellow tomatoes are not available for the chutney, use red ones.   6 SERVINGS

1   tablespoon cold-pressed corn oil
1   tablespoon grated fresh ginger
1   ancho chili, soaked for 3 hours, seeded, and chopped
⅓   cup grated fresh coconut
⅔   cup peeled and diced baking potato
5½   cups water
5   ears of corn (1½ pounds), kernels cut from the cob
1   tablespoon fresh lime juice
2   tablespoons finely chopped cilantro
     Salt
     Freshly ground pepper
     Yellow Tomato Chutney (recipe follows)

Heat the oil in a soup pot over moderate heat. Add the ginger, chili, coconut, potato, and ½ cup of the water. Cover and simmer for 10 minutes. Add the remaining water and bring to a boil. Add the corn, partially cover, and simmer until the potato is tender, up to 15 minutes.

Remove from the heat and cool slightly. Blend in a food processor until very smooth, allowing the machine to run for a good 3 minutes. Pass the soup through a fine-mesh sieve, pressing on the solids to extract as much puree as possible.

If necessary, reheat gently. Just before serving, stir in the lime juice and cilantro, and season with salt and pepper. Ladle into warm soup bowls, and serve with or without a spoonful of Yellow-Tomato Chutney.

Yellow Tomato Chutney

MAKES ABOUT 1½ CUPS

> 1 pint yellow cherry tomatoes, quartered
> ½ teaspoon cumin seeds
> ½ teaspoon fennel seeds
> 1 jalapeño chili, seeded and minced
>   Herb salt
>   Freshly ground pepper
> 1 teaspoon cold-pressed corn oil

Combine all of the ingredients in a 2-cup Pyrex measuring cup. Partially cover and microwave on medium for 4 minutes. Alternately, cook in a saucepan over moderate heat, stirring occasionally, until the tomato softens into a chunky puree, 10 to 12 minutes.

LIGHT SOUPS

Asparagus Tip Soup with Jalapeño Cream

The built-in body of in-season asparagus allows this soup to stand on its own without thickeners or cream. The predominating flavor is that of asparagus, with a supporting cast of cilantro, lime, coriander, and almonds—subtle and elegant.   6 SERVINGS

    1½ pounds thin asparagus, trimmed
     2 tablespoons clarified or unsalted butter
     5 cups Summer Vegetable Stock (page 77)
     2 tablespoons chopped cilantro
    ½ teaspoon ground coriander
     1 teaspoon fresh lime juice
        Salt
        Freshly ground white pepper
     3 tablespoons sliced almonds, pan-toasted until golden
        Jalapeño Cream (recipe follows)

Cut off the tips of the asparagus and set them aside. Cut the remaining spears into 1-inch pieces. Combine the asparagus, stock, cilantro, and coriander in a saucepan and bring to a boil. Reduce the heat and simmer until the asparagus is tender, 5 to 10 minutes.

Puree in a food processor until smooth. Pour through a fine-mesh sieve, pressing on the asparagus fibers to extract as much liquid as possible. If desired, reheat gently. Stir in the lime juice and season with salt and pepper.

Cook the asparagus tips in boiling water until tender, 1 to 2 minutes. Drain and distribute the tips equally among six warm soup bowls. Add the soup and garnish with a dollop of Jalapeño Cream and a few toasted almonds.

Jalapeño Cream

MAKES ABOUT ⅓ CUP

   3 tablespoons light cream cheese
   3 tablespoons nonfat yogurt
  ½ teaspoon jalapeño chili puree (see Note) or minced jalapeños
   1 teaspoon maple syrup
   1 teaspoon fresh lime juice

Combine the ingredients in a small bowl and stir until thoroughly mixed.

Note: To make jalapeño puree, grate the tip of a large jalapeño chili across the surface of a Japanese ginger grater; avoid grating the seeds.

Iced Cucumber-Lime Soup with Mint Yogurt

This summer soup was inspired by the Indian cucumber-yogurt salad called *raita*. It is light, refreshing, and easy to make — a perfect chilled soup for the dog days of summer.   6 SERVINGS

> 2 tablespoons chopped pistachio nuts
> 2 cups plain nonfat yogurt
> ½ cup chopped fresh mint leaves
> 1 medium cucumber, peeled, seeded, and coarsely shredded
> 1 teaspoon dry-roasted crushed cumin seeds
> ½ teaspoon grated lime zest
> 2 teaspoons fresh lime juice
> Salt
> Freshly ground white pepper
> Mint sprigs for garnish

In a blender, pulse the nuts until powdered. Add ¼ cup yogurt and the mint leaves and blend until smooth. Force through a fine-mesh sieve, pressing to extract as much liquid as possible. Set aside.

Squeeze the cucumber with your hands to extract the juice, then drain on paper towels. In a bowl, combine the cucumber with the cumin seeds, zest, and juice, and stir to mix. Season with salt and pepper and chill well for at least 3 hours. Garnish with a spoonful of mint yogurt and mint sprigs.

Mulligatawny Soup with Toasted Spices and Nuts

On my first trip to Madras, a chef informed me that "there are more variations of Mulligatawny in India than sandalwood trees in the Malaya Hills." Indeed, I found countless chefs extolling the virtues of their favorite recipes and regaling me with stories of their origins. (The name itself is derived from *mullaga,* meaning "pepper," and *tanni,* meaning "broth" or "water.") This vegetable-laden version, which gets its rich flavor from cashew nuts and South Indian–style toasted spices, is an outstanding light soup.   8 SERVINGS

    1 cinnamon stick, about 3 inches long
    6 cloves
    4 cardamom pods
    1 teaspoon black peppercorns, preferably Malabar
    1 tablespoon grated fresh ginger
    2 tablespoons chopped cashews or almonds
    3 cups chopped vegetables (mixture of carrots, cauliflower,
         potatoes, zucchini, peppers, in any proportion or combination)
    6 cups vegetable stock
    ½ teaspoon curry powder

South Indian Seasoning
    1 teaspoon mustard seeds
    1 teaspoon cumin seeds
    1 tablespoon unsalted butter or olive oil
       Salt
       Freshly ground pepper
    2 tablespoons chopped cilantro

Break the cinnamon stick into pieces. Combine the cinnamon, cloves, cardamom pods, and peppercorns; tie the spices in a piece of muslin. In a soup pot, combine the spice bag, ginger, nuts, vegetables, stock, and curry powder. Bring to a boil; reduce the heat and simmer, covered, until the vegetables are tender, about 30 minutes.

Remove the spice bag, then puree the stock and vegetables in a blender or food processor. Pass the mixture through a fine-mesh sieve, pressing to extract as much liquid as possible. (Thin with additional stock if desired.) If necessary, reheat the soup gently.

For the seasoning, warm a small pan over moderate heat. Add the mustard seeds; cover and cook until they pop and turn gray. Remove the pan from the heat. Add the cumin seeds and butter and let the spices cool. Pour the spice seasoning into the soup, stirring to mix. Season with salt and pepper, and serve in soup bowls, garnished with cilantro.

Chilled Vegetable-Yogurt Soup with Fried Mustard Seeds

You can use almost any variety or combination of vegetables in this light soup. My rough formula is two parts diced, raw vegetables to three parts buttermilk. You may come up wtih a ratio you like better. The toasted-mustard-seed garnish gives the soup a pleasantly nutty flavor.   6 SERVINGS

    3   cups buttermilk
    1   jalapeño chili, seeded and slivered
    3   tomatoes, peeled, seeded, and diced
   ½   European cucumber, peeled, seeded, and diced
    1   red bell pepper, seeded, deribbed, and diced
   ⅔   cup defrosted petite peas
      Salt
      Freshly ground pepper
   ½   tablespoon mustard seeds
      Paprika
  1½   tablespoons chopped cilantro

Combine the buttermilk, chili, and vegetables in a serving bowl and stir to mix. Season with salt and pepper. Cover and chill well.

At serving time, warm a small pan over moderate heat. Add the mustard seeds; cover and cook until they pop and turn gray. Pour the seeds over the soup; sprinkle with paprika and garnish with cilantro.

Indian Ratatouille Soup with Toasted Pumpkin Seeds

Aromatic fresh ginger, toasted cumin, and briefly cooked vegetables distinguish this variation on ratatouille. This is a fix-it-fast soup, good for lunch or dinner, hot or cold.   6 SERVINGS

- 2 tablespoons olive oil, preferably French
- 1 teaspoon grated fresh ginger
- 1 celery stalk, diced
- 6 large ripe tomatoes, peeled, seeded, and chopped
- 1 medium zucchini, diced
- 1 red bell pepper, seeded, deribbed, and diced
- 5 cups vegetable stock or a blend of 2½ cups water and 2½ cups tomato-vegetable juice
- 2 tablespoons chopped cilantro
  Salt
  Cayenne
- ½ cup pumpkin seeds, pan-toasted until golden
- 1 teaspoon cumin seeds, pan-toasted until golden and crushed

Warm the oil in a heavy casserole over moderately low heat. Stir in the ginger, celery, tomato, zucchini, and bell pepper. Cook, stirring occasionally, for 10 minutes. Add the broth and simmer for 10 minutes. Stir in the cilantro and season with salt and cayenne to taste. Ladle into bowls and sprinkle with pumpkin seeds and cumin seeds.

Yellow Tomato Soup with Vegetable Salsa

This all-occasion soup is good hot or iced, especially if you have access to bumper-crop garden tomatoes. (Out-of-season, low-juice, thick-walled, card-board tomatoes just can't compare to their juicy, rich, just-picked cousins, still warm from the sun.) Because the soup is cooked for only about 15 minutes, the flavor is fresh and intense. Delicious with oven-toasted chapati wedges.

6 SERVINGS

  2 tablespoons extra-virgin olive oil
  1 poblano chili, seeded and chopped
  1 teaspoon cumin seeds
 10 medium-size ripe yellow tomatoes (about 2½ pounds), peeled, seeded, and chopped (if yellow tomatoes are unavailable, substitute red)
  5 cups vegetable stock
  2 tablespoons chopped cilantro or fresh marjoram
  1 teaspoon maple syrup
    Salt
    Freshly ground pepper
    Vegetable Salsa (recipe follows)

Place half of the oil in a large saucepan over moderate heat. When hot, add the chili and cumin seeds and fry until the seeds darken slightly. Stir in the tomato and cook for 5 minutes. Add the stock, half of the cilantro, and maple syrup and cook for another 8 to 10 minutes. Season with salt and pepper, and stir in the remaining herbs and olive oil. To serve, ladle the soup into bowls and top each serving with a spoonful of Vegetable Salsa.

Vegetable Salsa

MAKES ABOUT 1¼ CUPS

½ cup peeled, seeded, and diced cucumber
¼ cup diced red bell pepper
¼ cup diced yellow bell pepper
½ cup peeled and diced jícama
1 teaspoon fresh lime juice
1 teaspoon grated fresh ginger
½ tablespoon extra-virgin olive oil
 Salt
 Freshly ground pepper

Mix all of the ingredients except the salt and pepper in a small bowl. (Can be made 8 hours ahead, covered, and stored in the refrigerator; drain before using.) Season with salt and pepper before serving.

Vegetable Bouillabaisse with Cilantro Pistou

This Bengali-style soup is reminiscent of its Provençal cousin. A trio of aromatics — saffron, mustard, and fennel seeds — infuse the vegetables with flavor. Cold-pressed mustard oil, available in gourmet and natural-food stores, gives the broth an added nose-tingling warmth. Delicious with or without a spoonful of Cilantro Pistou.   8 SERVINGS

1½ pounds new red or white potatoes
½ tablespoon mustard seeds
1 teaspoon fennel seeds
4 teaspoons mustard oil
¼ teaspoon saffron threads
6 cups Salt-Free Vegetable Stock (page 79) or water
⅓ cup chopped cilantro
    Salt
    Freshly ground pepper
1 pound zucchini, cut into ½-inch cubes
6 ounces snow peas, trimmed
    Virgin olive-oil spray
    Cilantro Pistou (recipe follows)

If the skins are more than paper-thin, peel the potatoes. Cut them into finger-sized pieces. Heat a large heavy-bottomed casserole over moderate heat. Add the mustard seeds; cover and cook until they pop and turn gray. Add the fennel seeds and mustard oil and fry until the fennel seeds darken slightly. Add the potatoes, saffron, stock, and half of the cilantro. Season with salt and pepper and bring to a gentle boil. Reduce the heat to low, cover, and cook for 10 minutes.

Add the zucchini, cover, and cook for about 20 minutes more, or until the vegetables are tender. Three or four minutes before serving, add the snow peas and cook until they are barely wilted and still bright green.

At serving time, stir in the remaining cilantro. Ladle into serving dishes, and if desired, spray with olive oil for added flavor. Garnish the soup with a spoon of Cilantro Pistou or serve it on the side. (The pistou is also delicious spread on toasted chapati or pita wedges.)

Cilantro Pistou

MAKES ABOUT ¾ CUP

    ½ **cup blanched almonds**
    1 **jalapeño chili, seeded and chopped**
  1½ **cups loosely packed cilantro leaves**
    ½ **cup water**
    1 **teaspoon virgin olive oil**
      Salt
      Freshly ground pepper

Place the nuts in a blender or food processor and pulse until finely chopped. Add the remaining ingredients and process until pureed, scraping down the sides of the jar or work bowl when necessary. (The pistou can be made 2 days ahead and kept refrigerated. Thin with water as necessary and serve at room temperature.)

Golden Gazpacho with Avocado Cream

On a hot summer day, there are few soups easier to make or more refreshing to eat than gazpacho. This version, made with yellow tomatoes, which are more sweet than acidic, is a feast for both the eye and the palate.

6 GENEROUS SERVINGS

2 pounds ripe yellow tomatoes, peeled, seeded, and coarsely chopped (about 4 cups)

1½ cups coarsely chopped yellow or orange bell pepper

1 cup coarsely chopped peeled and seeded English cucumber

1 jalapeño chili, seeded and chopped

1 teaspoon coriander seeds, pan-toasted until golden

2 tablespoons fresh lemon juice

2 tablespoons extra-virgin olive oil

1 tablespoon chopped cilantro

Salt

Freshly ground pepper

Avocado Cream (recipe follows)

Combine the ingredients except the Avocado Cream in a bowl. Place half the mixture in a food processor and puree. Add the other half and pulse until the vegetables are diced. Season with salt and pepper. Chill for at least 4 hours or overnight. Serve in iced goblets, with or without Avocado Cream.

Avocado Cream

MAKES ABOUT ⅔ CUP

½ avocado

½ tablespoon fresh lemon juice

½ cup white grape juice

Seed the avocado and scrape the flesh into a blender. Add the lemon and grape juice and puree until creamy.

Entrees

A MULTITUDE OF GRAINS

Rice

Rice is the most widely consumed grain in the world, a daily staple for more than half of the world's population. Of the thousands of strains cultivated, long-grain Indian basmati is regarded by connoisseurs as the finest long-grain rice.

If you haven't tried basmati rice yet, you're in for a real treat. The long, pointed grains are delicately perfumed. They cook up light and fluffy, with almost perfect shape retention.

Most of America's basmati is grown in California and Texas and is marketed as Calmati or Texmati rice. Arkansas organic basmati rice is hard to find outside the Southeast, though it is available through the mail-order sources listed in the Appendix. Brown basmati rice, available in gourmet and natural-food stores, has a different character than its white relative — robust, chewy, and nutty. Try several types of rice to discover your personal favorites.

A Word About Whole Grains

The grains that are gaining popularity today have been prominent staples in Mediterranean, Far Eastern, and Central and South American diets for mil-

lennia: millet, quinoa, barley, teff, buckwheat, and several strains of brown rice. Most of these grains appear somewhere in this recipe collection.

Nutritionists offer us myriad reasons to eat whole grains. As complex carbohydrates, they are excellent sources of essential vitamins, minerals, and fiber. They are essential to good nutrition. But an equally compelling reason is taste. The flavor of whole grains is unique, earthy, satisfying, exciting, and varied. In the last decade, whole-grain dishes have begun turning up in some of the nation's most fashionable restaurants. We are only beginning to uncover the potential and flavors of these grains. Two dishes that follow have been inspired by the creations of noted New York chefs Bert Greene and Michael Romano.

A Word About Quality

Several companies listed in the Appendix are marketing whole grains of uncompromising quality. Wholesome integrity is their credo. I place as much emphasis on the source of ingredients as I do on recipe development and kitchen technique. Outstanding cuisine relies on freshness, purity, and cleanliness.

All of the grains in these recipes are available at gourmet or natural-food stores. A few brand names and mail-order grain sources are listed in the Appendix. If you are unfamiliar with them, give them a try—they may open new doors.

A MULTITUDE OF GRAINS

Basmati Rice Pilaf

Instead of writing several rice recipes with minor variations, I've included a list of suggested seasonings in this recipe. Experiment with them, singly or in combination.   ABOUT SIX ½-CUP SERVINGS

    1¼ cups basmati rice
     ½ tablespoon butter or virgin olive oil
    2¼ cups water or vegetable stock
     ¼ teaspoon salt (optional)

Suggested Seasonings (use up to three in any combination)
    6 to 8 cloves; 1 cinnamon stick; 4 to 6 cardamom pods; 6 to 8
    peppercorns; 1 teaspoon cumin, mustard, sesame, or coriander seeds,
    pan-toasted until golden; a few sprigs of cilantro, fresh curry leaves,
    mint, or Italian parsley; 2 bay leaves; a strip of orange zest and a slice
    of fresh ginger; a strip of lemon or lime zest with 1 jalapeño chili;
    ¼ cup grated coconut and a pinch of dried crushed chilies.

If using Indian basmati, sort it on a plate to remove any foreign matter. Rinse under running water in a strainer. Soak in water or stock for 10 minutes to relax the grains; drain and reserve liquid. If using American basmati, follow package instructions.

Place the rice and butter in a heavy-bottomed saucepan over moderate heat. Fry the rice until the grains become slightly translucent, 2 to 3 minutes. Add the reserved liquid and salt if desired. Bring to a boil, stirring once or twice. Reduce the heat to very low, add one or two suggested seasonings if desired, and cover. Cook until the rice is tender and the liquid has been absorbed, 15 to 20 minutes (30 to 40 minutes for brown rice). Remove the pan from the heat and set aside for 5 to 10 minutes. Uncover and fluff with a fork.

Creamy Basmati Rice Pilaf with Broiled Tomatoes

This dish can be served at room temperature or chilled. It is as creamy as a savory rice pudding but lighter and lower in fat. It makes an excellent lunch meal, accompanied by a green salad.   6 SERVINGS

1½ **cups white or brown basmati rice**
 8 **cups water**
 ½ **tablespoon mustard seeds**
1½ **cups plain nonfat yogurt**
 1 **teaspoon fresh ginger puree (grated on a Japanese ginger grater) or ¼ teaspoon ground ginger**
 2 **tablespoons minced fresh herbs: cilantro, parsley, chervil, or mint**
    Herb salt
    Freshly ground pepper
    Broiled Tomatoes (recipe follows)

If white basmati rice is used, clean, rinse, and soak the rice in water for 10 minutes, then drain. Bring the water to a boil in a saucepan. Stir in the rice and gently boil until tender (10 to 12 minutes for white rice and about 20 to 25 minutes for brown rice). Pour the rice into a strainer, drain, and transfer to a bowl to cool.

Place the mustard seeds in a saucepan; cover and toast over moderate heat, shaking the pan, until the seeds pop and turn gray. Pour the toasted seeds into the rice; add the yogurt, ginger, and herbs, and stir to mix. Season with salt and pepper. Chill for at least 2 hours or serve at room temperature.

Spoon onto plates and serve with Broiled Tomatoes or Slow-Baked Tomatoes (page 240). (Keeps well for 1 to 2 days, refrigerated and covered.)

Broiled Tomatoes

6 SERVINGS

   3 firm, large tomatoes
  ⅓ cup buttermilk
  ¼ cup grated coconut
     Herb salt
     Freshly ground pepper
     Olive-oil spray (optional)

Preheat the oven to 400°F. Halve the tomatoes and remove the seeds. Drizzle about 1 tablespoon of buttermilk on each tomato half. Sprinkle with coconut, herb salt, and pepper. Bake on a nonstick cookie sheet for 12 to 15 minutes, then broil until topping is golden-brown. If desired, spray finished tomatoes with olive oil for flavor.

Pecan Rice and Summer Squash Tian

A *tian* is a baked vegetable gratin from Provence, traditionally made in a red-glazed earthenware pot, also known as a *tian*. In this grain-and-vegetable *tian*, a pecan-studded pilaf serves as the crust for a Delhi-style sauté of summer squash and tomatoes. As the dish bakes, the sweet vegetable juices caramelize into the crusty rice.

You can use any type of summer squash—patty pan, crookneck, or yellow or green zucchini.

Pecan rice, an increasingly popular grain grown in the Southeast, is available in many grocery and natural-food stores. It has a flavor redolent of its namesake, pecans, and is quite delicious. If it is not available, use Texmati, Calmati, basmati, or your favorite long-grain rice.

Depending on the season, finish the meal with a creamy hot or cold soup.   6 SERVINGS

2⅔ cups vegetable stock
1½ cups pecan or other long-grain rice
  3 tablespoons chopped pecans, pan-toasted until golden
     Olive-oil spray
  ½ tablespoon cumin seeds
  1 tablespoon coriander seeds
  ½ teaspoon ground turmeric
  3 tablespoons water
  2 tomatoes, peeled, seeded, and chopped
  1 pound summer squash, sliced
     Salt
     Freshly ground pepper
  2 tablespoons chopped cilantro or fresh parsley
  ¼ cup buttermilk or evaporated skim milk
  3 tablespoons Neufchâtel cheese

In a medium saucepan, bring the broth to a boil. Stir in the rice, cover, and reduce the heat to low. Simmer the rice for 15 to 20 minutes (about 40 minutes for brown rice), or until the broth has been absorbed and the rice is tender. Fold in 2 tablespoons of nuts. Spray a *tian*, quiche dish, or baking sheet with olive oil and press the rice mixture into a 12-inch circle or square.

Combine the remaining nuts, cumin and coriander seeds, turmeric, and water in a blender and process until smooth. Pour the seasoning mixture into a large, heavy, nonstick frying pan and place it over moderate heat. Stir in the tomato and cook for 4 to 5 minutes. Add the squash, reduce the heat slightly, and stir-fry for about 15 minutes, or until the vegetables are tender. If the liquid from the squash cooks off, add sprinkles of water; do not allow the vegetables to brown.

Preheat the oven to 375°F. Season the vegetables with salt and pepper and fold in the cilantro. Spoon the vegetables over the rice, drizzle with buttermilk, and dot with pieces of cheese. Bake until the top browns, 20 to 25 minutes. Let stand for 5 to 10 minutes before cutting into wedges. For additional flavor, spray the *tian* with olive oil just before serving.

Pine Nut and Orange Wild Rice

I created this pilaf in 1989 for a dinner at Govinda's restaurant celebrating "The Book and the Cook," hosted by the city of Philadelphia. The rice was served with a sauté of mixed baby vegetables and Cheese Fricadelle with Two Chutneys (page 193), and generated recipe requests from many of the journalists and food professionals present.   6 SERVINGS

3⅓	cups water
½	cup wild rice
1	cup basmati, Calmati, or Texmati rice
1	tablespoon extra-virgin olive oil
⅓	cup dried currants
¼	cup pine nuts, pan-toasted until golden
2	tablespoons chopped fresh Italian parsley
1	tablespoon grated orange zest
2	tablespoons fresh orange juice
1	teaspoon salt
	Freshly ground pepper
1 to 2	serrano chilies, seeded and finely slivered
	Italian parsley sprigs for garnish

Bring 1⅔ cups of water to a boil in a saucepan. Stir in the wild rice; reduce the heat, cover, and simmer until the grains are tender, about 25 minutes. Do not allow the grains to split. Transfer the rice to a sieve and drain off any excess liquid.

If basmati rice is used, clean, rinse, and soak in water for 10 minutes. Drain the rice in a strainer. Heat the oil in a saucepan over moderate heat. Add the rice, currants, pine nuts, parsley, and orange zest. Cook for 3 to 4 minutes, stirring occasionally. Add the remaining 1⅔ cups water to the saucepan and bring to a boil. Reduce the heat, cover, and cook for about 15 minutes. Remove from the heat and set aside for 10 minutes. Fluff the rice with a fork. Add the orange juice, wild rice, salt, pepper, and chilies and gently mix. Serve hot, garnished with parsley sprigs.

Brown Basmati Moussaka

Moussaka, a comforting Greek vegetable casserole, is the inspiration for this layered brown rice–and–eggplant dish. In this variation, chewy brown basmati pilaf is layered with butter-soft sliced eggplant. Instead of a traditional rich custard topping, this dish is finished with a light Indian-inspired sauce.
8 SERVINGS

>   2   medium eggplants (2 pounds), cut crosswise into ½-inch slices
>   Olive-oil spray

Pilaf
>   ½   tablespoon mustard seeds
>   2   tomatoes, peeled, seeded, and diced
>   ½   teaspoon ground cinnamon
>   ⅓   cup chopped cilantro or fresh parsley
>   2¼ cups water
>   1½ cups diced red bell pepper
>   1⅓ cups long-grain brown rice, preferably basmati

Sauce
>   3   tablespoons all-purpose flour or sifted garbanzo flour
>   ¼   teaspoon salt
>   ¼   teaspoon freshly ground pepper
>   ½   cup evaporated skim milk or plain nonfat yogurt
>   1½ cups water
>   ½   teaspoon curry powder
>   3   tablespoons sesame seeds

Preheat the oven to 375°F. Place the eggplant slices on nonstick baking sheets and spray them with olive oil. Cover with foil and bake for 15 minutes. Turn the slices over and bake, uncovered, until tender and lightly browned, about 15 minutes.

To make the pilaf, place a heavy-bottomed nonstick saucepan over moderate heat. Add the mustard seeds; cover. Shaking the pan, fry until the seeds sputter and pop. Stir in the tomato, cinnamon, and half the cilantro and cook

for 5 minutes. Add the water, bell pepper, and rice; stir and bring to a boil. Reduce the heat to low, cover, and simmer until the liquid has been absorbed, about 40 minutes. Remove from the heat and fluff after 5 minutes.

To make the sauce, combine the flour, salt, and pepper in a saucepan. Add the evaporated milk and whisk until smooth; stir in the water. Whisking constantly, cook over moderately high heat until the sauce thickens. Off the heat, stir in the curry powder and 1 tablespoon of the sesame seeds.

To assemble the moussaka, spray a shallow casserole or 13 × 9 × 2½-inch nonstick baking pan with olive oil. Spread one-third of the eggplant slices on the bottom of the pan; top with one-third of the rice and one-third of the sauce. Repeat the process two more times, finishing off with sauce. Sprinkle with the remaining cilantro and sesame seeds and spray with olive oil.

Bake, uncovered, in a 375°F oven until the top is golden-brown, 30 to 40 minutes. Set aside for 10 to 15 minutes before serving.

Garden Vegetable–Semolina Pilaf

Uppma, a succulent semolina pilaf, is one of India's hidden culinary treasures. Its texture ranges from light and fluffy to thick and polenta-like. Because only the latter type holds well in warming trays, it is the only type available in most restaurants. This vegetable-laden version is the former type—fluffy, moist, and quite irresistible. This pilaf makes a perfect workday one-pot meal.
6 SERVINGS

   1 cup fine-grained semolina (pasta flour)
  ½ tablespoon mustard seeds
1½ tablespoons melted butter or virgin olive oil
   2 red bell peppers, seeded, deribbed, and cut into thin strips
   3 small zucchini, cut into 2 × ¼-inch strips
  20 snow peas, tailed and cut in half lengthwise
  ½ teaspoon ground turmeric
   1 teaspoon salt
   2 cups water
   2 tablespoons chopped cilantro
   2 tablespoons fresh lime juice

Place the semolina in a large heavy frying pan over moderate heat. Stir-fry for 6 to 8 minutes, or until the grains darken a few shades. Transfer to a Pyrex measuring cup and set aside.

Place the mustard seeds in a large nonstick casserole over moderately high heat. Cover and fry until the seeds crackle and pop. Remove the pan from the heat; add ½ tablespoon butter and the vegetables. Stir-fry until the vegetables are tender-crisp, 4 to 5 minutes.

Add the turmeric, salt, and water and bring to a boil. While stirring, slowly sprinkle in the semolina. Reduce the heat to low, and stirring occasionally, cook until the semolina absorbs the liquid and the texture is light and fluffy. Fold in the cilantro. Serve on warm plates, drizzled with the remaining butter and lime juice.

Millet Pilaf in Peppers

Millet is an inviting grain with a mild, nutty taste, distinctive without being unusual. To bring out its flavor, toast the tiny yellow grains before use. Here, millet, corn, and tomatoes are simmered in a cilantro-lime stock and transformed into a fluffy, light pilaf. It is spooned into blanched peppers, topped with Swiss cheese and pumpkin seeds, and baked until the cheese is golden and bubbly. Serve with a green salad.   6 SERVINGS

    1 to 2 **serrano chilies, seeded**
      ½ **tablespoon chopped fresh ginger**
      ¼ **cup cilantro leaves**
      2 **tablespoons fresh lime juice**
    2½ **cups water**

Stuffing
      1 **tablespoon virgin olive oil**
    1¼ **cups millet**
      1 **yellow bell pepper, seeded, deribbed, and diced**
      ½ **cup frozen corn kernels, defrosted**

1 **cup coarsely chopped tomato**
¼ **teaspoon salt**
¼ **teaspoon freshly ground pepper**

6 **well-shaped red bell peppers**
½ **cup shredded low-fat Swiss cheese (optional)**
3 **tablespoons pine nuts or pumpkin seeds**

Combine the chili, ginger, cilantro, and lime juice in a blender or food processor and process until smooth. Add the water and set the stock aside.

Heat the oil in a saucepan over moderate heat. Add the millet and diced pepper and stir-fry until the millet darkens a few shades, 3 to 4 minutes. Add the stock, corn, tomato, salt, and pepper. Bring to a boil; reduce the heat to low, cover, and cook until the liquid has been absorbed, about 20 minutes. Set aside for 5 minutes, then fluff with a fork.

Preheat the oven to 375°F. To prepare the peppers, halve them lengthwise, derib them, and remove the seeds. Blanch for 4 minutes in boiling water; drain and pat dry. Mound the pilaf into the pepper halves. Sprinkle with cheese and pine nuts. Bake for 20 to 25 minutes, or until the topping ingredients are golden.

Couscous Molds with Garden Vegetables and Saffron Cream

Inspired by a creation of New York chef Michael Romano, this entree features a mint-scented couscous pilaf. It is seasoned like its Indian cousin, *uppma*.

For a holiday dinner or other special meal, you might add Almond-Crusted Cheese Sticks with Lime-Horseradish Mayonnaise (page 192). For a weekday meal, you need little more than a green salad.   4 SERVINGS

Couscous

½	tablespoon extra-virgin olive oil
1	teaspoon cumin seeds
⅓	cup diced red bell pepper
¼	teaspoon cayenne
¼	teaspoon ground cinnamon
1½	cups vegetable stock or water
1¼	cups quick-cooking couscous
	Salt
	Freshly ground pepper
2	tablespoons chopped fresh mint or cilantro
	Olive oil

Vegetables

2	teaspoons extra-virgin olive oil
4	carrots, scraped and cut into fine julienne
4	small zucchini, cut diagonally into ¼-inch slices
16	thin asparagus spears, trimmed, peeled, and cut diagonally into ½-inch pieces
1	cup vegetable stock or water
¼	teaspoon saffron threads, crushed
	Saffron Cream (recipe follows)
	Cilanto leaves for garnish

To prepare the couscous, heat the oil in a saucepan over moderate heat. Add the cumin seeds and fry until golden-brown. Stir in the bell pepper,

cayenne, and cinnamon and sauté until just tender, about 3 minutes. Add the stock and bring to a boil. Stir in the couscous, cover, and remove from the heat. Let stand for 5 minutes or until the grains swell and the liquid has been absorbed. If any liquid remains, place the saucepan over low heat until it has been absorbed. Season with salt and pepper; add the mint and gently mix.

Brush four ½-cup straight-sided *katoris* or ramekins with olive oil. Divide the couscous among them, pressing down with the back of a spoon. Cover each one tightly with foil and transfer to a baking tray. Set aside in a warm oven. (Can be prepared ahead of time and refrigerated. Before serving, add ½ inch boiling water to the baking tray. Place the tray in a preheated 350°F oven for 15 minutes.)

To prepare the vegetables, heat the oil in a large nonstick skillet over low heat. Add the trimmed vegetables and cook until the colors intensify and they just begin to soften, 2 to 4 minutes. Add the stock and saffron and gently "water-fry" until the vegetables are tender-crisp. Drain the vegetables in a strainer, reserving the saffron liquid, and set the strainer over simmering water to keep the vegetables hot while you make the Saffron Cream. Boil the reserved saffron liquid until it is reduced to 3 tablespoons.

At serving time, carefully unmold the couscous onto warm serving plates and surround with vegetables. Spoon Saffron Cream over the couscous and vegetables and garnish with whole cilantro leaves.

Saffron Cream

MAKES ABOUT 1¼ CUPS

> ¼ cup Neufchâtel cheese
> 1 cup plain nonfat yogurt, at room temperature
> Reserved saffron liquid, reduced to ¼ cup
> Salt
> Freshly ground pepper

Place the cheese in a blender and process until smooth. Add the yogurt and warm (not hot) saffron liquid. Season with salt and pepper.

Buckwheat-Potato Cake with Almond Chutney

Inspired by a Bert Greene potato-rice dish, this cake is prepared in a similar fashion. Though it looks like potatoes Anna on the outside, the buckwheat pilaf nestled inside is revealed when the cake is cut. Buckwheat groats, also called kasha, are sold in supermarkets and natural-food stores.

The Almond Chutney is a terrific accompaniment, though salsa would also be good. To round out the meal, accompany this Indian Ratatouille Soup with Toasted Pumpkin Seeds (page 101) or Four-Greens Salad with Yellow Tomato Vinaigrette (page 48).   4 SERVINGS

Pilaf
      2 teaspoons virgin olive oil
      2 tablespoons sesame seeds
     ⅛ teaspoon crushed red-pepper flakes
     ½ cup buckwheat groats (kasha)
      1 cup water
     ⅓ cup light cream cheese or pureed low-fat cottage cheese

      2 teaspoons softened butter
         Olive-oil spray
     ¾ pound pared baking potatoes, peeled and thinly sliced
         Salt
         Freshly ground pepper
      2 tablespoons chopped cilantro or fresh parsley for garnish
         Almond Chutney (recipe follows)

Heat the olive oil in a heavy saucepan over moderate heat. Add the sesame seeds, pepper flakes, and buckwheat groats, and fry until the kernels darken a few shades. Add the water and bring to a boil. Cover, reduce the heat to very low, and cook for about 25 minutes, or until the liquid has been absorbed. Remove from the heat and set aside for 10 minutes. Fluff with a fork and gently fold in the cream cheese.

Preheat the oven to 375°F. Coat a nonstick 9-inch pie pan with butter, then spray with olive oil. Lay half of the potato slices over the bottom and sides of the pan, barely overlapping. Season with salt and pepper. Distribute the buckwheat pilaf evenly over the potatoes, pressing down with a spatula. Spray with olive oil.

Cover the pilaf with the remaining potato slices, barely overlapping. Spray with olive oil and cover with foil. Bake until the potatoes are almost tender, about 40 minutes. Remove the foil and bake for 10 minutes longer.

Let stand for 5 to 10 minutes before inverting onto a serving plate, garnishing with cilantro, and cutting into wedges; accompany with a spoonful of Almond Chutney.

Almond Chutney

MAKES ABOUT ½ CUP

    3 tablespoons sliced almonds, pan-toasted until golden
    ⅔ cup cilantro leaves, loosely packed
    ½ cup buttermilk
    1 serrano chili, seeded
       Salt to taste
       Paprika to taste

Combine all of the ingredients in a food processor or blender and process until smooth.

Quinoa Macaroni and Cheese with Vegetables

I first created a version of this dish in the fall of 1969, while residing at John Lennon and Yoko Ono's Tittenhurst country estate in England. One September evening Yoko popped into the kitchen with a case of organic whole-wheat macaroni and pleaded for a quick treat. Within minutes, I came up with this vegetable-macaroni casserole.

This recipe features high-protein quinoa macaroni, a relative newcomer on the market, sold primarily in gourmet natural-food stores. Like corn macaroni, this pasta has a low gluten content and quickly breaks down into a mush when overcooked. Be forewarned! (You can also use wheat, corn, or semolina macaroni.)   6 SERVINGS

½	cup petite peas
⅔	cup diced carrot
1	cup diced zucchini
1	cup diced string beans
8	ounces quinoa macaroni
	Olive-oil spray
1	tablespoon virgin olive oil
1	teaspoon mustard seeds
2½	tablespoons whole-wheat or garbanzo flour
2	cups skim milk
½	tablespoon ground coriander
One	7-ounce jar roasted red peppers, drained and diced, or 4 roasted red bell peppers (page 288), peeled, seeded, and diced
1	cup finely shredded low-fat sharp cheddar or jalapeño Jack cheese

Steam the vegetables until tender-crisp and set aside. Cook the quinoa macaroni according to the package directions and drain. Spray a casserole with olive oil. Distribute the pasta and vegetables evenly in the casserole and gently mix.

Heat the oil in a saucepan over moderate heat. Add the mustard seeds; cover and fry until they sputter and pop. Add the flour, and using a wire whisk, stir until smooth; cook for 1 minute. Remove the pan from the heat, and while whisking, gradually add the skim milk. Bring to a gentle boil and, whisking frequently, cook for 5 minutes. Remove from the heat; stir in the coriander, diced pepper, and ¼ cup of cheese.

Preheat the oven to 375°F. Pour the sauce evenly over the vegetable-macaroni mixture, and gently mix. Sprinkle with the remaining cheese and bake until browned, about 20 minutes.

Millet and Quinoa Hash with Sautéed Swiss Chard

This is one of my favorite grain entrees. Make it whenever Swiss chard is available, or substitute any mild leafy green or vegetable in season, from spinach or kale to broccoli or string beans. If you want a sauce with the hash, try the Lemon Yogurt Sauce below.   6 SERVINGS

Hash

1	tablespoon sunflower oil
1 to 2	minced jalapeño chilies
½	tablespoon mustard seeds
2	cups diced red or yellow bell pepper
2	cups diced zucchini
½	cup millet
½	cup finely chopped cilantro or fresh parsley
1⅔	cups water or vegetable stock
¼	cup quinoa
	Salt
	Freshly ground pepper
⅔	cup dry-curd cottage cheese or 1 cup shredded low-fat jalapeño Jack cheese
	Sautéed Swiss Chard (recipe follows)
	Lemon-Yogurt Sauce (optional; recipe follows)

Place the oil, chilies, and mustard seeds in a nonstick skillet over moderately high heat. Cover and shake the pan until the mustard seeds pop and turn gray. Stir in the pepper, zucchini, and millet, and, stirring frequently, fry until the millet darkens a few shades, about 5 minutes. Add half of the cilantro and water and bring to a boil. Cover, reduce the heat to low, and simmer for 5 minutes. Add the quinoa; stir gently, cover, and continue cooking until the liquid has been absorbed, about 15 minutes. Set aside for 5 minutes, then fluff with a fork. Season with salt and pepper. Add the remaining cilantro and cheese; stir and serve immediately, with a dollop of Lemon Yogurt Sauce. if desired.

Variation: To make pan-fried hash patties, increase the quantity of Jack cheese to 1½ cups and add ½ cup pureed tofu or Neufchâtel cheese to the mixture. When cool enough to handle, moisten hands and divide the mixture into six portions. Press into patties about 3 inches in diameter. Dip on both sides in bread crumbs. Using 1 to 2 tablespoons of oil, pan-fry over moderate heat on a nonstick griddle until golden-brown, turning once.

Sautéed Swiss Chard

4 TO 6 SERVINGS

    18 to 20 large Swiss chard leaves (see Note)
    1 teaspoon coriander seeds, crushed
    Juice of 1 tangerine or lime
    Salt
    Freshly ground pepper
    Virgin olive-oil spray or a dribble of virgin olive oil

Remove the chard stems and steam the leaves for a few minutes, until bright green and flexible. When cool, coarsely chop and press out excess liquid.

Just before serving, toast the coriander seeds in a large nonstick skillet

over moderate heat. When they darken slightly, add the tangerine juice and chard and stir-fry until hot. Season with salt and pepper, spray or dribble with oil, and serve hot.

Note: You can also use 2 pounds of trimmed spinach, or 3 to 4 cups small broccoli florets or string beans cut into ½-inch pieces, steamed until tender-crisp.

Lemon-Yogurt Sauce

MAKES 1½ CUPS

> 1½ cups plain nonfat yogurt
> 1 tablespoon tomato paste
> 1 teaspoon grated lemon zest
> 1 tablespoon fresh lemon juice
> 1 teaspoon ground coriander

Combine in a bowl and whisk until blended.

Mixed Grain and Vegetable Stir-Fry with Almonds

I came up with this recipe for a cooking demonstration. It features a mixed grain product called Kashi—made with cracked oats, rye, wheat berries, barley, triticale, buckwheat, and sesame seeds—sold in supermarkets and natural-food stores. The herbed pilaf is served with a terrific vegetable stir-fry, glazed with a mixture of slivered ginger, lemon juice, and maple syrup.

Any leftovers make good salad toppers. Sprinkle them over mixed greens and top with zippy black onion sprouts (available at natural-food stores).
6 SERVINGS

Pilaf

1	tablespoon virgin olive oil
1 to 2	jalapeño chilies, seeded and slivered
One	3-inch piece cinnamon stick
4	cloves
½	tablespoon curry powder
1½	cups Kashi or other uncooked cracked-grain mixture
2¾	cups vegetable stock
⅓	cup minced fresh parsley
	Salt

Vegetables

One	½-inch piece peeled fresh ginger, slivered
5	cups small broccoli florets (1 large bunch)
4	cups finely sliced carrot (5 to 6 medium)
	Finely julienned zest and juice of 1 lemon
¼	cup water
1	tablespoon virgin olive oil
3	red bell peppers, seeded, deribbed, and cut into ¼-inch strips
1½	tablespoons maple syrup
	Salt
	Pepper
3	tablespoons sliced almonds, pan-toasted until golden

Heat 1½ teaspoons of the oil in a nonstick saucepan over moderate heat. Add the chilies, cinnamon stick, and cloves and fry for 1 minute. Stir in the curry powder and Kashi and fry until coated with oil. Pour in the stock and bring to a boil. Reduce the heat; cover and cook until the liquid has been absorbed, about 35 minutes. Set aside. Add the parsley, season with salt, and fluff with a fork. Drizzle with the remaining oil, cover, and keep warm.

Place the ginger, broccoli, carrot, lemon zest, juice, and water in a nonstick wok or large skillet over moderately high heat. Cover and cook for about 4 minutes, stirring once or twice. Add the oil and bell pepper, and stir-fry until the liquid has evaporated. Stir in the maple syrup and cook briefly. Remove from the heat and season with salt and pepper.

To serve, transfer the pilaf to individual warm plates or a platter. Spoon the vegetables over the pilaf and garnish with almonds.

NEW WAYS WITH CRÊPES

CRÊPE INGREDIENTS

The egg-free crêpes in the recipes that follow are thin and flexible but not fragile or flimsy. Unlike classic Indian crêpes made from thickish batters of ground whole beans and rice, most of the recipes that follow are made from flour and water. And unlike classic crêpes that take up to three days from start to finish, these are as easy to put together as pancake batter, and cooked immediately. Body, texture, and color vary according to the liquid and dry ingredients used. You don't need to purchase exotic ingredients to make them. You probably have most of the necessary dry ingredients handy in your pantry — whole-wheat, buckwheat, and chickpea flour, cornmeal, Cream of Wheat, split peas, and rice. Liquid ingredients are equally commonplace. The only things you may have to purchase are a bottle or two of spices.

BATTER CONSISTENCY AND SHAPING TECHNIQUES

Since recipe yields and success rest on the proper batter consistency, you'll likely have to fine-tune and adjust the flour-liquid ratio in the recipes. If you cook the crêpes immediately after making the batter, the recommended liquid amount will suffice. But keep in mind that even during cooking, you'll need to add splashes of additional water. All during cooking, the batter should remain bold, pourable, somewhere between the consistency of light and heavy cream. Once made, the batter can be kept in the refrigerator for several days but must be thinned before being used again. Cooked crêpes, stacked between pieces of waxed paper and placed in an airtight container or wrapping, will keep in the refrigerator for several days and can be frozen for several weeks.

Here are a few pointers. For ease in shaping, keep your equipment near the cooking surface. To cut cooking time in half, work with two griddles. The single most important element in crêpemaking is nonstick cookware. Silverstone has been found to be the easiest to use. The pans are nonstick, but not too slick, and light enough to lift and tilt with ease.

VERSATILE CRÊPES

Like tortillas, crêpes can be used in a number of ways. You can use plain crêpes as wrappers for pieces of fruits or vegetables that need to be used, bound together with Neufchâtel cheese or herbed yogurt. Or you might place a crêpe on a hot, oiled griddle, sprinkle it with shredded cheese, cilantro leaves, and strips of roasted bell pepper, and top it with a second crêpe. Pan-fried until golden and crisp on both sides, this makes a terrific quesadilla-sandwich.

Feel free to come up with your own stuffed, folded, rolled, or stacked crêpe creations.

Cream of Wheat Crêpes with Sesame Potatoes and Green Pea Chutney

Unless you've dined in a restaurant specializing in South Indian cuisine, you're unlikely to have sampled anything that faintly resembles these potato-stuffed crêpes. They are a standard favorite in some parts of India, much like griddle cakes with hash browns are here.

I'm pleased with this light version of a classic. In my last cookbook a similar recipe called for ¾ cup of *ghee* (clarified butter). This version relys primarily on olive-oil spray and calls for a mere 1 tablespoon of oil.

Serve these at any meal, from breakfast to a late-night dinner. You need little more than a seasonal soup or salad to finish the meal.   4 SERVINGS

Crêpes

- ⅔ **cup quick Cream of Wheat cereal**
- ⅔ **cup unbleached white flour**
- 1 **tablespoon extra-virgin olive oil**
- 2¼ **cups water, or as needed**
- ½ **teaspoon mustard seeds**
- ½ **teaspoon salt**
- ⅛ **teaspoon baking powder**

Potato Filling

    2 **tablespoons sesame seeds**
    1 **small jalapeño chili, seeded and minced**
  2⅔ **cups coarsely mashed potatoes**
  1½ **tablespoons fresh lime juice**
       Salt
       Freshly ground pepper
       Virgin olive-oil spray
       Green Pea Chutney (recipe follows)

To make the crêpe batter, mix the Cream of Wheat and flour in a bowl then whisk in the oil and 2 cups of water. Cover and set aside.

To make the potato filling, place the sesame seeds in a nonstick skillet over moderate heat. Pan-toast them until they begin to darken and jump. Stir in the chili and potatoes and fry for 3 minutes. Sprinkle with lime juice, season with salt and pepper, and toss to mix. Remove from the heat and spray with olive oil. (Can be made up to 1 day ahead, covered, and refrigerated. Bring to room temperature before assembling the crêpes.)

Place the mustard seeds in a small pan, cover, and toast. When the seeds turn gray and pop, pour them into the crêpe batter. Add salt and baking powder and mix well. (The batter should be thin, similar to cold half-and-half. If necessary, add water by tablespoons to adjust the consistency.)

Place one or two large nonstick crêpe pans or griddles over moderate to moderately high heat for 3 minutes. Working one pan at a time, remove from the heat and spray with oil. Stir the batter and pour ⅓ cup around the bottom of the pan. Immediately lift and tilt the pan so the batter spreads out into a 10-inch crêpe. The edges will be lacy, with tiny holes on top. Cook for 3 to 4 minutes, or until the bottom is brown and crisp. Flip and cook for another 1 to 2 minutes. Slip onto a plate and set aside. Repeat with the remaining batter, stirring well each time. When cool, stack the crêpes between waxed paper.

Preheat the oven to 375°F. Line a shallow ovenproof dish with parchment paper and spray with oil. Lay each crêpe on a work surface and spoon about ⅓ cup of the potato filling down the center of each. Roll them into logs and transfer them to the baking sheet. Spray with oil and bake 10 to 12 minutes.

Place two crêpes on a warm plate and spoon Green Pea Chutney down the center. Repeat with the remaining crêpes.

Green Pea Chutney

MAKES ABOUT 1¼ CUPS

⅓ cup chopped almonds, pan-toasted until golden
1 cup frozen peas, defrosted
1 teaspoon grated fresh ginger
1 teaspoon minced jalapeño chili
⅔ cup water
¼ cup cilantro leaves
   Salt
   Freshly ground pepper

Place the almonds in a food processor and pulse to mince. Add the remaining ingredients and process until smooth.

Vegetable and Split Pea Crêpes with Yellow Pepper Sauce

Though they feature humble split peas, these full-flavored crêpes are positively elegant—lacy and thin. Each one is spread with a chunky vegetable–and–coconut-yogurt mixture, folded in half, and then into quarters. The stuffed crêpes are baked until warm and bubbly and served in a pool of warm Yellow Pepper Sauce.

    This is a good make-ahead entree for entertaining. All you have to do is warm the crêpes before serving. Accompany them with a salad of Bibb lettuce tossed with a mint vinaigrette.

    If you have access to baby (miniature) vegetables, try the alternate presentation at the end of the recipe. The slender vegetables are left whole, so you need about four per person for this version.　8 SERVINGS

Crêpes

    1   cup yellow split peas, soaked overnight in 4 cups water
  One   ½-inch piece peeled fresh ginger, sliced
 1 to 2 serrano chilies, seeded
   3⅓   cups water, or as needed
    1   cup whole-wheat pastry flour or unbleached all-purpose flour
    ½   tablespoon arrowroot
    ¼   teaspoon salt
    ¼   teaspoon baking powder
    3   tablespoons chopped cilantro, fresh parsley, or basil
        Olive- or vegetable-oil spray

Filling

    3   cups of one seasonal vegetable combination:
            Spring: diced asparagus, carrots, and peas
            Summer: diced zucchini, bell pepper, and jícama
            Autumn: diced broccoli, cauliflower, and pumpkin
            Winter: diced potato, parsnip, and celery root
    1   cup shredded part-skim jalapeño Jack cheese
    ⅔   cup plain nonfat yogurt
    2   tablespoons grated fresh or dry coconut, unsweetened
        Salt
        Cayenne
        Olive- or vegetable-oil spray
        Yellow Pepper Sauce (recipe follows)

To make the crêpe batter, drain the split peas and transfer them to a food processor fitted with a metal blade. Add the ginger, chilies, and ½ cup water and process into a thick paste. Scrape down the sides of the container as necessary. Pour in ¾ cup water and process until smooth, 2 to 3 minutes. Add the remaining ingredients and process briefly to mix. Transfer the batter to a jar or bowl; cover and set aside. (The batter should resemble chilled heavy cream. Adjust the consistency with flour or water as necessary.)

To make the filling, steam or microwave the vegetables until just tender;

pat dry. Place the cooked vegetables in a food processor, and pulse 5 to 6 times to chop coarsely. Transfer the vegetables to a bowl; add the remaining ingredients and mix well. (Can be made up to 1 day ahead, covered, and refrigerated. Bring to room temperature before assembling the crêpes.)

Heat one or two nonstick griddles or 8-inch crêpe pans over moderately high heat. Working one pan at a time, spray it with oil. Stir the batter and pour ⅓ cup around the bottom of the pan. Immediately lift and tilt the pan so that the batter flows into an 8-inch crêpe. (If the batter is too thick, ⅓ cup will not flow to make an 8-inch crêpe. Adjust the quantity of liquid if necessary. The pan is the correct temperature when the top of the crêpe is covered with tiny holes and the color lightens within 30 seconds.) Cook until the top firms up and the bottom turns golden-brown, 3 to 4 minutes. Flip over and cook for another 1 to 2 minutes. Slide onto a plate and set aside. Repeat to make the remaining fifteen crêpes. When cool, stack the crêpes between waxed paper. (They can be refrigerated for 2 days and frozen for 1 month.)

Preheat the oven to 375°F. Line two nonstick baking sheets with parchment paper and spray with oil. With the smooth side down, spread about 3 tablespoons of filling over a crêpe; fold in half, then fold again into a quarter-circle. Transfer to the baking sheet. Assemble the remaining crêpes and spray them with oil. Loosely cover with foil and bake about 10 minutes.

Place two crêpes on each of eight warmed plates and spoon a little Yellow Pepper Sauce around them.

Variation: An alternate, more substantial presentation pairs the crêpes with whole baby (miniature) vegetables. You need slender vegetables for this visual dynamo—a total of about 4 pounds of tiny mixed vegetables for 8 servings: carrots, corn, green beans, or trimmed asparagus spears. The vegetables are steamed until tender-crisp and divided into eight portions.

For one serving, fold two crêpes into quarter-circles, and distribute one portion of the vegetables into each of the four pocket folds. Carefully place one of the crêpes in the center of an ovenproof dinner plate and the other one toward the edge. Allow the vegetable spears to fan out over the empty portion of the plate. Place a portion of the yogurt-cheese mixture in the top pocket fold of each crêpe. To serve, cover each plate with foil and bake until heated through. Spoon a little warm pepper sauce around the crêpes.

Yellow Pepper Sauce

MAKES ABOUT 1½ CUPS

    3 yellow bell peppers
    1 cup vegetable stock
       Salt
       Freshly ground pepper
    1 tablespoon fresh lime juice

Quarter, seed, and derib the peppers. Grill or broil the peppers until the skins blister and char. Transfer them to a bowl, cover, and set aside for 20 minutes. Rub off the skins and coarsely chop.

Combine the peppers and stock in a small saucepan and simmer until soft, 5 to 7 minutes. Puree in a food processor or blender, then press through a fine-mesh sieve into a saucepan. Season with salt and pepper and stir in the lime juice. Serve warm. (May be made up to 2 days in advance and refrigerated in a sealed jar.)

Gâteau of Buckwheat Crêpes with Kasha and Red Pepper Mousse

In this entree, delicate buckwheat crêpes and cabbage-studded kasha pilaf are layered to form an impressive savory torte, the whole bound together with melted cheese. The flavors jump off the plate in harmonious layers, first distinctive and then supportive. Use any kind of cheese you like — my favorites are part-skim smoked Swiss, jalapeño Jack, and peppered Gouda. Buckwheat flour and groats, also called kasha, are available in grocery or natural-food stores.

Serve a wedge of the gâteau with a spoon of light Red Pepper Mousse and a soup, or salad.　6 SERVINGS

Crêpes

    1¼ cups buckwheat flour
    ⅔ cup unbleached all-purpose flour
    ½ teaspoon salt
    1 cup cold water
    2 cups boiling water
    1 teaspoon baking powder
      Olive- or vegetable-oil spray

Kasha

    2 teaspoons butter
    ¼ teaspoon crushed red-pepper flakes
    3 cups finely shredded savoy cabbage
    ¾ cup roasted buckwheat groats
    1½ cups water or stock
    3 tablespoons chopped cilantro
      Salt
      Freshly ground pepper
    8 ounces finely shredded Swiss, Jack, or Gouda cheese
      Red Pepper Mousse (recipe follows)

To make the crêpe batter, combine the flours and salt in a food processor. Add the cold water and process until smooth. Add enough boiling water to yield a batter with a pourable consistency, similar to heavy cream. Transfer to a container; stir in the baking powder and stir until bubbly.

Heat one or two large nonstick sauté pans or griddles over moderately high heat. Working one pan at a time, remove from the heat and spray with oil. Pour ⅓ cup of batter around the bottom of the pan. Immediately lift and tilt the pan so the batter flows into an 8-inch crêpe. Cook until the edges begin to curl up and the bottom turns light brown, 2 to 3 minutes. Flip and cook for about 2 minutes. (If the batter is too thick, ⅓ cup will not flow to make an 8-inch crêpe. Adjust the quantity of liquid if necessary. The pan is the correct temperature when the top of the crêpe is covered with tiny holes and the color lightens within 20 seconds.) Slide the crêpe onto a plate and repeat the process to make the remaining eleven crêpes. When cool, stack the crêpes, separating them with waxed paper. (They can be refrigerated for 2 days and frozen for up to a month.)

Place the butter and pepper flakes in a skillet over moderately high heat. When the butter froths, add the cabbage and stir-fry until it wilts. Add the groats and water and bring to a boil. Reduce the heat, cover, and cook until the water has been absorbed, 10 to 15 minutes. Add the cilantro and a touch of salt and pepper; fluff with a fork to mix. Divide both the kasha and cheese into eleven equal portions on a baking sheet.

Spray an ovenproof serving plate with oil. Lay down the first crêpe and cover the surface with a portion of pilaf. Sprinkle with a portion of cheese. (Distribute the filling and cheese in an even layer all the way to the edges.) Continue to layer crêpes, pilaf, and cheese, ending up with a crêpe, "pretty" side up. Spray the gâteau liberally with olive oil.

Preheat the oven to 350°F. Loosely cover the gâteau with aluminum foil and bake until heated through, 10 to 12 minutes. Serve hot, cut into wedges, accompanied by a few tablespoons of Red Pepper Mousse.

Red Pepper Mousse

MAKES ABOUT 1⅓ CUPS

   3 **large red bell peppers, roasted, peeled, and coarsely chopped**
 ⅓ **cup water**
 ⅛ **teaspoon hot paprika or cayenne**
     Salt
 ⅓ **cup chilled heavy cream or ⅔ cup whipped light cream cheese,**
     at room temperature

Place the peppers and water in a small saucepan and simmer until softened, about 5 minutes. Transfer to a food processor and puree. Force the puree through a fine sieve, extracting as much liquid as possible. Add the paprika and season with salt. (May be made up to 2 days in advance.)

Just before serving, place the cream or cheese in a bowl. Whip the cream into light peaks or whisk the cream cheese until light and fluffy. Fold the pepper puree into the cream or cheese and serve immediately.

Cheesy Corn–Stuffed Crêpes with Ancho Chili–Tomato Sauce

This crêpe entree marries elements of North Indian and Tex-Mex cuisines. The stuffing is equally delicious rolled in soft blue cornmeal tortillas instead of corn crêpes. All of the elements in this presentation are outstanding, but the ancho chili–and–pumpkin seed tomato sauce is exceptional. This is a terrific make-ahead dish for a weekday or weekend dinner; it even seems to improve the second day. Serve with soup or a salad.   6 SERVINGS

Crêpes

1   cup cornmeal, preferably stone-ground
1   tablespoon ground ancho chilies or chili powder
1   teaspoon salt
2   cups boiling water
1⅓   cups cold water
½   cup skim milk
2½   tablespoons cold-pressed corn oil
1½   cups whole-wheat pastry or unbleached all-purpose flour
1½   tablespoons baking powder
     Olive-oil spray

Cheesy Corn Stuffing

1   cup part-skim ricotta cheese
⅓   cup cilantro leaves
½   tablespoon ground coriander
1½   cups diced cooked potato
2½   cups cooked corn kernels
½   cup diced low-fat jalapeño Jack cheese
    Salt
    Freshly ground pepper

Ancho Chili–Tomato Sauce (recipe follows)

To make the crêpe batter, place the cornmeal, ground chilies, and salt in a food processor. Pour in the boiling water and pulse to mix. Let the batter sit for 10 minutes. Add the remaining crêpe ingredients to the processor and blend until smooth. Set the batter aside.

To make the filling, place the ricotta cheese, most of the cilantro (leave a few sprigs aside for garnish), and the ground coriander in a food processor and blend until pale green and smooth. Transfer the mixture to a bowl. Add the potato, 2 cups of the corn, and the jalapeño cheese; stir to mix. Season with salt and pepper.

Heat one or two large nonstick sauté pans or griddles over moderate to moderately high heat. Working one pan at a time, remove from the heat and spray with oil. Pour ⅓ cup of batter around the bottom of the pan. Immediately lift and tilt the pan so the batter flows into an 8-inch crêpe. (If the batter is too thick, ⅓ cup will not flow to make an 8-inch crêpe. Adjust the quantity of liquid if necessary. The pan is the correct temperature when the top of the crêpe is covered with tiny holes and the color lightens within 20 seconds.) Cook until the edges begin to curl up and the bottom turns light brown, 3 to 4 minutes. Flip and cook for another 1½ to 2 minutes. Slide the crêpe onto a plate; repeat the process to make the remaining eleven crêpes. When cool, stack the crêpes, separating them with waxed paper; cover and refrigerate. (Can be refrigerated for 2 days and frozen for one month.) Alternately, wrap twelve tortillas in foil and warm them in a preheated 300°F oven for 10 minutes.

Preheat the oven to 375°F. Spray a shallow baking dish with oil. Lay each crêpe or softened tortilla flat on a work surface and spoon a portion of the corn mixture down the center. Roll up to enclose the filling and transfer to the baking dish. Repeat. Spray the crêpes with oil and bake until the stuffing is heated through, 12 to 15 minutes. Let stand for 5 minutes before serving.

To serve, spoon some sauce onto the bottom of a warm plate and place two stuffed crêpes in the center. Garnish the sauce with a generous tablespoon of the remaining corn kernels and a few cilantro leaves.

Ancho Chili–Tomato Sauce

      1 teaspoon cumin seeds
     ¼ cup raw pumpkin seeds
  2 or 3 ancho chilies, stemmed and seeded
    1½ pounds Roma (plum) tomatoes, peeled, seeded, and chopped
      1 cup water
     ½ cup cilantro leaves
      1 teaspoon extra-virgin olive oil
     ½ tablespoon fresh lime juice

Place the cumin and pumpkin seeds in a dry skillet over low heat. Stir-fry until lightly toasted; set aside. Repeat the process with the ancho chilies, then transfer them to a bowl of water. Soak until soft, about 20 minutes; drain.

Combine the tomato, water, and cilantro in a saucepan. Bring to a boil, reduce the heat, and simmer for 20 minutes. Transfer to a food processor or blender; add the chilies, cumin, and pumpkin seeds. Process until smooth and pour into a saucepan. Bring to a boil, reduce the heat, and simmer for 10 to 15 minutes. Pass the sauce through a sieve into a clean saucepan and stir in the oil and lime juice. Keep warm.

Rice and Pea Griddle Cakes with Green Beans and Cilantro Yogurt

Typically South Indian, these thin griddle cakes are made from a batter of soaked long-grain rice and split peas. You can use almost any dry-textured green vegetable for the stuffing. In this instance, the griddle cakes are speckled green, the yogurt is pistachio green, and the beans are a vibrant green.

Try this for an informal verandah or dining room dinner. Aficionados of these full-bodied but delicate griddle cakes find it hard to stop at one, and since leftovers are great for brown-bag lunches, it's a good idea to double the recipe. Serve with hot or chilled soup, according to the season.　　8 SERVINGS

Griddle Cakes

- ½ cup basmati rice, soaked overnight in water and drained
- ⅔ cup green split peas, soaked overnight in water and drained
- 2 jalapeño chilies, seeded
- ½ teaspoon chili powder
- ½ teaspoon salt
- 1¾ to 2 cups water, or as needed
- ⅓ cup unbleached all-purpose flour
- ¼ cup cilantro leaves
- Olive- or vegetable-oil spray

Green Beans

- 1½ pounds green beans, cut into ½-inch pieces
- ½ tablespoon unsalted butter or corn oil
- 1 tablespoon chopped fresh dill or ½ teaspoon dried
- Salt
- Freshly ground pepper or cayenne
- Cilantro Yogurt (recipe follows)

To make the batter, place the rice in a food processor and process until it resembles cornmeal, scraping down the sides of the work bowl as necessary. Add the split peas, jalapeños, chili powder and salt, and continue to process until coarsely ground. Pour in the water, flour, and cilantro and process until the mixture is reduced to a grainy batter.

Heat one or two large nonstick sauté pans or griddles over moderate heat. Working with one pan at a time, remove from the heat and spray with oil. Scoop up ⅓ cup of batter and pour it in a small circle in the center of the pan. Immediately lift and tilt the pan so that the batter flows into a griddle cake roughly 7 inch round. Within seconds the bottom will set; with the bottom of a soup spoon, ease the surface batter to extend the diameter to about 8 inches. (If the batter is too thick, ⅓ cup cannot be eased into an 8-inch crêpe. Add water as necessary.) Cook until the edges begin to curl up and the bottom crisps to golden-brown, about 3 minutes. Spray the top surface with oil, flip, and cook for another 1½ minutes. Slide onto a plate and repeat the process to make seven more griddle cakes. Stack them, separating them with waxed

paper. When cool, seal in plastic wrap. (Can be refrigerated for 2 days and frozen for 1 month.)

Steam the cut beans until barely tender. In a nonstick skillet, melt the butter over low heat until nutty brown. Stir in the dill and beans and cook until heated through. Season with salt and pepper or the barest trace of cayenne.

To serve, place a griddle cake on the plate and spoon about ⅔ cup of beans on one half, so that they spill onto the plate. Fold over the top half. Drizzle with Cilantro Yogurt.

Cilantro Yogurt

MAKES ABOUT 1½ CUPS

> 1½ cups plain nonfat yogurt
> ¼   cup chopped cilantro
>   Scant ½ teaspoon chili blend or chili powder
> 1   tablespoon tomato paste
> 1   teaspoon avocado oil

Combine the first four ingredients in a bowl and mix well. Swirl in the oil. (For a pistachio-green chutney, process in a blender for 1 to 2 minutes.)

Chickpea Crêpes with Asparagus and Sesame Cream Sauce

The first time I tasted Deborah Madison's creative cuisine was at a restaurant dinner hosted by the city of Philadelphia: the 1988 "Book and the Cook." We were the only vegetarian chefs present. This is an egg-free version of her asparagus-stuffed crêpes.

The flavor of spring asparagus plays with the sweetness of feather-light chickpea crêpes and a delicate sesame sauce. If asparagus isn't available, use any julienned steamed vegetable in season. The crêpes freeze well.

8 SERVINGS

Crêpes

>   3 large roasted red bell peppers (page 288), peeled, or use one
>   7-ounce jar roasted red bell peppers, drained and rinsed
>   3⅓ cups water, or as needed
>   2⅓ cups chickpea flour (scooped and leveled)
>   1 to 2 jalapeño chilies, seeded and chopped
>   1 teaspoon salt

Filling

>   2½ pounds pencil-thin asparagus, trimmed, blanched, and divided
>   into 16 bundles
>   6 ounces finely shredded part-skim jalapeño Jack cheese
>   2 tablespoons chopped cilantro
>   Sesame Cream Sauce (recipe follows)

To make the crêpe batter, combine the red peppers and 1 cup water in a food processor and puree. Add the remaining water, flour, jalapeños, and salt, and process for several minutes until smooth and creamy. Pour the batter through a fine-mesh sieve, pressing to force through all usable parts of the pepper. Transfer to a storage container; loosely cover and set aside.

To make the crêpes, heat one or two large nonstick sauté pans or griddles over moderate heat. Working one pan at a time, remove from the heat and spray with oil. Pour ⅓ cup of batter around the bottom of the pan, and immediately lift and tilt so that the batter flows into a 8-inch crêpe with tiny holes on the top. (If ⅓ cup of batter does not flow to make an 8-inch crêpe, adjust the quantity of liquid or flour as necessary.) Cook until the edges begin to curl up and the bottom turns pale gold through the red hue, 2 to 3 minutes. Flip and cook for another 2 to 3 minutes. Slide out onto a plate. Repeat the process to make the remaining fifteen crêpes. Stack them, separating them with waxed paper. When cool, seal in plastic wrap. (Can be refrigerated for 2 days and frozen for 1 month.)

To assemble, place one crêpe, smooth side down, on a work surface. Sprinkle with 2 tablespoons of cheese. Place a bundle of asparagus at one edge and gently roll the crêpe around it. Repeat with the remaining crêpes.

Preheat the oven to 400°F. Spray a nonstick baking sheet with oil. Place

the crêpes in a single layer, seam side down, on the pan. Spray the surface with oil and bake until heated through, 8 to 10 minutes.

To serve, spoon hot Sesame Cream Sauce on the bottom of a warmed plate, top with two hot crêpes, and sprinkle with cilantro.

Sesame Cream Sauce

MAKES ABOUT 2 CUPS

½   tablespoon sesame seeds
2   cups skim milk
3   tablespoons Cream of Rice cereal
    Salt
    Cayenne

In a heavy-bottomed saucepan, toaste the sesame seeds over moderate heat until golden-brown. Pour in the milk and bring to a boil. Stir in the Cream of Rice, and, stirring frequently, boil until thickened, 4 to 5 minutes. Remove the pan from the heat and set it aside for 5 minutes. Using a wire whisk, whisk until smooth. If necessary, gently reheat just to the point of boiling. Season with salt and cayenne to taste.

Lacy Lemon Crêpes with Spinach Filling and Mustard Sauce

Two forms of mustard bring this crêpe dish to life. Toasted whole seeds lend a nutty flavor to the crêpes, while grainy mustard brings warmth to the light cheddar sauce. In the center of it all is a vibrant spinach–and–bell pepper filling. This light entree is ideal for a hot-weather brunch, perhaps accompanied by Indian Summer Tomatoes (page 49).   8 SERVINGS

Crêpes

   1 tablespoon mustard seeds
  ⅔ cup Cream of Rice cereal
1⅔ cups unbleached all-purpose flour
   2 tablespoons grated lemon zest
  ¼ cup fresh lemon juice
4¼ cups water, or as needed
   1 teaspoon salt
   1 tablespoon baking powder
    Vegetable-oil spray

Filling

   4 pounds fresh spinach, washed and stemmed
   2 teaspoons extra-virgin olive oil
   1 tablespoon grated fresh ginger
   1 jalapeño chili, seeded and slivered
   2 large red bell peppers, seeded, deribbed, and cut into thin strips
  ½ cup farmer cheese or light cream cheese
   3 tablespoons chopped cilantro
    Salt
    Freshly ground white pepper
   3 tablespoons dry whole-wheat bread crumbs
    Mustard Sauce (recipe follows)

To make the crêpe batter, place the mustard seeds in a saucepan over moderate heat. Shaking the pan, cook until they crackle and pop; remove the pan from the heat. Add the Cream of Rice and, stirring occasionally, lightly toast while the pan cools. Add the flour, zest, juice, water, and salt and whisk until smooth. Cover the pan and set aside for 1 hour to let the grains soften.

To cook the crêpes, heat one or two large nonstick sauté pans or griddles over moderate heat. Working one pan at a time, remove from the heat and spray with oil. Pour ⅓ cup of batter around the bottom of the pan. Immediately lift and tilt so that the batter flows into an 8-inch crêpe with tiny holes on the top. (If ⅓ cup of batter does not flow to make an 8-inch crêpe, adjust the quantity of liquid or flour as necessary.) Cook until the edges begin to curl up and the bottom turns golden-brown, 2 to 3 minutes. Flip and cook for another

2 to 3 minutes and slide onto a plate. Repeat the process to make the remaining fifteen crêpes. Stack them, separating them with waxed paper. (When cool, seal in plastic wrap. Can be refrigerated for 2 days and frozen for 1 month.)

To make the filling, place the spinach in a large pot of boiling water for 2 to 3 minutes. Drain, rinse under cold water, squeeze dry, and chop fine.

Place the oil, ginger, and jalapeño in a large nonstick skillet or wok and sauté over moderately high heat. When the seasonings sizzle, add the bell pepper and sauté until it is wilted, about 5 minutes. Remove the skillet from the heat and stir in the spinach, farmer cheese, and cilantro. Season with salt and pepper and divide into sixteen portions.

To assemble and bake the crêpes, preheat the oven to 375°F. Spray a nonstick baking pan with olive oil. Lay each crêpe on a work surface and spoon a portion of the filling down the center. Roll crêpes and transfer them, seam side down, to the baking pan. Sprinkle with bread crumbs and spray with oil. Bake about 10 minutes. To serve, place two hot crêpes on a dinner plate and spoon Mustard Sauce on the side.

Mustard Sauce

MAKES ABOUT 2¼ CUPS

2 tablespoons cornstarch
¼ teaspoon curry powder
¼ teaspoon freshly ground pepper
2½ cups skim milk
1 bay leaf
3 tablespoons grainy mustard
¼ cup finely shredded sharp cheddar cheese
¼ teaspoon salt

Combine the cornstarch, curry powder, pepper, and ½ cup of milk in a bowl and blend well. Bring the remaining milk and bay leaf to a boil in a saucepan. Pour the heated milk into the cornstarch mixture, whisking constantly, then return to the saucepan. Cook over moderately high heat, stirring constantly, until it has thickened slightly, 3 to 4 minutes. Remove the pan from the heat and discard the bay leaf. Stir in the mustard, cheese, and salt; serve.

LEGUME MAINSTAYS

Legumes — dried split peas, beans and lentils — are some of the most exciting foods on the horizon. They can be served in every course of a meal, from appetizer through dessert. For much of the last twenty years, I have used them in some way on a daily basis, and the following legume-based entrees I have developed will give you a sense of their versatility.

In India, legumes have been respected for their nutritional benefits since ancient times. Containing only a trace of fat, they are one of the best sources of cholesterol-lowering fiber. They are also excellent sources of complex carbohydrates, high-quality protein, vitamins, and minerals. Simmered in water with aromatic seasonings, and a vegetable or a grain, you end up with a distinctive one-pot meal. Eaten in this way, with a few turns of the pepper mill and a garnishing spray of good oil, legumes are ideal weight-loss and weight-maintenance entrees.

Legumes are widely available in three forms: dried, frozen, and cooked. When you want a pot of slow-cooking soup, chili, or stew simmering on the back burner, start with dried beans. Cooked or frozen beans may be more convenient when you need only a small amount for a recipe. Natural-food stores offer a good selection of dried bulk and packaged beans, and cooked organic beans are available in both bottles and cans. Supermarkets offer a wider selection of prepared beans, available frozen, bottled, and canned.

NEWCOMERS ON OUR PANTRY SHELVES:
OLD-WORLD BEANS

At the turn of the century, bean pots were common on wood-burning stoves from Boston to San Francisco. Easy to store and transport, legumes were common staples at the general store. Sold in burlap bags, the variety was exciting; beans had evocative names like French navy beans, Christmas limas, Jacob's Cattle, Scarlet Runners, European soldier beans, and Appaloosas.

Though most old-world legumes fell out of popularity, they are finding their way onto grocers' shelves in the nineties. (See Appendix for sources.) As beautiful to behold as they are uniquely delicious, these beans are patterned dramatically, black and white or mottled purple and scarlet. Even more

inviting, they do not require a presoaking, only a brief parboiling, to quicken cooking time and enhance digestibility.

Old-world legumes can be used interchangeably with other more common legumes, and with slightly adjusted cooking procedures, both will yield excellent results. A brief description of familiar, and perhaps unfamiliar, legumes used in the book are listed in the Glossary.

Split Pea Soup with Cardamom-Saffron Rice Cakes

A cup of this velvety smooth, light soup is as good as it gets. Though it's made with only water, vegetables, split peas, and a touch of rice, the body of the soup is exceptional, with a distinctive flavor from the toasted spice oil. Vary the character of the soup by using other legumes such as split mung beans, lima beans, or navy beans. Let this recipe serve as a formula for exploring a myriad of delicate legume-based soups.

Good on its own for a light lunch. For a simple dinner, add a composed salad and the Cardamom-Saffron Rice Cakes.   6 SERVINGS

Soup

¾   cup yellow split peas, soaked in water for 2 hours and drained
2   tablespoons long-grain rice
7   cups water or stock
1   tablespoon grated fresh ginger
1 to 2   jalapeño chilies, seeded and minced
½   teaspoon ground turmeric
2   cups of one of the following: chopped tomatoes, sliced carrots, cubed zucchini, chopped cauliflower, shredded spinach or chard
    Salt
    Freshly ground pepper

Toasted Spice Oil

  1 **teaspoon mustard seeds**
  1 **teaspoon cumin seeds**
  1 **tablespoon cold-pressed nut or seed oil**
  3 **tablespoons chopped cilantro, mint, basil, or parsley**

Cardamom-Saffron Rice Cakes (recipe follows)

Combine all of the soup ingredients (including one of the vegetables) in a large heavy-bottomed pot. Bring to a boil; partially cover and reduce the heat to low. Briskly simmer until the split peas fall apart, 1 to 1½ hours. Cool slightly, then puree in batches in a food processor and return to the cooking pan. Season with salt and pepper; gently reheat.

Place the mustard seeds in a small pan over moderate heat. Cover and toast until they pop and crackle. Add the cumin seeds and oil; cook for about 5 seconds, then swirl the toasted spice oil into the soup.

To serve with Cardamom-Saffron Rice Cakes, carefully unmold a rice cake in the center of a shallow soup bowl. Pour about ¾ cup soup into the bowl; garnish with herbs and serve piping hot.

Cardamom-Saffron Rice Cakes

6 SERVINGS

  5 **cups water**
  1½ **cups long-grain rice, preferably basmati**
  One **3-inch cinnamon stick**
  2 **bay leaves**
  Salt
  Olive-oil spray
  ½ **teaspoon cardamom seeds, crushed**
  Large pinch saffron threads

In a large saucepan, bring the water to a boil over high heat. Stir in the rice, cinnamon stick, bay leaves, and a pinch of salt. Cook for 10 minutes. Transfer to a strainer and rinse under cold running water. Discard the cinnamon stick and bay leaves.

Preheat the oven to 450°F. Generously spray six 3- to 4-inch nonstick tart pans with olive oil. Sprinkle cardamom seeds and saffron threads over the bottom of the pans. Distribute the rice evenly among the pans and pack it down firmly. Spray with olive oil.

Bake for 12 minutes. Carefully unmold and serve hot.

Lima Beans with Grilled, Vegetable-Stuffed Vine Leaves

In this dish, stuffed grape-leaf parcels are briefly grilled before they are set atop a bed of vegetable-studded lima beans seasoned with a delicate jalapeño-mustard seasoning. Made with old-world Christmas limas, the flavor is exceptionally vibrant. The grape leaves — stuffed with a simple mixture of diced vegetables and farmer cheese — are light and delicious. Feel free to use other seasonal vegetable combinations that complement your menu. This is a late-August vegetable blend.   8 SERVINGS

Stuffed Grape Leaves

32 large, bottled grape leaves
⅔ cup cooked chopped spinach, pressed dry
⅔ cup roasted red bell peppers, chopped into ¼-inch dice
⅔ cup zucchini, grilled or steamed, chopped into ¼-inch dice
⅔ cup yellow squash, grilled or steamed, chopped into ¼-inch dice
5 ounces farmer cheese, crumbled
3 tablespoons chopped cilantro
2 tablespoons fresh lime juice
   Salt
   Hot Hungarian paprika
   Olive-oil spray

Lima Beans

1½ cups dried lima beans, preferably Christmas limas soaked over-
    night, or three 15-ounce cans grand limas, drained

8 cups water

1 bay leaf

2 tablespoons extra-virgin olive oil

½ tablespoon mustard seeds

1 to 2 jalapeño chilies, seeded and slivered

1 red bell pepper, seeded, deribbed, and cut in 1-inch squares

1 cup peeled, seeded and chopped tomato
   Salt
   Freshly ground pepper

3 tablespoons chopped fresh parsley

3 tablespoons chopped fresh mint

Soak the grape leaves in cool water for 10 minutes. Rinse them under running water. Place the leaves, vein sides up, on paper towels. (Cut away the tough stems with kitchen scissors.)

Combine the vegetables, farmer cheese, and cilantro in a bowl. Add half of the lime juice and season with salt and paprika. Place about 1 tablespoon of the mixture on each leaf, ¾ inch from the stem end. Fold the stem end of the leaf over the filling; then fold in the sides and roll the leaf into a firm packet.

Soak four or five long wooden skewers in water for 10 minutes. Thread the stuffed grape leaves onto the skewers, spacing them about 1 inch apart. (May be made 1 day ahead and kept refrigerated.)

Drain the beans and combine them with the water, bay leaf, and ½ tablespoon of oil. Bring to a boil; reduce the heat and simmer until nearly tender, about 1½ hours. Remove skins that have floated to the surface; drain.

About 15 minutes before serving, heat a grill or broiler. Spray the grape leaves with olive oil and grill until darkened a few shades, 5 minutes a side.

Heat the remaining oil in a large skillet over moderately high heat. Add the mustard seeds; cover and cook until they pop and turn gray. Add the jalapeño and bell pepper and stir-fry about 2 minutes. Add the tomato and cook for another 2 minutes. Stir in the beans, season with salt and pepper, and fold in the herbs. Spoon the beans onto a warmed platter or individual plates and top with the grape leaves. Sprinkle with the remaining lime juice.

Appaloosa Beans with Saffron Cream and Grilled Okra

Appaloosa beans are very receptive to aromatic Indian seasonings, making this dish as delicious as it is aromatic. The old-world, kidney-shaped beans are mottled white-and-purple-brown, the same colors as the speckled horse bearing the name, and are available at specialty and natural-food stores. If you can't find them, use Anazaki or pinto beans instead. Serve the entree with a vegetable side dish or salad and flame-toasted chapatis.   6 SERVINGS

Beans

1	teaspoon cumin seeds
½	tablespoon coriander seeds
1	teaspoon dried oregano
1	teaspoon ground ancho chilies or chili powder
1½	tablespoons extra-virgin olive oil
1	teaspoon grated fresh ginger
2½	cups dried Appaloosa (not soaked but parboiled according to package instructions) or pinto beans, soaked overnight, then drained
6 to 8	cups water
	Salt
2	tablespoons chopped cilantro or fresh parsley

Saffron Cream

10 to 12	saffron threads
⅔	cup low-fat cottage cheese
3	tablespoons buttermilk

Grilled Okra (recipe follows)

Combine the cumin, coriander, oregano, and ground chilies in a mortar; coarsely crush the seeds with a pestle. Heat the oil in a large soup pot over moderate heat. Stir in the spice blend and ginger and fry for about 1 minute.

Add the beans and 6 cups of water and bring to a boil. Reduce the heat, partially cover, and simmer until the beans are tender (1 to 1½ hours), adding water if necessary. Season with salt and fold in the cilantro.

While the beans are cooking, toast the saffron in a warm pan until the threads are brittle. Grind to a powder with the back of a spoon. Transfer to a blender along with the cottage cheese and buttermilk. Process until creamy smooth and scrape into a bowl.

Serve the beans on warm dinner plates, with Grilled Okra and Saffron Cream on either side.

Grilled Okra

If you've never tasted okra before, this dish, a slightly amended version of one devised by Philip Steven Shultz, is a terrific introduction. When you don't have a wood fire stoked up, a stovetop grill or a broiler works just fine.
6 SERVINGS

> 1¼ **pounds medium okra, tops lightly trimmed**
>   1 **cup peeled, seeded, and chopped tomato**
>   1 **tablespoon virgin olive oil**
>   ½ **tablespoon ground cumin**
>   ½ **tablespoon ground coriander**
>   2 **tablespoons chopped cilantro**
>   **Salt**
>   **Cayenne**
>   **Olive-oil spray**

Spear the okra lengthwise on long wooden skewers and place them in a single layer in a shallow dish. Combine the tomato, oil, cumin, coriander, cilantro, and a pinch of salt and cayenne in a blender. Process until smooth, then pour over the okra. Set aside for 1 hour, covered.

Preheat a grill over moderately high heat or preheat a broiler. Grill the okra, basting frequently with any remaining marinade, until well browned on all sides. Serve the skewers piping hot, sprayed with olive oil.

Black Bean Chili with Orange-Pepper Sauce and Wheat Chips

Though the first black bean soup I tasted was rather dull, I quickly envisioned it jazzed up with warm aromatics such as fresh ginger, serrano chilies, and toasted spice seeds. This version is a current favorite, and like other chili dishes, it's warm and welcome on a cold day. Serve with or without Orange Pepper Sauce and Wheat Chips.   8 TO 10 SERVINGS

        3 cups dried black beans (about 1¼ pounds), sorted, rinsed, and
           soaked overnight in water
        8 cups water
        2 jalapeño chilies, seeded and minced
      One ½-inch piece peeled fresh ginger, minced
        1 bay leaf
        1 cup cilantro leaves, lightly packed
        1 tablespoon cumin seeds
        2 tablespoons ground ancho chilies or chili powder
        ½ tablespoon oregano
        ½ cup chopped sun-dried tomatoes (not oil-packed), 10 to 12
        4 cups peeled, seeded, and chopped plum tomato or one 28-ounce
           can plum tomatoes, chopped
        ⅓ cup coarse bulgur
        ½ cup boiling water
           Salt
           Freshly ground pepper
        ½ tablespoon mustard seeds
        ½ teaspoon fennel seeds
        2 tablespoons extra-virgin olive oil or olive-oil spray
           Orange-Pepper Sauce (recipe follows)
           Wheat Chips (recipe follows)

    Drain the beans. Place the beans and water in a soup pot and bring to a boil. Skim off the foam that rises to the surface. Add the chilies, ginger, bay

leaf, and half of the cilantro and bring to a boil again. Reduce the heat to low; cover and gently boil until the beans are tender, 1½ to 2 hours.

Meanwhile, place a heavy-bottomed saucepan over moderately high heat. Add the cumin seeds and toast until they darken a few shades, 1 to 2 minutes. Add the ancho chilies or chili powder, oregano, sun-dried tomatoes, and fresh or canned tomatoes and their juice. Stir and bring to a boil. Reduce heat to low, cover, and simmer for 30 minutes, stirring frequently. In a separate pan, add the bulgur to the boiling water, cover and allow it to soak and soften.

When the black beans are tender, remove 1 cup and puree it in a food processor with some of the cooking liquid. Combine the puree, remaining whole beans, tomato sauce, and bulgur in the soup pot. Season with salt and pepper and gently simmer for 10 minutes.

Place the mustard seeds in a saucepan over moderate heat. Cover and cook until the seeds begin to sputter. Drop in the fennel seeds, cover, and shaking the pan, cook until the popping sound stops and the fennel darkens a few shades. Pour the seeds into the chili. Add the remaining cilantro and oil; stir to mix. Alternately, spray each serving with olive oil. Garnish individual bowls with Orange-Pepper Sauce and accompany with Wheat Chips.

Orange-Pepper Sauce

MAKES ABOUT 1¼ CUPS

   4 **large orange bell peppers or 2 green and 2 red bell peppers**
      (1½ pounds), roasted, peeled, and coarsely chopped
   ½ **cup water**
   ½ **tablespoon avocado oil or light sesame oil**
      Herb salt
      Cayenne

Place the peppers in a food processor and process to a chunky paste. Add the water and continue to blend until the color lightens. Drizzle in the oil, season with salt and cayenne, and set aside until ready to serve.

Wheat Chips

Chapatis, also called wheat tortillas, are available in most natural-food stores. A recipe for homemade chapatis is given in the Appendix. Though they can be flame-toasted and buttered like toast, when oven-baked they become crunchy, like baked tortilla chips.　MAKES 36 CHIPS, ABOUT 9 SERVINGS

> 6　**whole-wheat chapatis**
> 　　**Water**
> 　　**Hungarian paprika or herb salt**

Preheat the oven to 400°F. Using a sharp knife or scissors, cut each chapati into six triangles to yield thirty-six wedges. Lay the wedges on nonstick baking sheets in single layers, without overlapping. Spray or brush the wedges with water and sprinkle with paprika or salt.

Bake until lightly brown and crisp, 8 to 10 minutes. Cool and store in airtight containers or freeze in plastic bags. Four chips equal 1 serving.

Lentil Ravioli with Gingered Tomato Sauce

I like to use old-world French lentils in this stuffing for ravioli. The slate-green lentils have a rich distinctive flavor, a little more pronounced than many domestic varieties. Still, you can use virtually any lentil you like. Won ton wrappers streamline the ravioli-making process. For a workday meal, serve with hot French bread and Sautéed Spinach and Eggplant Salad (page 60).
6 SERVINGS

Filling

> ½　**teaspoon ground cumin**
> 1　**teaspoon ground coriander**
> ¼　**teaspoon ground turmeric**
> ¼　**teaspoon ground cinnamon**

2⅔ cups water
 1 tablespoon olive oil
¼ cup minced bulb fennel or celery
 1 teaspoon grated fresh ginger
¾ cup dried lentils, cleaned and rinsed
 2 tablespoons chopped cilantro
    Salt
    Cayenne
30 trimmed fresh cilantro leaves

 3 tablespoons grated coconut
60 round or square won ton wrappers (available at supermarkets
    and Oriental markets), defrosted if frozen
    Gingered Tomato Sauce (recipe follows)

Mix the ground spices in a small dish with 3 tablespoons of water. Heat the oil in a large saucepan over moderate heat. Add the fennel and ginger and cook for 3 to 4 minutes. Pour the spice mixture into the pan and cook until the liquid has evaporated. Add the lentils and the remaining water and bring to a boil. Reduce the heat slightly, cover, and gently boil for 30 minutes. Uncover and, stirring frequently, cook until almost all of the liquid has evaporated. Stir in the cilantro and season with salt and cayenne. (Can be prepared 2 days ahead and refrigerated. Bring to room temperature before use.)

Place four won ton wrappers on a work surface. Mound 1 tablespoon of filling in the center of a wrapper, and top with a single cilantro leaf. Brush the edges with water and top with a second wrapper. Using your fingers, press firmly around the filling, removing any air bubbles, and seal. With a fluted pastry wheel, cut into roughly 2½-inch squares or rounds. Remove scraps and set the ravioli aside on a dry towel. Repeat for the remaining ravioli.

Bring a kettle of salted water to a gentle boil and cook the ravioli in batches for 2 minutes, or until they rise to the surface. (Ravioli will break open if cooked in rapidly boiling water.) Transfer them to a buttered baking pan. Keep covered in a preheated 200°F oven while cooking the remaining ravioli.

Spoon some of the sauce on each of six heated plates. Arrange five ravioli on each plate, with the cilantro leaf visible on top. Drizzle with the remaining sauce and sprinkle with coconut.

Gingered Tomato Sauce

MAKES ABOUT 1½ CUPS

1½ tablespoons grated fresh ginger
3 pounds tomatoes, quartered, or one 28-ounce can plum
   tomatoes, drained and chopped
1 tablespoon chopped fresh mint or cilantro
   Salt
   Freshly ground pepper
1 to 2 tablespoons extra-virgin olive oil

Place the ginger and tomato in a deep heavy skillet over moderately low heat. Cover and cook for 30 minutes. Force the stewed tomatoes through a fine-mesh sieve to remove skins and seeds. Transfer to a food processor and puree, in batches if necessary. Add the mint and season with salt and pepper. Just before serving, drizzle with oil and stir. (Can be made 2 days ahead and refrigerated. Reheat slowly before serving.)

Mung Bean and Basmati Rice Stew with Vegetables

Indian *kitcheree* — a rice, bean, and vegetable stew — has many faces. It can be thick-textured or thin and creamy, made with only a few ingredients or as many as two dozen. This version is somewhere in between — a baked stew that takes just minutes to assemble and almost cooks by itself. Use the recipe as inspiration for your own favorite versions. This is an ideal slow-cooker meal year-round. Serve with a green salad and toasted flat bread chapatis. Hearty appetites seem to increase when this entree appears, so make plenty of it. Leftovers seems to improve on the second day.   8 SERVINGS

Stew

                1 cup dried whole mung beans
               ⅔ cup white or brown basmati rice
                1 tablespoon grated fresh ginger
       ¼ to ½ teaspoon cayenne
                1 tablespoon ground coriander
                1 teaspoon ground turmeric
             1½ cups chopped plum tomato (1 pound)
                6 cups water or stock
             1½ teaspoons salt
                4 tablespoons chopped fresh cilantro, dill, basil, or chervil
        One of the following seasonal vegetable combinations:
                   Summer Vegetables (cut in ½-inch pieces)
                     2 cups zucchini or yellow crookneck squash
                     1½ cups green beans
                     1½ cups cut red, green, or yellow bell pepper
                   Winter Vegetables
                     1½ cups sliced carrot or radish
                     3 cups small cauliflower florets
                     4 cups torn spinach or Swiss chard leaves

Seasoned Oil

                1 tablespoon mustard seeds
                2 tablespoons cold-pressed corn oil or olive-oil spray

                   Freshly cracked black pepper

Preheat the oven to 375°F. Sort through the beans and rice and remove any foreign matter. Combine them in a strainer and rinse under running water. Transfer to a large, heavy casserole along with the spices, tomato, water, salt, and half of the fresh herbs. Cover and bake for 20 minutes. Stir in one of the seasonal vegetable combinations. Partially cover and bake until most of the liquid has been absorbed and the beans, rice, and vegetables are butter-soft, about 45 minutes. Remove from the oven and set aside.

Place the mustard seeds in a small pan over moderate heat. Cover, and

shaking the pan, fry until they sputter and pop. When the pan is silent, remove it from the heat and add half of the oil.

Just before serving, stir the remaining 2 tablespoons fresh herbs and seasoned oil into the stew. Adjust the seasoning and add a few grinds of pepper. Drizzle individual servings with the remaining oil or spray with olive oil.

Herbed Bean Sauce and Sautéed Tomatoes over Rice

This second *kitcheree* recipe is a recent invention focusing on three elements, presented in layers—a rice pilaf, a chili-like bean sauce, and caramelized sautéed tomatoes. I have made the sauce with several varieties of beans and ended up with too many favorites to mention here.

Use the recipe as a formula to explore bean sauces. Beans of like size and/or color will have similar flavors. You might try China Yellow beans, French navy beans, Great Northern, Jacob's Cattle, or Anazaki beans. Each will lend the sauce a unique body, character, and flavor. 6 SERVINGS

Bean Sauce

  1 cup dried white beans, soaked overnight and drained
1 to 2 serrano chilies, seeded and chopped
  ½ tablespoon grated fresh ginger
  1 bay leaf
  ¼ teaspoon ground turmeric
  4 cups water
 1⅓ cups vegetable stock
  ¼ cup cilantro leaves
   Salt
   Freshly ground pepper
  2 tablespoons chopped pecans, pan-toasted until golden

Tomatoes

- 2 tablespoons extra-virgin olive oil
- 4 tomatoes, peeled, seeded, and diced
- 1 teaspoon ground ancho chilies or chili powder
- 1 tablespoon chopped fresh marjoram or thyme leaves
- 1 teaspoon maple syrup

Rice

- 5 cups water
- 1½ cups long-grain rice, preferably basmati
- 2 carrots, finely shredded
- One 3-inch cinnamon stick
- ½ tablespoon extra-virgin olive oil

To make the bean sauce, combine the drained beans, chilies, ginger, bay leaf, turmeric, and water in a large saucepan. Bring to a boil; reduce the heat to low, cover, and gently boil until the beans are tender, 1½ to 2 hours. Discard the bay leaf and drain the beans. Place the cooked beans, stock, and cilantro in a food processor and pulse into a chunky sauce. Season with salt and pepper. (May be prepared 1 day ahead and refrigerated. Thin to original consistency before use.) Add the pecans and reheat gently.

To make the tomatoes, combine the oil, tomato, chili powder, marjoram, and maple syrup in a nonstick sauté pan. Season with salt and pepper and stir-fry over moderate heat until the tomato begins to caramelize and brown, about 10 minutes. Keep warm on low heat.

To make the rice, bring the water to a boil. Stir in the rice, carrot, and cinnamon stick. Cook on high heat until the rice is tender, 10 to 12 minutes for white rice and 20 to 25 minutes for brown rice. Drain in a strainer, discard the cinnamon, and rinse briefly under running water. Return to the pan and toss with the oil.

To serve, spoon the rice onto warm plates, top with bean sauce, and scatter with tomatoes.

Mung Bean–Cabbage Cakes with Bengali Tomato Chutney

Slight variations of this dish are found in Indian village kitchens from Amritsar to Calcutta; however, all of them are deep-fried. I much prefer this lighter pan-fried version. During the recipe-testing process, dinner guests familiar with Indian cuisine renamed them "vegetarian crab cakes." If you are on a fat-restricted diet, use olive-oil spray on the pans and finished cakes for flavor. For an entree, accompany with a green salad and minted peas with carrot ribbons. Leftovers are great in sandwiches.
4 ENTREE SERVINGS; 6 FIRST-COURSE SERVINGS

> One 1-inch piece peeled fresh ginger
> 1½ cups dried mung beans, soaked overnight and drained
> ½ cup water
> 2 tablespoons fresh lemon juice
> 1 teaspoon salt
> ½ tablespoon ground coriander
> ¼ cup chopped fresh parsley
> ¼ cup chopped cilantro
> 5 cups finely shredded cabbage
> ½ teaspoon dried red chili flakes
> ½ teaspoon baking powder
> 3 tablespoons extra-virgin olive oil or olive-oil spray
> Bengali Tomato Chutney (recipe follows)
> ¼ cup plain nonfat yogurt, stirred until smooth

With the food processor running, drop the ginger through the feed tube and mince. Add the drained beans and process until coarsely chopped. Pour in the water and process until pureed. Add the lemon juice, salt, coriander, and ⅓ cup of herbs (equal parts parsley and cilantro) and process until the herbs are minced. Transfer to a bowl; stir in the cabbage, chili flakes, and baking powder, and mix well.

Preheat the oven to 250°F. Preheat a nonstick griddle over medium heat

and brush with ½ tablespoon of oil or spray with oil. Place ⅓ cup of cabbage batter on the griddle and spread into a cake about ⅓-inch thick, shaping four at a time. Cook until brown on the bottom, 3 to 4 minutes. Spray with oil or drizzle with ½ tablespoon of oil, flip, and cook the second sides until brown. Transfer to a baking sheet and keep warm. Shape and cook the remaining eight cakes, using the remaining 2 tablespoons of oil.

To serve, place three cakes on a hot dinner plate. Spoon Bengali Tomato Chutney at the base of each, drizzle with yogurt, and sprinkle with the remaining herbs.

Bengali Tomato Chutney

This is the book's first recipe tested in a microwave, one of a handful of chutneys and salsas. I prepare it in a small 500-watt combination microwave oven–toaster oven; it takes 5 minutes to cook to perfection. If your machine is more powerful, it should be finished in just 3 or 4 minutes.

To make a stovetop version, toast the spices in a dry saucepan and simmer all of the ingredients over low heat for 15 to 20 minutes.

MAKES ABOUT 1¼ CUPS

    ½ teaspoon fennel seeds
    ¼ teaspoon cumin seeds
    3 ripe tomatoes, chopped
    ¼ cup tomato puree
    ⅛ teaspoon cayenne
       Salt
       Freshly ground pepper
    1 teaspoon extra-virgin olive oil
    1 tablespoon chopped fresh mint or cilantro

Place the spice seeds in a folded paper towel and microwave until fragrant and lightly toasted, 1 to 2 minutes (depending on your oven's wattage). Combine the toasted spices, tomato, puree, and cayenne in a 4-cup microwave-proof dish. Cook for 5 minutes on full power. Season with salt and pepper; stir in the olive oil and mint. Serve warm or at room temperature.

Oven-Baked Black Bean, Potato, and Corn Cake

At a 1990 PETA (People for Ethical Treatment of Animals) benefit in Washington, D.C., executive chef Peter Schaffrath of The Willard prepared a shallow-fried version of this bean entree. I wanted to try my hand at a lighter version, and he kindly shared his recipe with me. The bean-vegetable cakes have a texture somewhere between crispy potato pancakes and diner hash browns. Slow oven-baking allows them to brown evenly and uses very little oil. Make them in small tart pans for individual round servings or in round cake tins for sliced wedges.

You can serve these cakes as an entree, accompanied by Dilled Carrot Puree and Steamed Spinach, or as a starter or side dish, with lime wedges or fresh chutney on the side.   8 SERVINGS

    4   large baking potatoes (2½ pounds)
    2   tablespoons butter, melted
    1   tablespoon extra-virgin olive oil
    1   tablespoon crushed coriander seeds
    ¼   teaspoon crushed red-pepper flakes
    1½ cups cooked black beans or adzuki beans, drained
    ½   cup diced zucchini
    1   cup fresh or frozen corn kernels, defrosted and drained
        Salt
        Freshly ground pepper
        Dilled Carrot Puree and Steamed Spinach (recipe follows)

Preheat the oven to 450°F. Spray two nonstick 8-inch round cake pans or eight 3-inch tart pans with olive-oil spray.

Fit a medium shredding disk in the food processor. Peel the potatoes and cut them so that they fit horizontally in the feed tube. Shred them lengthwise, applying medium pressure. Plunge the shreds in cold water; drain and pat dry.

Combine the butter, oil, coriander seeds, and pepper flakes in a large bowl. Add the potato shreds and the remaining ingredients. Season with salt and pepper and toss to mix. Press the mixture lightly into the prepared pans and bake until browned, 45 to 50 minutes. (Prepare the carrot puree and spinach while the potato cakes are baking.)

To unmold the cake, run a knife around the edge of the pan and invert the cake onto a plate. Invert again onto a serving plate and cut large cakes into quarters. (May be kept warm for 10 minutes in a 250°F oven if necessary.)

To serve, spoon a bed of spinach onto each of eight warmed plates. Top with an individual potato cake or wedge. Surround the spinach with hot carrot puree and serve immediately.

Dilled Carrot Puree and Steamed Spinach

8 SIDE-DISH SERVINGS

1½ **pounds carrots, peeled**
1 **bay leaf**
4 **stems dill (about 4 inches long), trimmed and minced**
   Salt
   Freshly ground pepper
2 **pounds spinach leaves, washed, stems removed, and torn in pieces**

Place the whole carrots and bay leaf in a medium saucepan. Cover with cold water and bring to a boil over high heat. Reduce the heat to low, cover, and simmer until the carrots are tender, about 20 minutes. Drain, and puree in a food processor or blender. Transfer to a saucepan. Add the dill, season with salt and pepper, and keep warm over low heat.

With the water still clinging to leaves, place the spinach in a large saucepan over moderately low heat. Cover and cook until tender, about 5 minutes. Remove from the heat and drain.

Chickpea–Red Pepper Cutlets with Mustard Cream Sauce

Green herbs, red bell peppers, and yellow corn give this cutlet striking visual appeal. Bedded on wilted romaine lettuce and blanketed with a fragrant mustard cream sauce, this is an impressive entree for entertaining. If you use canned chickpeas and roasted red peppers, it takes less than half an hour to make.

For a meal with more substance, double the sauce recipe and fold half the sauce into a 6-cup mixture of cooked whole-wheat fettuccine and sliced vegetables.   6 SERVINGS

4	cups finely shredded romaine lettuce leaves
One	7-ounce jar roasted red peppers or 3 roasted red bell peppers (page 288), peeled, seeded, and diced
⅓	cup fresh or frozen corn kernels, defrosted and drained
2	cups cooked chickpeas, rinsed and drained
¼	cup cilantro leaves
¼	cup fresh mint leaves
½	tablespoon chopped peeled fresh ginger
1 to 2	jalapeño chilies, seeded and chopped
½	teaspoon ground coriander
1	teaspoon salt
⅔	cup fresh whole-wheat bread crumbs
	Olive-oil spray or 2 tablespoons virgin olive oil
	Mustard Cream Sauce (recipe follows)

Steam the romaine for about 30 seconds or until it is barely wilted and the color has intensified. Scatter it over the bottom of a serving dish. Cover and keep warm over simmering water.

Rinse the roasted peppers under running water; drain and pat dry on paper towels. Cut the peppers into 1-inch squares; place them in a dish and mix with the corn.

Combine the chickpeas, fresh herbs, ginger, chilies, coriander, and salt in a food processor and pulse until coarsely chopped. Scrape down the sides of the work bowl as necessary to keep the ingredients toward the blades. Add the bread crumbs and process to a paste. Add the peppers and corn and pulse until the vegetables are coarsely chopped. Transfer the mixture to a plate. With moistened palms, shape into twelve balls and flatten each into a 2-inch patty.

Spray an 8-inch nonstick skillet with oil and warm over moderately high heat. Spray the surface of six patties with oil. Place them on the griddle and fry until well browned, 3 to 4 minutes per side. Arrange the patties over half of the lettuce and repeat the process for the second batch. (Alternately, brown each batch of patties in 1 tablespoon of oil.)

To serve, pour a thin stream of Mustard Cream Sauce over both patties and lettuce to form a lattice pattern, or serve the sauce separately.

Mustard Cream Sauce

This makes enough sauce for the cutlets and lettuce. If you serve the entree with pasta or rice and steamed vegetables, double the recipe.
MAKES ABOUT 1¾ CUPS

    1   teaspoon mustard seeds
    2   cups skim milk
    2½ tablespoons Cream of Rice cereal
        Salt
        Freshly ground pepper

Place the mustard seeds in a saucepan; cover and place over moderately high heat. Shaking the pan, toast the seeds until they sputter and pop. Pour in the milk, and, stirring constantly, bring to a boil. Sprinkle in the Cream of Rice, and, continuing to stir, boil until the sauce is thick enough to coat the spoon with a thin film, 4 to 5 minutes. Using a wire whisk, beat until smooth; season with salt and pepper.

Adzuki Bean Cakes with Pepper Cream and Tomato-Cilantro Concasse

Laced with herbs, red bell pepper, and yam bits, these bean cakes are speckled with green, red, and orange hues. If you are a newcomer to adzuki beans, this is a good choice. They are available at gourmet and natural-food stores. You can also use supermarket black beans with excellent results. When served as an entree, the Pepper Cream and Tomato-Cilantro Concasse are perfect accompaniments. You need little more than a green salad and a grain pilaf to make a meal.   8 SERVINGS

2½	cups dried adzuki beans or black beans (1 pound)
6	cups cold water
5	cups Summer Vegetable Stock (page 77)
1½	cups finely chopped carrot
1½	cups finely chopped yam
½	tablespoon cumin seeds
1	tablespoon coriander seeds
¼	cup tomato paste
1	teaspoon salt
	Cayenne
1	cup fresh whole-wheat bread crumbs
½	cup lightly packed cilantro leaves
3	large roasted yellow bell peppers (page 288), peeled and seeded, or one 7-ounce jar roasted red peppers
½	tablespoon chili powder
½	cup whole-wheat flour
	Olive-oil spray
	Pepper Cream (recipe follows)
	Tomato-Cilantro Concasse (recipe follows)

Sort through the beans and place them in a saucepan. Add the water and set aside for 8 hours or overnight.

Drain the beans and add the vegetable stock. Bring to a boil; cover and reduce the heat. Briskly simmer until the beans are tender, 1 to 1½ hours. Drain in a sieve, rinse under cold water, and set aside.

Steam the carrot and yam for 3 minutes and set aside to drain. Place the cumin and coriander seeds in a pan and toast over moderate heat until they darken a few shades. Combine the toasted spices, drained beans, tomato paste, salt, a touch of cayenne, and the bread crumbs in a food processor. Process until the ingredients are reduced to a paste, scraping down the sides of the bowl as necessary. Add the cilantro, bell peppers, carrot, and yam, and pulse until the peppers are coarsely chopped.

Preheat the broiler. Mix the chili powder into the flour. Divide the bean mixture into ¼-cup portions, and with moistened hands, flatten into 2½-inch cakes. Roll the cakes in the seasoned flour to coat them. Generously spray the cakes with olive oil and set them on a broiling rack about 5 inches from the heat. Broil until they are browned and crisp, 4 to 5 minutes per side. Serve hot, drizzled with Pepper Cream and a spoonful of Tomato-Cilantro Concasse on the side.

Pepper Cream

MAKES 1 CUP

   ⅓ **cup low-fat cottage cheese**
   ⅔ **cup buttermilk**
   ½ **teaspoon freshly cracked pepper**
   2 **tablespoons chopped fresh parsley**

Puree the cottage cheese and buttermilk in a blender until creamy. Stir in the pepper and parsley.

Tomato-Cilantro Concasse

MAKES ABOUT 2 CUPS

    8 plum tomatoes (1 pound), peeled, seeded, and chopped
    1 tablespoon maple syrup
    1 tablespoon fresh lime juice
  ¼ cup cilantro leaves
    2 tablespoons tomato paste
  ½ teaspoon cumin seeds, pan-toasted until a darker shade
      Salt or herb salt

Combine all of the ingredients in a food processor and process until the mixture is reduced to a coarse puree.

Eggplant, Potato, and Chickpea Stew

In 1976 I had my first taste of eggplant-potato stew. I can remember the appearance of the dish as if it were yesterday—chunky vegetables glistening in a buttery tomato glaze. To sample the dish, I was instructed to break off a piece of toasted chapati, and using my fingers, scoop up a bite of succulent stew and pop it into my mouth. The flavor wowed me, and I was hooked from the first bite.

Some one hundred stews later, this low-fat version is my current favorite. Try it with chapati or a salad.   8 SERVINGS

  ½ tablespoon mustard seeds
  ½ tablespoon grated fresh ginger
    1 pound tomatoes, chopped
  ½ cup chickpeas (garbanzo beans), soaked overnight in water and
      drained
    5 cups water

½ teaspoon ground turmeric
3 tablespoons chopped cilantro
1½ pounds firm, ripe eggplant
1½ pounds red potatoes
  Olive-oil spray
½ tablespoon ground coriander
1½ tablespoons fresh lime juice
  Salt
  Freshly ground pepper
1½ tablespoons virgin olive oil or melted butter

Place the mustard seeds in a heavy casserole over moderate heat. Cover and dry-fry until the seeds sputter and pop. Add the ginger, tomato, chickpeas, water, and turmeric and half of the cilantro. Bring to a boil; reduce the heat slightly and gently boil for 1 to 1½ hours, or until the chickpeas are soft.

While the beans are cooking, roast the vegetables: Preheat the oven to 375°F. Cut the eggplant and potatoes into 1-inch pieces and toss to mix. Spray two nonstick cookie sheets with olive oil. Spread the vegetables out in the pans and spray with olive oil. Sprinkle with coriander and bake for about 45 minutes, or until crisp and golden-brown. Sprinkle the hot vegetables with lime juice.

Fold the vegetables into the hot stew and season with salt and pepper. Cover and barely simmer for 10 to 15 minutes. Sprinkle with the remaining cilantro and drizzle with oil or butter.

SAVORY PASTRIES

In this volume, my approach to pastries is to maximize lightness and ease of preparation. The savory pastries that follow are baked. Most are made with phyllo dough, a few with puff pastry.

ABOUT PHYLLO

Phyllo dough (also called phyllo leaves) is a wonderful alternative to a richer, high-fat dough. Prepared from only gluten-rich flour and water, the dough is paper-thin and cooks up crisp. I have a French friend who makes her own phyllo and swears it is not difficult to master, but I have yet to find the knack. Since it is inexpensive, widely available, and ready to use, I always use commercially prepared phyllo. It is sold in well-sealed boxes (about twenty sheets of pastry per box) in the frozen-food section of most supermarkets and specialty food stores.

HOW TO PREPARE PHYLLO FOR USE

Frozen phyllo dough should be defrosted in the box, overnight, in the refrigerator. Once unwrapped, phyllo dries out quickly. The defrosted leaves should be kept stacked and protected with a barely damp kitchen towel or plastic wrap to preserve their moistness. Keep unused dough in the refrigerator, well wrapped.

On more than a few occasions I have opened a new box only to find all of the sheets stuck together and impossible to separate. When this happens, either the phyllo has previously been defrosted, during transport or in storage, or it is defective. A call to the point of purchase will usually result in a refund.

LAYERING PHYLLO FOR BAKING

Phyllo is delicate and dries out quickly. To make flaky layers of phyllo, the leaves are traditionally separated with a film of melted *ghee* or butter, usually with a pastry brush. When stacked or folded, the buttered layers swell apart

and crisp as they bake. Until recently, I never thought to use oil to separate, moisten, and flavor the layers.

OIL SPRAYS AND PHYLLO

Today I use oil sprays, commercial and homemade, to flavor and moisturize phyllo. They are clean, quick, and easy to use. I use extra-virgin olive-oil spray for much of my cooking, though you will see a few other selections in the pastry recipes. Several brands of spray are on the market, but many use characterless refined oils, with a boost from propellants and preservatives. All oils are not the same. At least two brands of extra-virgin olive-oil spray are available. Recommended brands and mail-order sources are listed in the Appendix.

It is easy to make high-quality sprays at home. Purchase small bottles of unrefined, expeller-pressed or organic oils at gourmet natural-food stores and store them in spray bottles, the kind used for misting plants, available at garden supply stores. Keep a few homemade flavor-infused oils in spray bottles as well. It is hard to describe the subtle distinction of pastries sprayed with ancho chili oil, sun-dried tomato oil, or curry oil.

ASSEMBLY AND STORAGE OF PASTRIES

All of the fillings can be made ahead of time and kept refrigerated. Phyllo pastry is best assembled just before baking to assure a crisp crust. Because the stuffings have a higher moisture content than the phyllo, the leaves soften when they cool to room temperature. Clearly, the closer to baking time the pastry is assembled, the crispier it will be.

A FEW WORDS ABOUT PUFF PASTRY

Puff pastry can be assembled a few hours before serving and kept refrigerated until baked. Frozen puff pastry is sold tightly wrapped, usually two sheets per package. Remove as many sheets as you will need, and thaw them at room temperature before unfolding. Rewrap unused pastry and return it to the freezer. Keep the pastry dough cold to the touch while working with it, and handle it as little as possible. Use sharp cutting utensils.

Bengali-Style Potato-Pea Samosas with Dried Fruit Chutney

Bengali *samosas*, also called *singhara*, are mouthwatering, deep-fried, savory pastries. While most *samosas* are shaped into triangular parcels, Bengali pastries are rolled into logs. These baked *samosas* are a breeze to make, assembled like potato strudel, using phyllo dough.

There are many approaches to Indian *samosa* stuffings. This is an example of one of the simplest, combining flavor and heat from the chilies, a hint of sweetness from the maple syrup, and the headiness of fresh herbs. It is sure to be appealing to the Western palate.   6 SERVINGS

>   3 large baking potatoes (1½ pounds), peeled, coarsely shredded,
>   and steamed for 5 minutes
>   1 cup defrosted petite peas
>   ½ teaspoon ground ancho chilies or paprika
>   2 tablespoons fresh lemon juice
> 1½ tablespoons maple syrup
>   3 tablespoons chopped cilantro or fresh mint
>   ½ tablespoon mustard seeds
>   Salt
>   Freshly ground pepper
>   12 phyllo dough sheets, about 14 × 18 inches
>   Olive- or walnut-oil spray
>   ½ cup toasted wheat germ
>   Dried Fruit Chutney (recipe follows)

Combine the potato, peas, ground chili, lemon juice, maple syrup, and cilantro on a platter. Place the mustard seeds in a small pan over moderate heat. Cover and cook until the seeds turn gray and pop. Add to the potato mixture, season with salt and pepper, and gently mix. Divide into twelve portions.

Preheat the oven to 375°F. Stack the phyllo sheets between waxed paper

and cover with a barely dampened kitchen towel. Place one phyllo sheet, with the short side facing you, on a work surface. Spray or brush with a film of oil and sprinkle with ½ tablespoon wheat germ. Lift up the bottom end of the phyllo sheet and fold it in half. Spray or brush the folded sheet with oil and strew one portion of the potato mixture over the dough, leaving 1 inch on all sides. Fold over the sides and roll into a log from bottom to top.

Place, seam side down, on a nonstick baking sheet and spray or brush with oil. Shape and spray the remaining *samosas* and bake until golden, 35 to 40 minutes.

Serve with the chutney, allowing two *samosas* per person.

Dried Fruit Chutney

MAKES ABOUT 1½ CUPS

  1 **cup mixed dried fruit (6 ounces)**
1½ **cups apple juice**
  1 **tablespoon grated fresh ginger**
⅛ **teaspoon cayenne**
⅛ **teaspoon ground cinnamon**
⅛ **teaspoon ground cloves**
  2 **tablespoons fresh lemon juice**
  2 **tablespoons fresh orange juice**
  1 **tablespoon finely chopped cilantro or fresh mint**

In a small heavy saucepan, combine the fruit, apple juice, ginger, and spices and bring to a boil. Reduce the heat, cover, and simmer for 30 minutes. Transfer to a food processor and blend until smooth. Force through a fine sieve into a bowl. Stir in the citrus juices and cilantro.

Ratatouille Spirals with Red Pepper–Tomato Sauce

These strudel spirals are beautiful on the dinner plate, served with a few spoonfuls of a brilliant red sauce and colorful seasonal vegetables. A few favorite side dishes are Swiss Chard with Toasted Sesame Seeds (page 234), Oven-Roasted Okra (page 244), and Deviled Corn on the Cob (page 249).

8 SERVINGS

> ½   tablespoon mustard seeds
> Virgin olive-oil spray
> 2   medium eggplants (1½ pounds), peeled, cubed, and steamed until soft
> ½   tablespoon grated fresh ginger
> 1 to 2 jalapeño chilies, seeded and minced
> 1   cup cooked chopped spinach, well drained
> 1½   cups cooked chickpeas, drained
> 2   roasted red bell peppers (page 288), peeled, seeded, and chopped
> ½   cup cilantro leaves
> Salt
> Freshly ground pepper
> 16   phyllo sheets, about 12 × 18 inches
> Red Pepper–Tomato Sauce (recipe follows)

Place the mustard seeds in a small pan. Cover and toast over moderate heat until the seeds sputter and pop. Remove from the heat and set aside.

Place a large nonstick skillet over moderate heat and spray with olive oil. When hot, add the eggplant, ginger, and chilies. Stirring constantly, fry until the eggplant begins to brown and stick to the pan. Stir in the spinach, chickpeas, bell peppers, and cilantro and fry for another 3 to 4 minutes. Cool slightly. Transfer the mixture to a food processor, pulse 4 or 5 times, then process until reduced to a coarse-textured paste. Add the mustard seeds, season with salt and pepper, and pulse twice to mix. (Can be made 1 day ahead.) Spoon the vegetable mixture into a pastry bag fitted with a No. 8 plain tube.

Cover the phyllo sheets with waxed paper and a damp dishtowel to prevent them from becoming brittle. Place one phyllo sheet on a piece of waxed paper and spray the surface with olive oil. Fold in half lengthwise to make a 6 × 18-inch sheet, and spray with olive oil. Leaving 1 inch at either end, pipe a band of eggplant filling 1 inch from the folded long edge. Fold over the short ends, then lift the folded long edge over the filling and roll into a cylinder. Turning the cylinder seam side down, gently wind into a loose, flat spiral, like a coil of rope. Spray with olive oil and transfer to a parchment-lined baking tray. To secure the end of the coil in place, insert a toothpick from the outer end toward the center of the spiral. Cover loosely with plastic while assembling the remaining pastries. Gentle handling is of the essence throughout.

Preheat the oven to 350°F. Remove the plastic wrap and bake the spirals until they are golden-brown, about 45 minutes. Remove the toothpicks before serving. Serve hot or warm (two per person), accompanied with sauce.

Red Pepper–Tomato Sauce

This is a terrific sauce for many things — rice, pasta, pizza, vegetables, and casseroles. It has a texture somewhere between that of cooked Indian tomato chutney and Italian marinara sauce. It is one of the first dishes I ever tried to make in a microwave oven — a quick 15 minutes versus about half an hour on the stove. Both yield good results.   MAKES ABOUT 1⅓ CUPS

   2 **large red bell peppers**
   ½ **tablespoon coriander seeds**
   1 **pound ripe tomatoes, preferably Italian plum, chopped**
   ½ **cup shredded carrot**
      Salt
      Freshly ground pepper
   ½ **tablespoon virgin olive oil**

Preheat a broiler or stovetop grill over moderate heat. Char the peppers on all sides until the skins blacken. Transfer to a bowl, cover, and cool for 15 minutes. Rub off the charred skins, seed, derib, and coarsely chop.

Place the coriander seeds in a 2-quart microwave dish; cover and microwave on medium for 2 minutes. Add the pepper, tomato, and carrot. Cover and microwave on full power for 6 minutes, stirring once during cooking. Alternately, toast the seeds in a dry pan over moderate heat. Add the pepper, tomato, and carrot, and cook over moderately low heat for 25 minutes, or until the sauce is thick and the excess liquid has evaporated. Force the sauce through a coarse sieve; season with salt and pepper and drizzle with oil.

Kale and Corn Strudel with Light Tomato Sauce

If you are a newcomer to kale, this dish may be the one that makes you a convert. The kale is paired with sweet corn, ricotta, and coconut and laced with warm jalapeños and fresh ginger. For added texture and a nutty flavor, the phyllo leaves are sprinkled with toasted mustard seeds and wheat germ as they are folded. Serve with soup, salad, or a side-dish vegetable.   6 SERVINGS

Filling

8	ounces kale, trimmed, steamed, and finely chopped
1½	cups cooked corn kernels
3	tablespoons grated fresh or dry coconut
1	cup part-skim ricotta cheese
1	jalapeño chili, seeded and minced
1	teaspoon grated fresh ginger
	Salt
	Freshly ground pepper

½	tablespoon mustard seeds
⅓	cup raw wheat germ
8	phyllo dough sheets (5 to 6 ounces)
	Olive-oil spray
	Light Tomato Sauce (recipe follows)

In a mixing bowl, combine all of the filling ingredients. Season with salt and pepper. Divide into twelve portions and shape each into a 3-inch-long log.

Place the mustard seeds in a pan over moderate heat. Cover and toast, shaking the pan, until the seeds begin to pop. Stir in the wheat germ and, still shaking the pan, toast until the wheat germ turns golden; set aside.

Preheat the oven to 375°F. Stack the phyllo sheets, separating them with layers of waxed paper, and cover with a dampened towel. Cut through the sheets into 6-inch pieces, yielding forty-eight squares. Transfer twelve squares to a work surface and spray them with olive oil. Top each with another phyllo square and sprinkle with half of the wheat-germ mixture. Top with a third phyllo square, spray with oil, and top with a final square. You should have twelve four-layer stacks. Top with the remaining wheat-germ mixture.

Position a cylinder of stuffing diagonally across a phyllo stack. Fold over opposite corners to cover the filling, and tuck over the ends to form a packet. Place seam side down on a nonstick baking tray. Repeat the process for the remaining pastries.

Bake until the pastries are golden-brown, 30 to 35 minutes. Spoon warm sauce on each plate and top with two pastry parcels while they are hot.

Light Tomato Sauce

When tomatoes are abundant, I make a large pot of this simple tomato sauce and freeze it in 1½-cup portions in zipper-lock freezer bags. It's great in almost any Mexican, Italian, Asian, or American dish calling for tomato sauce.   MAKES ABOUT 1½ CUPS

> 1½ **pounds ripe tomatoes, peeled, seeded, and chopped**
> 1 **teaspoon chopped fresh ginger**
> ⅛ **teaspoon crushed red-pepper flakes**
> 1 **tablespoon virgin olive oil**
>   **Salt**
> 2 **tablespoons chopped cilantro**

Combine the tomato, ginger, and pepper flakes in a saucepan and simmer for 30 minutes. Transfer to a food processor and puree. With the machine running, drizzle the oil through the feed tube. Season with salt and add the cilantro.

Dinner-Size Chickpea Kachori with Chickpea Chutney

Kachori are special-occasion Indian pastries—rich, savory, and elegant. Perhaps the most difficult fried pastry to master, *kachori* come in various shapes and sizes, a legume or vegetable stuffing nestled under flaky layers of buttery crust. They are served from midmorning to late supper as finger foods when feasting is in the air.

This *kachori* variation takes center stage as a dinner entree, and is large enough to master on a first try. It is assembled and baked like a French *pithiviers*, though the vegetable and chickpea stuffing more resembles one used in an Italian calzone. When I want to make the dish for weekday company, I use frozen puff pastry, bottled chickpeas, and bottled roasted red bell peppers, though you could make all from scratch. Serve a wedge of chickpea *kachori* with generous portions of grilled seasonal vegetables and Chickpea Chutney. Accompany with soup or salad to round out the meal.   6 TO 8 SERVINGS

Filling

- 1 medium yellow zucchini (8 ounces)
- 2 large red bell peppers
- 1 jalapeño chili, seeded and chopped
- 1⅓ cups cooked chickpeas
- ¼ cup cilantro leaves
- 1 teaspoon mustard seeds
  Salt
  Freshly ground pepper

- 8 ounces fresh or frozen puff pastry (one 10 × 10-inch sheet)
  Olive-oil spray
  Chickpea Chutney (recipe follows)

Cut the zucchini crosswise into ¼-inch slices. Stack the rounds five at a time and cut them into ¼-inch julienne. Steam the zucchini until tender-crisp and pat dry on paper towels.

Quarter the bell peppers; seed and derib them. Broil them until the skins blacken. Transfer to a bowl, cover, and set aside for 15 minutes. Remove the charred skins and dice. Set aside one-fourth of the pepper for the chutney.

Place the jalapeño, chickpeas, and cilantro in a food processor and pulse until evenly chopped, about 10 times. Combine the chickpea mixture, zucchini, and remaining diced pepper in a bowl. Toast the mustard seeds over moderate heat in a covered pan until they pop and turn gray. Add the seeds to the filling, season with salt and pepper, and mix well. (Can be made several hours ahead and refrigerated, covered.)

Thaw the frozen pastry for about 20 minutes before unfolding. Keep fresh or defrosted pastry cold to the touch and roll, on a lightly floured surface, into a 12 × 23-inch rectangle. Using the bottom of a 12-inch springform pan, cut out a circle of pastry. Place it on a baking tray lined with parchment paper. Cut out a top "lid" 1 inch larger than the bottom.

Using your hands, mound the filling smoothly on the bottom pastry round, leaving a 1-inch border around the edges. The filling should be about 1½ inches high in the center and taper to nothing toward the rim. Moisten the border of the bottom pastry round with water. Fold the top pastry round in half, align it on one side of the bottom round, then unfold to cover the mound of filling, pressing around the moistened edges to seal. Trim off uneven edges with a sharp knife. With the tip of the knife, draw lines radiating out from the center of the top pastry round. To decorate the edges of the crust, notch them decoratively with the dull side of the knife without cutting through the dough. Freeze the *kachori* for at least 15 minutes, or cover and refrigerate for up to 6 hours.

Preheat the oven to 400°F. Bake the *kachori* for 10 minutes; reduce the heat to 375°F and bake until the pastry is well risen and golden-brown, 20 to 30 minutes. Remove and cool for a few minutes. Using a sharp serrated knife, cut into six or eight portions depending on appetites, and serve with generous spoons of chutney.

Chickpea Chutney

MAKES ABOUT 1½ CUPS

  ½ to 1 jalapeño chili, seeded and chopped
      1 cup plain nonfat yogurt
     ⅔ cup cooked chickpeas (garbanzo beans), well drained
     ½ cup cooked spinach, well drained
      2 tablespoons chopped cilantro
         Reserved roasted red bell pepper from previous recipe
      1 teaspoon cumin seeds
         Salt
         Freshly ground pepper

Combine the chili and yogurt in a food processor and process until the chili is minced. Add the chickpeas and spinach and process until the chickpeas are finely chopped, 30 to 45 seconds. Transfer to a bowl; add the cilantro and red pepper. Place the cumin seeds in a pan over moderate heat and toast until they darken slightly. Add to the chutney; season with salt and pepper and stir to mix.

Stuffed Pepper Pastries with Yellow Pepper Sauce

Red bell peppers are stuffed with vegetables, farmer cheese, coconut, and cilantro — a rich blend of colors, textures, and flavors. Thin puff-pastry lids are fitted on the peppers, and as they bake, they rise into artful sculptures. If you want to avoid the puff pastry altogether, sprinkle the vegetable stuffing with pumpkin or sesame seeds. Served in a pool of smoky-flavored Yellow-Pepper Sauce, this entree is elegant and simple.   8 SERVINGS

    8 large red bell peppers (3 to 3½ pounds)
   ½ tablespoon mustard seeds
    8 ounces fresh or frozen puff pastry

Filling

- 3 medium zucchini (1¼ pounds)
- 3 medium yellow squash (1¼ pounds)
- 1 cup diced green beans
- 1 cup corn kernels
- 2 carrots, coarsely shredded
- 4 ounces farmer or hoop cheese
- 3 tablespoons grated fresh or frozen coconut
- 3 tablespoons chopped cilantro
- Salt
- Cayenne

Yellow Pepper Sauce (recipe follows)

Halve the peppers lengthwise; seed, derib, and pat dry. Place the mustard seeds in a pan over moderate heat. Cover and toast until the seeds turn gray and pop; set them aside.

Thaw the frozen pastry for about 20 minutes before unfolding. Keep fresh or defrosted pastry cold to the touch. Sprinkle the mustard seeds on the pastry and roll, on a floured surface, into a 12 × 22-inch rectangle. Arrange the peppers, cut sides down, on the pastry and, using a sharp knife, cut out shapes ½ inch larger than the peppers. Transfer them to a parchment-lined baking tray; refrigerate. Parboil the peppers for 5 minutes in boiling water; drain and invert on paper towels.

Cut the zucchini and yellow squash crosswise into ¼-inch slices. Stack five rounds at a time and cut into ¼-inch julienne. Set up a large steamer; add the green beans, cover, and steam for 2 minutes. Add the corn, carrot, zucchini, and yellow squash; cover and steam for 4 minutes. Transfer the vegetables to a bowl. Add the cheese, coconut, and cilantro and gently mix. Season with salt and cayenne.

Preheat the oven to 350°F. Fill the peppers with the mixture; arrange them on a baking pan with 3 tablespoons of water in the bottom of the pan. Top the peppers with the pastry cutouts, pressing the edges firmly along the walls of the peppers. Bake for about 30 minutes, or until the pastry is golden.

To serve, pour about ¼ cup of pepper sauce on the bottom of a warmed dinner plate and top with two pepper halves.

Yellow Pepper Sauce

If yellow peppers are not available, substitute half green and half red—the flavor will still be exceptional. This rich, smoky-flavored sauce is also good on everything from mashed potatoes to salads.   MAKES ABOUT 2¼ CUPS

 1¼ **pounds yellow or orange bell peppers (3 large)**
 ⅔ **cup water**
 ½ **tablespoon herbed or plain olive oil**
 2 **tablespoons tahini**
 1 **teaspoon mustard seeds**
  Herb salt

Quarter the peppers; seed and derib them. Broil them until the skins blacken; set aside in a closed container for 15 minutes. Rub off the charred skins and roughly chop. Place the peppers in a food processor and process to a chunky paste. Add the water and continue to blend until the color lightens. Add the oil and tahini and process until creamy and slightly thickened.

Place the mustard seeds in a saucepan over moderate heat. Cover and toast until the seeds pop and turn gray. Pour the sauce into the pan; season with salt, stir, and keep warm.

Vegetable Pie with Watercress Cream Sauce

This is a light version of one of my childhood favorites—vegetable pot pie. The recipe gives directions for making one large pie, but you can also serve it in individual ramekins. Accompany it with soup or salad.   6 SERVINGS

Filling
 1½ **pounds Napa cabbage, leaves separated, washed, and trimmed**
 1 **cup fresh or frozen green beans, cut into ¼-inch dice**
 1 **cup fresh or frozen corn kernels**

 1 cup fresh or frozen peas
 1 cup diced red bell pepper
1¼ cups farmer or part-skim ricotta cheese
 3 tablespoons chopped cilantro
 ½ teaspoon curry powder
 ½ teaspoon salt
 ½ tablespoon mustard seeds
 1 tablespoon virgin olive oil
 ¼ teaspoon crushed red-pepper flakes

 6 phyllo dough sheets
   Olive-oil spray
 ¾ cup toasted wheat germ
   Watercress Cream Sauce (recipe follows)

Steam the cabbage until slightly wilted and softened, 2 to 3 minutes; set it aside to cool. Steam the fresh beans, corn, peas, and pepper for about 8 minutes; transfer to a large mixing bowl. (If using frozen vegetables, thaw in hot water, drain, and pat dry on paper towels.) Stack the cabbage leaves and cut them into thin slices. Add to the mixed vegetables, along with the ricotta, cilantro, curry powder, and salt.

Place the mustard seeds in a small pot over moderate heat. Cover and toast until the seeds pop and turn gray. Remove the pan from the heat and add the oil and pepper flakes. Add the seasoned oil to the vegetables and mix the ingredients well.

Preheat the oven to 375°F. Butter a 13 × 9-inch casserole dish.

Cut the phyllo sheets in half crosswise; stack them, separating the layers with waxed paper, and cover with a damp kitchen towel. Remove one piece of phyllo and place it on the bottom of the prepared dish. Spray with olive oil and sprinkle with 1 tablespoon of wheat germ. Add three more pieces of phyllo, spraying each one with oil and sprinkling each with wheat germ.

Spoon the vegetable mixture onto the pastry and level the surface. Cover with the remaining eight pieces of phyllo, following the same procedure as before. Using a sharp knife, score the top layer of phyllo to mark six servings.

Bake until golden-brown, 40 to 50 minutes. To serve, pour ¼ cup of sauce around the bottom of a serving plate and place a square of pie in the center.

Watercress Cream Sauce

MAKES ABOUT 2 CUPS

2⅔ cups skim milk
8 coriander seeds
8 peppercorns
1 bay leaf
2 long strips lemon zest
1 tablespoon butter
2½ tablespoons whole-wheat pastry flour
2 cups loosely packed watercress leaves, minced
   Salt

Combine the milk, spices, and lemon zest in a double boiler or heavy-bottomed saucepan. Scald the milk over boiling water or bring to a boil over moderate heat and set aside over the lowest possible heat for 20 minutes. Strain the milk and set aside. (You should have about 2½ cups of milk.)

Melt the butter over low heat. Stir in the flour and cook for 1½ to 2 minutes, stirring constantly. (Do not allow the flour to brown.) Remove from the heat and whisk in the hot milk. Add the watercress, season with salt, and cook over very low heat until thickened, about 20 minutes, stirring frequently.

Cheesy Artichoke Croustade

While this dish tastes extravagant, it's quick and easy to make, especially if you use bottled roasted red peppers. The cheese–and–artichoke bottom filling hints of heat from crushed red chilies. Layered phyllo leaves are sprinkled with toasted poppy seeds for added texture and flavor.

This is a perfect late-fall dinner entree, perhaps accompanied by Orange-Glazed Winter Vegetables (page 56) or Peanut Soup with Okra Croutons (page 90). As a starter or hors d'oeuvre, cool to nearly room temperature and slice into sixteen wedges.   8 MAIN-DISH SERVINGS; 16 APPETIZER SERVINGS

Filling

    ¾ cup (3 ounces) shredded fresh Parmesan
    1 cup (3 ounces) finely shredded Monterey Jack cheese
One 14-ounce can artichoke bottoms in water, rinsed and cut by hand
       into fine julienne
       Half of a 7-ounce jar roasted red peppers or 2 roasted red bell
       peppers (page 288) peeled, seeded, and finely chopped
    ½ cup eggless low-fat mayonnaise
    ¼ teaspoon crushed red-pepper flakes
    3 tablespoons chopped cilantro

1½ tablespoons poppy seeds
    8 sheets phyllo pastry
      Olive- or peanut-oil spray

Mix the filling ingredients in a large bowl. Place the poppy seeds in a saucepan over moderate heat. Cover and cook until the seeds pop and jump. Remove from the heat and set aside.

Stack eight phyllo sheets on a work surface, and cover with a barely dampened kitchen towel. Remove one sheet and place it on a piece of waxed paper. Spray the top lightly with olive oil and sprinkle with about ½ teaspoon of poppy seeds. Fold in half lengthwise; spray the top with olive oil. Place one end of the folded sheet in the center of a 12- or 14-inch nonstick pizza pan, extending it over the sides of the pan. Repeat with the remaining phyllo dough; arrange strips spoke-fashion evenly around the pan.

Preheat the oven to 375°F. Spread the filling around the pastry base to cover a circle about 10 inches in diameter. Lift the end of one folded phyllo strip and bring it toward the center of the filling. Twist the end into a loose coil to form a rosette that lies over the filling; generously spray with oil. Leave a 2-inch circle of filling visible in the center. Repeat with the remaining strips. Spray the entire pastry with oil. (May be made 2 to 3 hours before baking, covered with plastic wrap, and refrigerated.) Bake until crisp and golden, 35 to 40 minutes. Cool 10 minutes before cutting into wedges. Serve hot, warm, or at room temperature.

VERSATILE CHEESE DISHES

ABOUT HOMEMADE CHEESE

Whether known as Indian *panir*, or French *fromage blanc*, homemade cheese is a snap to make. It is simply the result of adding an acid element — fresh lemon or lime juice, soured whey, or a citric-acid solution — to freshly boiled milk. Within moments, a soft cheese curd forms. Drained of whey, the solid cheese curd has enough body to sauté, pan-fry, or bake, *without melting or disintegrating*, very much like tofu, and unlike any commercially available cheese.

If making homemade cheese is your kitchen Waterloo, these dishes are still within easy reach. All of the recipes have been tested using tofu, and the results are excellent. The instructions for tofu usage follow below.

ABOUT THE RECIPES

These cheese entrees are new creations — the refinements of older cuisines and vegetarian versions of nonvegetarian classics. The herbs and spices are kept simple, and though they sometimes chart new territory, they marry beautifully. My training in Indian cuisine has greatly influenced the seasoning technique, but never with a notion to overpower or mask the character of the core ingredients.

The dishes are good for entertaining or for family workday dinners, as most can be assembled ahead of time and conveniently baked or pan-fried at serving time. The cheese is transformed into a wide variety of dishes — croquettes, tarts, *galettes*, and *fricadelles*. Most of the entree selections are accompanied with a grain or vegetable side-dish selection and a sauce, chutney, salsa, or pesto.

FLAVOR-INFUSED CHEESES

Aside from a master recipe for plain, homemade White Cheese, there are recipes for several variations. Each recipe specifies a particular flavor of

cheese — French Herb, Tex-Mex, Jalapeño-Ginger, or Country Vegetable Cheese (pages 189). If you use plain cheese or tofu, you can simply add the cheese seasonings and come up with a flavor redolent of the flavor-infused homemade cheese version.

With a texture and body similar to French Boursin, homemade White Cheese is fine on its own. It is elegant with fruit, crudités, crackers, or toasted chapati wedges. You can marinate homemade cheese cubes or balls in flavored oil for holiday gift baskets.

THE TOFU OPTION

In recent years, creative restaurant and spa chefs have been redesigning the parameters for tofu use. Inspired by their work, I tried tofu for the first time last year. Today I have devised scores of recipes for it.

Tofu is analagous to homemade cheese in that it is the pressed curd of soy milk. Once found only in Asian and natural-food stores, it is now widely available. Cholesterol and lactose free, it is low in fat and nutritious. For purposes of comparison, 3½ ounces of tofu have 145 calories and about 9 grams of fat. The same amount of whole-milk homemade cheese has 265 calories and 20 grams of fat.

All commercial tofu is not the same. Some brands taste fresher than others, with better flavor and texture. I suggest buying tofu that is sold in vacuum-wrapped packages — you can check expiration dates. It is available in packages ranging in weight from 10.5 ounces to 16 ounces, depending on the brand.

Organic Nasoya tofu was used in recipe testing, both the firm and extra-firm varieties. Sample several brands, preferably organic, to find those that best suit your own taste. Before using tofu in the recipes, refer to the preparation instructions mentioned below.

TO PREPARE TOFU OR CHEESE FOR THE RECIPES

To drain tofu of excess moisture: Cut as directed in the recipe or in 1-inch slices, and place between several thicknesses of paper towels to absorb excess moisture. Repeat the process until all of the excess moisture has been absorbed.

Before pureeing cheese or tofu: Break the cheese or tofu into roughly 1-inch pieces, and press between several thicknesses of paper towels to absorb excess moisture. Transfer to a food processor, pulse, and then process into a fluffy powder. Transfer to a work surface and gather into a ball.

If the recipe calls for fillets or cutlets: Knead well-drained cheese or tofu on an oiled countertop until smooth. Divide into the number of pieces indicated in the recipe. Shape into crack-free patties — oval, round, or almond-shaped — ⅓ to ½ inch thick. (The patties may be shaped 1 day ahead. Lay them in a single layer on a tray, seal tightly, and refrigerate.)

These entree servings are not generous by some standards. I've seen hearty eaters finish off one-half pound of cheese or tofu at a sitting. Tofu and homemade cheese are high-protein foods, and the servings are based on 2 to 4 ounces per serving. Serve these entrees with generous helpings of vegetables, soup, and salad when appetites are substantial.

Master Recipe for White Cheese and Its Variations

White Cheese — similar to Indian *panir* and French *fromage blanc* — is the type of cheese used in all of the following entrees. You can use 2% or whole milk — the former yields less volume and a drier consistency, the latter a greater volume and creamier consistency.

To make one of the variations below, add any of the variation ingredients to the quantity of milk and citrus juice mentioned in this master recipe.   MAKES 1 TO 1¼ POUNDS

>   1 **gallon milk**
> ½ **cup fresh lemon or lime juice**
>   **Cheesecloth**

Place the milk (and optional variation ingredients) in a large, heavy-bottomed pot. Bring to a rolling boil, stirring frequently. Remove from the

heat, and gently stir in the lemon juice. If the milk does not immediately separate into whey and white cheese, place it momentarily over heat.

Drape a double thickness of cheesecloth over a colander resting in a sink. Using a slotted spoon, transfer the large curds to the colander, then pour the whey and smaller cheese bits through it. Gather the cheesecloth ends and rinse the cheese under warm running water.

Drain the cheese over a bowl for 4 hours or until it weighs 1 to 1¼ pounds. Alternately, place a 5-pound weight over the wrapped cheese and press for 1 hour on a slanted board. Store the cheese, tightly covered, in the refrigerator for up to 1 week.

Variations: French Herb Cheese: 2 tablespoons each: minced chervil, tarragon, parsley, and chives; ½ teaspoon herb salt; and ½ teaspoon cracked white pepper

Jalapeño-Ginger Cheese: ⅓ cup finely chopped cilantro; 1 tablespoon minced, seeded jalapeño chili; 1 tablespoon minced fresh ginger; and ½ teaspoon herb salt

Oriental Sesame Cheese: 2 tablespoons toasted sesame seeds; ⅓ cup minced fresh parsley; and 1 tablespoon Sesame-Cumin Salt (page 284) or a commercially prepared sesame herb-and-spice blend

Country Vegetable Cheese: ¼ cup each: finely diced carrots, celery, and red, green, and yellow bell peppers; 3 tablespoons chopped fresh parsley; and ½ teaspoon cracked black pepper or pepper blend

Mint–Fennel Seed Cheese: ¼ cup finely chopped mint; ½ tablespoon fennel seeds; ¼ teaspoon crushed red-pepper flakes; and ½ teaspoon herb salt

Poppy Seed–Orange Cheese: 3 tablespoons toasted poppy seeds; 1½ tablespoons grated orange zest; and 1 tablespoon orange flower water

Tex-Mex Cheese: 1 tablespoon toasted cumin seeds, crushed; ¼ to ½ teaspoon crushed red-pepper flakes; and 1 teaspoon dried oregano

Cheese Cutlets with Pineapple-Ginger Glaze and Basmati Rice

This dish is a double tribute to chefs from two great traditions. Bhavatarine "Pishima" Devi, one of my earliest Bengali teachers, is responsible for the cheese concept, and Jean-Georges Vongerichten is the inspiration behind the Bengali-style fresh-juice glaze.

In colder months, accompany the cutlets with the Basmati Rice. For warm-weather menus, serve them with Cucumber Noodles. To complete the meal, add a salad or vegetable dish.   6 SERVINGS

24	Jalapeño-Ginger Cheese cutlets (pages 188 and 189) or 1 pound extra-firm tofu and Jalapeño-Ginger Cheese seasonings
½	cup chopped pecans
2 to 3	tablespoons extra-virgin olive oil
	Pineapple-Ginger Glaze (recipe follows) or
	Basmati Rice or Cucumber Noodles (recipe follows)

If you use tofu, roughly break and press it between several layers of absorbent towels to extract all of the excess moisture. Place the tofu (and Jalapeño-Ginger Cheese seasonings) in a food processor and process until smooth. Shape into twenty-four crack-free cutlets and place on a tray. Sprinkle with pecans and press firmly into place.

Place 2 nonstick frying pans over moderate heat and warm ½ tablespoon of oil in each pan. Place twelve cutlets in each pan and cook until lightly browned, 5 to 6 minutes per side. Add the remaining oil when necessary. Keep warm over very low heat or in a 250°F oven.

To serve, place Basmati Rice or Cucumber Noodles on one half of a warm dinner plate. Place four cutlets, pecan side up, on the other half of the plate. Spoon Pineapple-Ginger Glaze over the cutlets.

Pineapple-Ginger Glaze

MAKES ABOUT 1½ CUPS

> 1 medium pineapple (about 2½ pounds)
> 1 tablespoon grated fresh ginger
> 1½ tablespoons butter or extra-virgin olive oil
> 3 tablespoons fruit-sweetened apricot jam
> 3 tablespoons fresh lime juice
>   Salt
>   Cayenne
> 3 tablespoons currants

Peel and core the pineapple. Put enough pineapple through a juice extractor to make 1½ cups. Cut the remaining fruit into ¼-inch dice (you should have about 1 cup). Combine the fresh juice and ginger in a nonreactive frying pan. Bring to a boil over high heat and reduce by half (you should have about ¾ cup). Remove from the heat and whisk in the butter, apricot jam, and lime juice. Season with salt and cayenne. Add the currants and remaining pineapple. Keep warm over low heat.

Basmati Rice or Cucumber Noodles

6 SERVINGS

> 1¼ cups basmati rice or 2 European cucumbers (see Note)
> 1 tablespoon unsalted butter or extra-virgin olive oil
>   Salt
>   Cracked pepper, preferably Malabar
> 2 tablespoons chopped cilantro

To make the rice, bring 6 cups of water to a boil in a saucepan. Stir in the rice and boil for 10 minutes. Drain in a strainer, and rinse under hot water. Return to the saucepan, add the butter, season with salt and pepper, and stir in cilantro.

To make the cucumber noodles, peel the cucumber and slice it on the diagonal into slices ⅛ inch thick. Stack four slices together, and cut into noodles ⅛ inch thick.

Heat the butter in a large nonstick frying pan over moderately low heat. Stir-fry the cucumber noodles until barely limp. Season with salt and pepper and toss in the cilantro.

Note: European cucumbers are long and slender with very few seeds — ideal for slicing into noodles. If they aren't available, you might try peeled zucchini.

Almond-Crusted Cheese Sticks with Lime-Horseradish Mayonnaise

This dish is ideal for a weekday dinner when time is short. If you are a newcomer to either homemade cheese or tofu, this is a great introduction — easy to make and delicious. If you like, substitute cashews or pecans for the almonds. Serve with generous portions of seasonal vegetables.   4 SERVINGS

　1　**pound French Herb Cheese fillets (pages 188 and 189) or 1 pound extra-firm tofu plus the French Herb Cheese seasonings**
　½　**cup almonds, ground medium-fine**
　½　**cup saltine cracker crumbs**
　1　**teaspoon paprika**
　⅛　**teaspoon cayenne**
　¼　**teaspoon herb salt**
　　　Olive-oil spray
　　　Lime-Horseradish Mayonnaise (recipe follows)

If you use tofu, cut it into twelve even-sized sticks. Press the tofu between several layers of paper towels to extract excess liquid.

Preheat the oven to 375°F. Combine the nuts, crumbs, paprika, cayenne, and herb salt in a shallow plate and mix. Spray both sides of the cheese or tofu

with olive oil. Press into the cracker mixture until completely coated, and place on a nonstick baking tray. Bake, turning once during cooking, until the fillets or sticks are golden and crisp, 25 to 30 minutes. Serve piping hot, three fillets or sticks per person, with the mayonnaise as a dipping sauce on the side.

Lime-Horseradish Mayonnaise

Rich and creamy, this is little more than dressed-up low-fat cottage cheese. The small amount of added mayonnaise goes a long way, in terms of both flavor and consistency, but it can be omitted.　MAKES ABOUT ¾ CUP

- ¾ **cup low-fat cottage cheese**
  Zest from 1 lime, minced
- ½ **tablespoon fresh lime juice**
- 2 **tablespoons calorie-reduced, egg-free mayonnaise (optional)**
- ½ **tablespoon peeled, freshly grated horseradish or 1 teaspoon powdered horseradish**
- ¼ **cup minced celery**

Place the cottage cheese in a food processor or blender and process until creamy-smooth. Add the remaining ingredients and pulse a few times to mix. (Can be made 2 days ahead of use and refrigerated, well sealed.)

Cheese Fricadelle with Two Chutneys

Fricadelle, like Indian *tikki,* are pan-fried cutlets. In France, the dish centers around various meats. This version highlights homemade cheese or tofu, with supporting color and texture from millet and bright diced vegetables. Inspired by a Jacques Pépin *fricadelle* recipe, this version is lighter, with less fat and cholesterol. Served with the accompanying duo of chutneys, this is a superb entree for entertaining. Try it with Pine Nut and Orange Wild Rice (page 113) and Sautéed Sugar Snap Peas and Radishes (page 235) for a special menu.
8 SERVINGS

1   tablespoon virgin olive oil
⅔   cup millet
1⅓ to 1½ cups water
1   cup finely diced carrot
1   cup finely diced zucchini
½   cup finely diced red bell pepper
½   cup finely diced yellow bell pepper
2   ounces trimmed spinach leaves, wilted, pressed dry, and
       finely chopped
1   pound Jalapeño-Ginger Cheese (page 189) or drained
       extra-firm tofu pureed with Jalapeño-Ginger Cheese
       seasonings
1¼   teaspoons salt
½   teaspoon medium-grind black pepper
2   cups fresh bread crumbs
       Virgin olive oil
       Cilantro Chutney (recipe follows)
       Lime Yogurt Chutney (recipe follows)

Combine 1 tablespoon of oil and the millet in a saucepan over moderate
heat, and while stirring, toast the grains until darkened a few shades. Add the
water and bring to a boil. Cover, reduce the heat to low, and cook until the
millet is tender and the water has been absorbed, about 20 minutes. Set aside
for 10 minutes, then fluff with a fork.

Individually steam the vegetables until tender-crisp. Pat the vegetables
between absorbent towels to remove excess liquid. Place the cheese or tofu
plus seasonings in a food processor and puree until smooth. Transfer to a bowl;
add salt and pepper, millet, and vegetables, and gently mix.

Moisten your hands and divide the mixture into sixteen flattened balls.
Sandwich each piece between plastic wrap, and flatten into crack-free patties,
just under ½ inch thick. Pat the patties in the bread crumbs so they are coated
on all sides. Set aside on waxed paper–lined trays. (Can be made 1 day ahead
and refrigerated. Bring to room temperature before cooking.)

To pan-fry the *fricadelles*, place two nonstick frying pans over moderately
high heat. Add oil to a depth of ⅛ inch and heat. Place eight *fricadelles* in each

pan and cook until lightly browned, 5 to 7 minutes per side. Keep warm over very low heat or in a 250°F oven.

To serve, place two *fricadelles* on each of eight heated plates. Drizzle with two chutneys. Serve with rice pilaf and vegetables.

Cilantro Chutney

MAKES ABOUT 1¼ CUPS

1⅓	cups cilantro leaves, lightly packed
¼	cup chopped almonds or cashews
1 to 2	jalapeño chilies, seeded and roughly chopped
One	⅛-inch-thick slice peeled fresh ginger
3	tablespoons maple syrup
½	cup fresh orange juice or water
	Pinch salt

Combine all of the ingredients in a food processor and puree until silky. Force through a fine strainer; discard roughage. Transfer to a squeeze bottle with a funnel top. (Can be prepared 1 to 2 days ahead and thinned to original consistency before using.)

Lime Yogurt Chutney

MAKES ABOUT 1¼ CUPS

1¼	cups plain nonfat yogurt, stirred
½	teaspoon freshly grated lime zest
1	tablespoon fresh lime juice

Combine the ingredients in a squeeze bottle with a cap. Shake vigorously to mix.

Vegetable and Cheese Ramekins with Yellow Pepper–Tomato Sauce

With a flavor almost like salmon cakes, this is a convenient make-ahead entree for company. Serve with Baked Vegetable Packets (page 248) for no-fuss entertaining.   6 SERVINGS

1	pound White Cheese (page 188) or firm tofu, drained
One	½-inch slice peeled fresh ginger
1 to 2	jalapeño chilies, seeded
1	red bell pepper, seeded, deribbed, and cut into 1-inch pieces
2½	cups finely shredded carrot
1½	cups finely shredded cabbage
⅓	cup whole-wheat pastry flour or seasoned bread crumbs
2	teaspoons baking powder
	Salt
	Freshly ground pepper
	Olive-oil spray or 2 tablespoons butter
	Yellow Pepper–Tomato Sauce (recipe follows)

Slice the tofu and press it between absorbent towels to extract all excess liquid. Break the drained cheese or tofu into pieces. Place the ginger and chili in a food processor and mince. Add the bell pepper and pulse to chop coarsely. Add the cheese or tofu and pulse, then process to a crumbly powder.

Preheat the oven to 350°F. Steam the carrot and cabbage until wilted. Add the vegetables, flour, and baking powder to the processor bowl and pulse until you have a coarse puree. Season with salt and pepper.

Generously spray or butter a nonstick 12-cup muffin tin. Distribute the mixture among the cups, and gently pack to smooth the surface. Bake until golden-brown, 35 to 45 minutes. Loosen the ramekins with a knife and carefully invert onto a cake rack.

Place two ramekins in the middle of each of six warm dinner plates. Surround with Yellow Pepper–Tomato Sauce and serve immediately.

Yellow Pepper–Tomato Sauce

You can also make this sauce with red or green bell peppers and red tomatoes.   MAKES ABOUT 1½ CUPS

   3 yellow bell peppers
   3 yellow or orange tomatoes, peeled, seeded, and chopped
   ½ tablespoon grated fresh ginger
   1½ tablespoons extra-virgin olive oil
   1 tablespoon chopped fresh dill
      Herb salt
      Cayenne

Preheat a broiler or stovestop grill over moderate heat. Char the peppers on all sides until the skins blacken. Transfer to a plastic bag and cool for 15 minutes. Rub off the charred skins. Seed, derib, and coarsely chop the peppers.

Combine all of the ingredients in a food processor and puree. Gently warm before serving (Can be prepared 1 day ahead. Cover and refrigerate.)

Tex-Mex Cheese Tostadas with Ancho Chili–Tomato Salsa

This is my version of Tex-Mex *tostadas*. It's accompanied by one of my favorite salsas, the smoky flavor of ancho chilies fusing into caramelized baked tomatoes. When I don't have time to make homemade chapatis, I use Alvarado Street Bakery sprouted wheat tortillas or Garden of Eatin' organic wheat tortillas—both of which are excellent for *tostadas* and pizza crusts. Ancho chilies are found in Latin American, specialty, and Southwestern markets.
4 SERVINGS

  10 ounces drained Tex-Mex Cheese (page 189) or drained extra-firm
       tofu plus Tex-Mex Cheese seasonings
    4 large flour tortillas or wheat chapatis
       Olive-oil spray
    4 ounces Neufchâtel cheese, diced
    1 ear of corn or ½ cup defrosted corn kernels
       Ancho Chili–Tomato Salsa (recipe follows)
    1 small avocado, pared, peeled, and diced
    8 oil-cured olives, pitted and chopped

Preheat the oven to 450°F. Break the cheese or tofu into roughly ½-inch pieces. (Toss the tofu in the seasonings.) Spray the tortillas with olive oil and place them on nonstick baking trays. Evenly distribute the cheese or tofu, Neufchâtel, and corn over the tortillas.

Bake until the toppings are browned, about 8 minutes. Spoon Ancho Chili–Tomato Salsa over the top. Sprinkle with avocado and olives; serve hot.

Ancho Chili–Tomato Salsa

MAKES ABOUT 1½ CUPS

    3 ancho or New Mexico chili pods
    5 vine-ripened tomatoes
    1 tablespoon virgin olive oil
    1 tablespoon maple syrup
       Salt
    3 tablespoons chopped cilantro

Soak the chilies in hot water until soft, about 20 minutes. Drain, stem, seed, and finely chop the chilies. Blanch the tomatoes in boiling water for 10 seconds, then peel, seed, and chop.

Preheat the oven to 400°F. Combine the chilies, tomato, oil, and maple syrup in an ovenproof pan. Season with salt and pepper. Bake until the tomatoes begin to caramelize and turn brown, about 20 minutes. Set aside and stir in the cilantro. (Can be made 2 or 3 days ahead, covered, and refrigerated.)

Herb Cheese Galette with Cashew Crust and Papaya-Cilantro Chutney

This cheese entree was inspired by a dish created by Dallas chef Dean Fearing. It is also delicious made with Mint-Fennel Seed or Oriental Sesame Cheese (page 189). The smooth and creamy texture of the herbed cheese, similar to that of French Boursin, is in marked contrast to the crispy cashew crust.

For a no-fuss, make ahead baked meal, accompany with Oven-Roasted Okra (page 244) and Baked Vegetable Packets (page 248).   4 SERVINGS

> 1 **pound French Herb Cheese (page 189) or 1 pound extra-firm tofu plus French Herb Cheese seasonings**
> 1 **cup buttermilk or soya milk**
> ¾ **cup unsalted cashews, ground medium-fine**
> ⅔ **cup dry fine bread crumbs**
> ⅛ **teaspoon cayenne**
> **Salt**
> **Olive-oil spray**
> **Papaya-Cilantro Chutney (recipe follows)**

If using tofu, cut into 12 equal slices and extract any excess liquid with paper towels. Combine the French Herb Cheese seasonings and buttermilk or soya milk in a flat dish and mix.

Preheat the oven to 375°F. Place the nuts, bread crumbs, and cayenne on waxed paper and mix. One by one, dip the cheese or tofu pieces into the milk mixture and then press into the nut mixture until completely coated. Seat aside on a separate sheet of waxed paper. When all pieces are breaded, liberally spray on both sides with olive oil. Bake, turning once, on a nonstick baking sheet until crisp and richly browned, 35 to 40 minutes.

Place three cutlets on each of four warm dinner plates. Serve with okra or a seasonal vegetable and Papaya-Cilantro Chutney.

Papaya-Cilantro Chutney

MAKES ABOUT 1½ CUPS

    1 large papaya (about 2 pounds), peeled, seeded, and coarsely
       chopped
    2 tablespoons julienned peeled fresh ginger
    2 tablespoons finely chopped cilantro
    3 tablespoons fresh lime juice
    2 tablespoons maple syrup
    ½ teaspoon salt
       Cayenne

Combine the first five ingredients in a bowl and mix. Cover and chill for
at least 1 hour or up to 4 hours. Before serving, add the salt and season with
cayenne to taste.

Cauliflower and Cheese Croquettes with Horseradish Potatoes

This is a light variation of two Bengali dishes—hot vegetable *kofta* balls and
room-temperature potato *tikki* balls. Here they are transformed into baked
vegetable–Swiss cheese croquettes and horseradish-laced whipped hot potatoes. This is a perfect workday family dinner or active weekend dinner; it
needs only a green salad to make a meal. Croquette leftovers are wonderful in
sandwiches.   6 SERVINGS

      3 cups finely shredded cauliflower (12 ounces)
    1½ cups finely shredded low-fat Swiss cheese (8 ounces)
      1 jalapeño chili, seeded
    One 1-inch piece peeled fresh ginger
      1 teaspoon coriander seeds

1   pound Jalapeño-Ginger Cheese (page 189) or extra-firm drained
    tofu plus Jalapeño-Ginger Cheese seasonings
⅔   cup whole-wheat or chickpea flour
1   teaspoon curry powder
1   tablespoon baking powder
1   teaspoon salt
1   teaspoon freshly ground pepper
    Olive-oil spray, preferably extra-virgin
    Horseradish Potatoes (recipe follows)

Preheat oven to 350°F. Combine the cauliflower and Swiss cheese in a
mixing bowl. Place the ginger, chili, and coriander seeds in a food processor
and process until minced. Add the homemade cheese or tofu and pulse, then
process until powdered. Sprinkle in the flour, curry powder, baking powder,
salt, and pepper. Pulse to mix.

Scrape the mixture into the mixing bowl and blend with the cauliflower
mixture. Spray a nonstick baking tray with olive oil. Divide the cauliflower
mixture into 12 portions (about ⅔ cup each) and shape into smooth almond-
shaped croquettes about ¾ inch thick. Bake until golden-brown, for about 45
minutes. Cool for 10 minutes in the pan, loosen with a knife, and invert onto a
wire rack. Serve two croquettes per person accompanied by whipped Horseradish Potatoes.

Horseradish Potatoes

6 SERVINGS

2½ pounds baking potatoes, peeled and cubed
⅔   cup buttermilk
⅓   cup freshly grated horseradish
1   teaspoon minced jalapeño chili
1   tablespoon butter or cold-pressed corn oil
    Salt
    Freshly ground white pepper

Place the potatoes in a saucepan, cover with cold water, and bring to a boil. Reduce the heat and simmer until the potatoes are soft, about 25 minutes. Drain in a colander and return to the saucepan. Add the remaining ingredients and mash until smooth and fluffy. Serve immediately or keep warm in the top of a double boiler over simmering water.

Four-Vegetable Tart with Two Pepper Sauces

I came up with this entree when catering a vegan meal served at the U.S. Capitol for National Meat-Out Day, hosted by PETA (People for Ethical Treatment of Animals). Congressmen, senators, and lobbyists raved about the presentation. Try it with New Potatoes with Lemon and Bay Leaves (page 247).   12 SERVINGS

   1 small cauliflower, trimmed and cut into florets
   2 small kohlrabi, pared and cubed
   2 carrots, cubed
   2 poblano chilies, seeded and cut into 1-inch pieces
   1 red bell pepper, seeded, deribbed, and cut into 1-inch pieces
   1 pound Country Herb Cheese (page 189) or firm tofu plus
      Country Herb Cheese seasonings, drained and cubed
1½ cups fresh wheat-bread crumbs, toasted
   1 teaspoon salt
   1 teaspoon freshly ground pepper
¼ cup minced fresh parsley
¼ cup minced cilantro
     Olive-oil spray
     Two Pepper Sauces (recipe follows)

In manageable batches, finely chop the cauliflower, kohlrabi, and carrot in a food processor. Microwave or steam the vegetables until half cooked. Transfer the vegetables to a large mixing bowl.

Combine the chili, bell pepper, and cheese or tofu in a food processor, and pulse until the chili and pepper are diced. Scrape the mixture into the vegetables; add the bread crumbs, salt, pepper, and herbs, and mix well. (Can be prepared 1 day ahead, covered, and refrigerated.)

Preheat the oven to 375°F. Spray twelve 4-inch tart pans or a large cookie sheet with olive oil. Divide the vegetable mixture into twelve equal portions; press into individual tart pans or shape into patties 1 inch thick and transfer to the cookie sheet. Spray with olive oil. Bake until golden brown, 40 to 50 minutes. Cool on the trays for 5 minutes, then carefully invert tarts for serving.

To serve, divide both sauces evenly on warmed dinner plates. Place one tart in the middle of the plate, straddling both sauces. Garnish each serving with a single cilantro leaf.

Variation: Spray a large nonstick cookie sheet with olive oil. Shape the mixture into a smooth loaf about 16 inches long. Spray with olive oil and bake until golden, 1¼ to 1½ hours. Cool the loaf for 15 minutes before slicing into twelve portions. Serve as above. Leftover thin, chilled slices are terrific in sandwiches.

Two Pepper Sauces

These simple sauces also go well with any number of entree, pilaf, or pasta dishes.   12 SERVINGS

>   3 large red bell peppers
>   3 large yellow bell peppers
>   2 poblano chilies
>   1 cup vegetable stock
>   2 tablespoons extra-virgin olive oil

Cut the peppers in quarters and the chilies in half. Core and derib them. Char them, skin sides toward the heat source, under a broiler or on a stovetop

grill. Place in a covered bowl for 15 minutes. Rub off the blackened skins, washing them if necessary.

In a blender or food processor, puree the red pepper, 1 chili, ½ cup of stock, and 1 tablespoon of oil. Clean the blender and process with the yellow pepper and remaining ingredients. Keep the sauces warm in separate double boilers.

White Cheese–Vegetable Pipérade

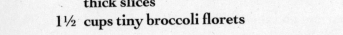

French *pipérade,* popular in the Basque country, is a mélange of vegetables and scrambled eggs. This Indian vegetarian counterpart is made with fresh white cheese instead of eggs, and I serve it as the French would, with hot, fresh bread.

This is one instance where I feel that tofu falls far short of cheese, but vegan friends love the dish made with silken firm tofu, and salsa instead of cream cheese—it's a matter of taste. Silken tofu has a smooth, custard-like consistency, with a bland flavor that is quite receptive to seasonings.

Serve with toast or, for a breakfast-type burrito, roll the *pipérade* up in flame-toasted chapatis and top with zesty salsa.   4 SERVINGS

> 1 **pound Country Vegetable Cheese, drained for only 1 hour
>   (page 189), or 1½ packages (10.5-ounce size) silken firm tofu plus
>   seasonings from Country Vegetable Cheese, patted dry**
> 1 **tablespoon butter or infused Curry Oil (page 293)**
> ¼ **teaspoon crushed red-pepper flakes**
> ½ **teaspoon curry powder**
> 1 **red bell pepper, seeded, deribbed, and cut into 1-inch squares**
> 1 **yellow bell pepper, seeded, deribbed, and cut into 1-inch squares**
> 1 **medium yellow squash, halved lengthwise and cut into ¼-inch-
>   thick slices**
> 1½ **cups tiny broccoli florets**

¼ **pound snow peas, trimmed and cut into thin julienne**
¼ **cup light cream cheese, diced**
   Salt
   Freshly ground pepper
2 **tablespoons chopped cilantro**

Break the cheese or tofu into pieces roughly 1 inch in diameter. Heat the butter in a large nonstick skillet or wok over moderately high heat. Add the pepper flakes and curry powder, and within seconds, add all of the vegetables. Stir-fry until the vegetables are tender-crisp, 5 to 8 minutes. Reduce the heat to moderate; gently stir in the cheese or tofu and pan-fry for 3 to 4 minutes. Remove from the heat, fold in the cream cheese, and season with salt and pepper. Sprinkle with cilantro and serve hot.

STACKED, STUFFED, LAYERED, AND SPIRALED CREATIONS

Like casseroles and bean pots, most of these dishes are good for feeding a crowd. Most can be prepared ahead of time, look good on a buffet, and multiply easily. Baked in tart pans, Tamale Pie (page 218) and Summer Vegetable Tart (page 219) are terrific to behold, and delicious at room temperature. All of them are good on their own as entertaining entrees, some for leisurely weekends and others for work nights.

Ratatouille Savarin with Tomato Coulis

Most cooks who have studied French breads have tried their hand at the ring-shaped cake called *savarin*. The first time I tried Faye Levy's vegetable savarin I knew the classic cake had a legitimate rival. Inspired by Faye's recipe, I came up with a wonderful East-West variation. The dish can be baked in either a ring-shaped French savarin pan or a loaf pan.

To make this even more elegant, fill the center with chilled Creamy Basmati Rice Pilaf (page 110).   6 SERVINGS

    2 pounds Japanese eggplant (each 6 to 7 inches long)
       Olive-oil spray
    1 teaspoon mustard seeds
 1½ tablespoons extra-virgin olive oil
    1 teaspoon fennel seeds
  ¼ teaspoon crushed red-pepper flakes
  ½ cup chopped fresh fennel bulb

  1 **large red and 1 large yellow bell pepper, seeded, deribbed, and cut into ½-inch pieces**
  1 **pound zucchini, cut in ½-inch dice**
  ¾ **pound tomatoes, peeled, seeded, and chopped**
  2 **tablespoons tomato paste, preferably sun-dried**
1½ **tablespoons cornstarch**
  ⅓ **cup chopped cilantro**
    Salt
    Tomato-Coulis (recipe follows)

Preheat the broiler. Remove the eggplant caps and cut off a slice lengthwise on both sides. Cut the center portion into lengthwise slices ¼ inch thick; you need about twenty-five slices. Cut the remaining eggplants and end slices into ½-inch dice and steam until tender; set aside.

Generously spray oil on both sides of the eggplant slices. Broil them about 3 inches from the heat source until lightly browned, 3 to 4 minutes per side. Line a 9½-inch savarin or 9 × 4 × 3-inch loaf pan with plastic wrap and spray with olive oil. Line the pan with eggplant slices, placing them crosswise, with the thick ends resting on the outer edge of the pan. Overlap the slices slightly so none of the pan is visible. Trim the eggplant slices level with the inside rim of the pan.

Place the mustard seeds in a nonstick sauté pan over moderate heat. Cover and cook until they pop. Add the olive oil, fennel seeds, and pepper flakes and cook briefly until they darken a few shades. Stir in the fresh fennel, pepper, and zucchini. Reduce the heat to low, cover, and stirring occasionally, cook for about 15 minutes.

Stir in the tomato, steamed eggplant, tomato paste, and cornstarch and cook for 3 to 4 minutes. Add the cilantro and season with salt. Transfer the mixture to the lined pan; even the top and cool for 30 minutes. Cover and refrigerate for at least 3 hours or overnight.

About ½ hour before serving, invert the *savarin* onto a 12-inch serving platter. Just before serving, remove the plastic wrap and spray the *savarin* with olive oil. Spoon Tomato Coulis around the outside of the *savarin*. Slice with a sharp serrated knife.

Tomato Coulis

6 SERVINGS

> 6 ripe tomatoes (about 2 pounds) peeled, seeded, and chopped
> 1 hot red chili pepper, fresh or dried
> 1 teaspoon ground coriander
> ½ teaspoon dried marjoram
> ¼ teaspoon salt
> 1 teaspoon extra-virgin olive oil

Combine all of the ingredients except the oil in a nonstick saucepan and bring to a boil. Reduce the heat to low, partially cover, and simmer for 30 minutes. Remove the chili pepper, and process the *coulis* in a food processor for 2 minutes. Pass through a fine strainer into a pan, swirl in the oil, and rewarm before serving. (Can be made 1 day ahead, covered, and refrigerated.)

Potato Croquettes

This is a light version of a Bengali dish called *aloo bonda*. The horseradish-spiked mashed potatoes are flecked with broccoli, cabbage, and bell pepper bits. Shaped into patties and rolled in cheesy saltine crumbs, the croquettes have a crisp exterior and creamy inside. Potato lovers might want to make a double batch and freeze individual portions for quick meals.

The croquettes need a sauce — something like a tomatillo salsa, catsup, or warm red-pepper sauce.   8 SERVINGS

> 16 regular or whole-wheat saltines
> 4 ounces shredded low-fat sharp cheddar or Swiss cheese
> 3 baking potatoes (about 1½ pounds), peeled and cut into ½-inch cubes
> 4 cups coarsely chopped broccoli florets

3 cups coarsely chopped savoy cabbage
½ cup diced red bell pepper
¼ cup freshly grated fresh horseradish or 2 tablespoons grated fresh
    ginger
¼ teaspoon freshly ground white pepper
1 teaspoon salt
1 teaspoon mustard seeds
    Olive-oil spray

Place the saltines in a sealable plastic bag; seal, and using a rolling pin, crush into fine crumbs. Add half of the cheese to the bag and toss to mix. Spread the crumbs evenly onto a large piece of waxed paper.

Steam the potatoes for 8 minutes. Move the potatoes to half of the steamer and add the broccoli, cabbage, and bell pepper to the other half. Steam for another 5 to 10 minutes, or until the potatoes are tender.

Transfer the potatoes to a large bowl and mash until smooth. Add the broccoli, cabbage, bell pepper, horseradish, white pepper, and salt. Place the mustard seeds in a saucepan and cover. Cook over moderate heat, shaking occasionally, until the seeds pop and turn gray. Add the seeds to the potato mixture, mix well, and divide into sixteen portions. Roll into balls or logs.

Preheat the oven to 325°F. Spray a large nonstick baking tray with oil. Flatten the balls into patties or ovals in the crumbs. coating all sides. Bake until golden, turning once, about 45 minutes. Serve with lemon wedges and your choice of sauce.

Vegetable Terrine with Grilled Tomato Sauce

This summertime terrine is not layered but marbled with a confetti of colorful vegetable nuggets. I rarely make it the same way twice, preferring to contrast seasonal vegetable combinations with various whole-grain selections.

After trying this recipe, use it as a guideline to explore your own favorite vegetable-grain-cheese combinations. Instead of the suggested brown rice, try

a brown-rice blend, millet, or white basmati rice. Or instead of smoked Gouda cheese, give Swiss, dilled Havarti, or sharp cheddar a try.

The terrine can be baked in any 9-cup pan, from a round soufflé dish to a deep-walled casserole.   8 SERVINGS

12 to 15 large Swiss chard or savoy cabbage leaves
          Olive-oil spray
      2   cups cooked brown rice
      3   tablespoons chopped fresh dill
      3   ounces Neufchâtel cheese
      6   ounces shredded smoked Gouda
     ½   teaspoon crushed red-pepper flakes
      2   cups diced carrot
      1   cup baby lima beans, fresh or frozen
      1   cup corn kernels, fresh or frozen
      7   cups finely chopped Swiss chard or cabbage
   1½   cups diced red bell pepper
   1½   cups diced green bell pepper
          Salt
          Freshly ground pepper
          Grilled Tomato Sauce (recipe follows)

Cut away the protruding chard or cabbage ribs from the whole leaves. Steam the whole leaves until bright green and flexible; cool slightly. Liberally spray a 9-inch soufflé dish, deep-walled casserole, or terrine dish with oil. Line the bottom and sides with most of the leaves, overlapping slightly, allowing them to hang over the top of the dish. Set aside.

Place the rice, dill, Neufchâtel, Gouda, and pepper flakes in a large mixing bowl and toss to mix. Set aside.

Place the carrot and lima beans in a large steamer and steam for 8 minutes. Add the corn and chard and steam for 5 minutes. Add the bell pepper and steam another 4 minutes. Cool slightly and stir into the rice mixture. Season with salt and pepper.

Preheat the oven to 350°F. Add the rice mixture to the prepared dish. Bring the overhanging leaves over the top; cover with the remaining leaves

and level. Cover with foil and place the pan in a larger roasting pan. Add enough hot water to come halfway up the sides of the dish. Bake for 50 to 60 minutes, then cool on a rack for 15 minutes. Unmold on a platter. To serve, cut into wedges and arrange with Grilled Tomato Sauce on the side.

Grilled Tomato Sauce

For a more intense, smoky-flavored sauce, use smoked instead of grilled tomatoes. They are easy to prepare using equipment such as the portable Weber Smoky Joe Picnic Grill or the larger Brinkmann Charcoal Grill Smoker. Follow the instructions for smoking, using a mild wood such as apple, alder, or basil. Soak wood chips in water for 10 minutes and drain. Add to dying coal embers to create aromatic smoke. Place the tomato halves on a clean, oiled rack above the heat source and smoke for 10 to 12 minutes to infuse with flavor. Coarsely chop and proceed as directed in the recipe.

This sauce freezes well and is an ideal way to use bumper-crop tomatoes and cilantro.   6 SERVINGS

    8 medium tomatoes (about 2½ pounds)
    ⅔ cup vegetable stock
       A few whole cilantro leaves
    1 teaspoon curry powder
   1½ tablespoons extra-virgin olive oil
       Salt
       Freshly ground pepper

Pierce a whole tomato with a long fork and grill it over direct gas or electric heat until evenly charred on all sides. Alternately, brush a grilling rack with oil and char over a preheated grill or medium coals. Repeat with remaining tomatoes. Coarsely chop the tomatoes, leaving the charred skins intact. Transfer to a saucepan along with the stock, cilantro, and curry powder. Bring to a boil, reduce heat, and simmer for 20 to 25 minutes. Force the sauce through a sieve to remove the seeds and skins. Whisk in the oil and season with salt and pepper. Serve hot or warm.

Potato Enchiladas with Ancho Chili–Tomato Sauce

This is my version of a Tex-Mex entree created by Houston chef Robert Del Grande. I use flavoring elements common to both new Southwest and new Italian cuisine — nuts, seeds, lime juice, cilantro, and hot chilies.

All you need is green salad, pistachio-laced yogurt, and refried beans to make a memorable meal.   6 SERVINGS

Sauce

3 to 4	ancho or New Mexico chilies
½	cup raw pumpkin seeds
½	tablespoon cumin seeds
½	cup lightly packed cilantro leaves
4	cups seeded, diced plum tomato
2	cups stock or water
1	tablespoon extra-virgin olive oil
	Salt
	Freshly ground pepper

Enchiladas

5	cups cubed (½ inch) cooked Idaho potatoes
1	tablespoon grated fresh ginger
1	teaspoon salt
1	teaspoon cracked black pepper
6	ounces crumbled White Cheese (page 188) or farmer cheese
½	tablespoon mustard seeds
	Olive-oil spray
1	dozen corn tortillas, preferably blue
4	ounces shredded low-fat sharp cheddar cheese

To make the sauce, fry the chilies in a warm skillet until lightly toasted. Soak them in hot water until soft, about 15 minutes, then strain. While they

are soaking, slowly dry-roast the pumpkin and cumin seeds until aromatic and lightly toasted. Transfer ¼ cup of the mixture to a food processor and set the remaining ¼ cup aside.

Stem and seed the chilies and tear them into bits. Add to the processor along with the cilantro, tomato, and stock. Process for 2 to 3 minutes and transfer to a saucepan. Bring to a boil. Reduce the heat to low, partially cover, and simmer for 30 minutes. Strain the sauce through a fine sieve and gently reheat with the oil; season with salt and pepper.

To make the enchiladas, combine the potato, ginger, salt, pepper and cheese in a bowl and toss to mix. Place the mustard seeds in a small pan over moderate heat. Cover, and shaking the pan, toast until they crackle and pop. Add to the potato mixture; mix well and spray with olive oil. Divide into twelve portions. Lightly spray the tortillas with olive oil; stack them and wrap them in plastic wrap. Steam until flexible, 3 to 4 minutes. Keep warm.

Preheat the oven to 350°F. Spray a large baking dish or six individual gratin dishes with olive oil. Place a portion of potatoes along the center of each tortilla, and roll into an enchilada. Place, seam side down, in the baking dish (two per gratin dish). When all twelve are assembled, spray with olive oil. Pour three-fourths of the sauce over the enchiladas and sprinkle with cheese. Bake until warm and bubbly, about 15 minutes.

Serve two enchiladas per person, garnished with the pumpkin-seed mixture and some of the remaining sauce.

Two-Potato Terrine with Warm Black-Eyed Peas

This terrine was inspired by a recipe from *Gourmet* magazine — red-orange yams and snowy white potatoes separated by paper-thin layers of red-pepper puree. The smooth-textured terrine is offset with a chunky-textured, warm bean dish.

This is a good make-ahead entree; it can be baked and warmed up just before serving. To round off the meal, add a salad or stovetop vegetable side dish.   8 SERVINGS

3	large red bell peppers
½	cup vegetable stock
1½	pounds new potatoes, peeled
1½	pounds yams or sweet potatoes, peeled
1 to 2	jalapeño chilies, seeded and minced
3	tablespoons evaporated skim milk
2	tablespoons minced candied or stem ginger
3	tablespoons fresh orange juice
	Salt
	Freshly ground pepper
	Butter
	Warm Black-Eyed Peas (recipe follows)

Quarter and seed the peppers. Broil or grill them until the skins are blistered and charred. Transfer the peppers to a bowl, cover, and set aside for 15 minutes. Rub off the skins. Combine the peppers and stock in a blender and puree. Pour the puree into a saucepan and cook it, stirring frequently, until it is reduced to a very thick paste, about 15 minutes. Set aside.

Keeping them separate, steam the potatoes and yams until fork-tender. When they are cool enough to handle, force the potatoes through a potato ricer into a bowl. Repeat the process for the yams. Mix the jalapeño and milk into

the potato mixture and the ginger and orange juice into the yams. Season both mixtures with salt and pepper.

Generously butter a 9 × 5 × 3-inch nonstick loaf pan. Evenly spread 1 cup of the yam mixture over the bottom. Spread 1 cup of the potato mixture over it and brush with half of the pepper puree. Continue to layer the terrine in the same manner, ending with a layer of the potato mixture. (May be made 1 to 2 days ahead, covered, and refrigerated.)

Preheat the oven to 375°F. Cover the loaf pan with foil and place it in a larger roasting pan. Add enough hot water to come halfway up the sides of the loaf pan. Bake for 1 hour, then cool on a rack for 15 to 20 minutes. Invert onto a serving platter and cut with a very sharp serrated knife, wiping it clean between each cut. Serve with Warm Black-Eyed Peas.

Warm Black-Eyed Peas

8 SERVINGS

2	tablespoons virgin olive oil
1 to 2	serrano chilies, seeded and chopped
1	tablespoon grated fresh ginger
1	teaspoon cumin seeds
2	cups diced yellow bell pepper
2	teaspoons maple syrup
2	tablespoons fresh lime juice
4	cups cooked black-eyed peas, drained
3	tablespoons chopped cilantro
	Salt
	Freshly ground pepper

Heat the oil in a large nonstick sauté pan over moderate heat. Add the chilies, ginger, and cumin and fry until the seeds darken a few shades. Add the bell pepper and sauté for 2 minutes. Add the maple syrup, lime juice, black-eyed peas, and cilantro and cook until heated through. Season with salt and pepper.

Rice Pilaf–Stuffed Eggplant with Mango Sauce

This is an ideal make-ahead entree for entertaining. Try it with a legume dish such as Appaloosa Bean Salad (page 73) or Black Bean Salad with Three Roasted Peppers (page 70). For a lighter meal, pair it with Asparagus Tip Soup with Vegetable Salsa (pages 96 and 103).　　8 SERVINGS

4　medium eggplants (about 1 pound each), unpeeled, stems cut off, halved lengthwise
Olive-oil spray

Rice Pilaf
1　cup long-grain rice, preferably basmati
1　tablespoon virgin olive oil
1　teaspoon cumin seeds
2　cups diced red bell pepper
2　cups water
¼　cup dried currants
Salt
Freshly ground pepper
⅓　cup sliced almonds, pan-toasted until golden

Mango Sauce (recipe follows)

Preheat the oven to 450°F. Spray a shallow baking pan with olive oil. Using the tip of a sharp paring knife, make a ¼-inch-deep cut around the inside of each eggplant half. Score the flesh 4 to 5 times in the center. Place the eggplant halves, cut sides up, in the prepared pan; spray with oil and sprinkle with salt. Bake until tender, 25 to 30 minutes. Set aside to cool.

If you use basmati rice, rinse it and soak it in water for 10 minutes; drain well. Heat the oil and cumin seeds in a nonstick saucepan over low heat for 2 minutes. Stir in the bell pepper and rice and fry for 2 to 3 minutes. Add the water, currants, salt, and pepper; stir, and bring to a boil. Reduce the heat to

low, cover, and cook until tender, about 18 minutes. Remove from the heat; set aside 10 minutes, then fluff with a fork.

Carefully scoop out the eggplant pulp, leaving the walls and skins intact. Pat the shells dry. Coarsely chop the eggplant pulp; add it to the pilaf and gently mix. Spoon the pilaf into the eggplant shells. (Can be made 1 day ahead, covered, and refrigerated. Bring to room temperature before baking.)

Preheat the over to 350°F. Spray oil in a shallow baking dish. Place the eggplants in the baking dish, cut sides up, and spray the tops with oil. Bake until heated through, 15 to 20 minutes.

To serve, place a stuffed eggplant on the left side of each of eight warm dinner plates and spoon a legume salad on the right. Surround the eggplant with warm Mango Sauce, sprinkle with almonds, and serve immediately.

Mango Sauce

8 SERVINGS

        1   teaspoon fennel seeds
        4   ripe mangoes, peeled, seeded, and coarsely chopped
    1 to 2 jalapeño chilies, seeded and chopped
       1½   tablespoons grated fresh ginger
        2   cups water
       1½   cups vegetable stock
        2   tablespoons maple syrup
        2   tablespoons dried currants
        3   tablespoons chopped cilantro
            Salt

Place the fennel seeds in a large skillet and toast them over moderate heat until darkened a few shades. Add all but 1 cup of the chopped mango, the chilies, ginger, water, stock, and maple syrup to the pan. Bring to a boil, reduce the heat to medium-low, and simmer until reduced by half.

Pour the mixture into a food processor and blend until smooth. Transfer to a saucepan, add the currants and cilantro, and season with salt. Add the remaining chopped mango and warm over low heat for 10 minutes. Serve warm.

Tamale Pie

A childhood love affair with corn tamales inspired this entree, which is essentially an open-faced tamale; the polenta crust relies on Indian seasonings for added interest. Assembled and baked much like a tray pizza, it is easier to prepare than individually wrapped tamale parcels. The cheesy vegetable mélange that tops the crust gets its superb flavor from lime-spiked cream cheese, earthy ancho chilies, toasted cumin seed, and cheddar cheese.

This dish can be served warm, at room temperature, or chilled, from breakfast to late supper.   8 SERVINGS

Crust

	Olive-oil spray
1	teaspoon mustard seeds
4½	cups water
½	teaspoon salt
1¼	cups yellow or white cornmeal

Filling

1	teaspoon cumin seeds
1	teaspoon extra-virgin olive oil
3	medium zucchini (12 ounces), diced
3	cups fresh corn kernels (3 large ears) or 1¼ pounds frozen corn kernels, thawed
3	red bell peppers, seeded, deribbed, and diced
½	tablespoon ground ancho chilies or chili powder
½	cup light cream cheese, at room temperature
1	tablespoon fresh lime juice
½	teaspoon salt
½	cup chopped cilantro
1	cup shredded low-fat extra-sharp cheddar cheese (4 ounces)
1 to 2	seeded jalapeño chilies, slivered
8	oil-cured or Niçoise olives, pitted and quartered
	Tomato or tomatillo salsa (optional)

Preheat the oven to 375°F. Spray a 15 × 10 × 1-inch pizza pan with olive oil.

Place the mustard seeds in a large saucepan; cover and cook over moderately high heat until they pop and turn gray. Add the water and salt and bring to a boil. Stirring constantly, sprinkle in the cornmeal and cook until all of the liquid has been absorbed, 5 to 8 minutes. The polenta should be thick enough to hold its shape. Pour the mixture into the prepared pan and spread out to a uniform thickness. Cover with foil and bake for 15 minutes.

Meanwhile, place the cumin seeds in a saucepan, and cook them over moderate heat until they darken a few shades. Transfer to a mortar and coarsely crush with a pestle.

Heat the oil in a large nonstick skillet over high heat. Stir in the zucchini and sauté for 2 minutes. Add the corn and bell pepper and cook for another 2 minutes. Remove the pan from the heat and fold in the toasted cumin, ground chilies, cream cheese, lime juice, salt, and half of the cilantro.

When the polenta crust is ready, spoon the vegetable mixture over it. Scatter with cheddar cheese, jalapeños, and olives.

Bake until the cheese is bubbly and golden, 25–30 minutes. Set aside for at least 15 minutes before cutting and garnish with the remaining cilantro. If desired, top with dollops of tomato or tomatillo salsa.

Summer Vegetable Tart

This tart has a wonderful semolina crust, filled with a colorful mélange of summer vegetables. It is easy to make and is great cold or at room temperature. When tomatoes are scarce, or you don't have time to whip up a salsa, I recommend Enrico's Hot Salsa for the topping.

This dish can be served at any meal. For a weekday meal, accompany it with a big salad. As part of a party buffet, contrast room-temperature tart wedges with squares of Tamale Pie (opposite).   6 SERVINGS

¾ cup quick Cream of Wheat cereal
1 teaspoon ground cumin
½ tablespoon chili powder
2 teaspoons extra-virgin olive oil
1 teaspoon salt
2 cups water or vegetable stock
2 cups diced zucchini (2 medium)
1 cup diced yellow crookneck squash (1 medium)
¾ cup diced red bell pepper
¾ cup diced orange bell pepper
1 teaspoon curry powder
½ cup part-skim ricotta cheese
½ cup chopped cilantro
1 cup shredded low-fat jalapeño Jack cheese (4 ounces)
½ cup tomato salsa

Spray a 10½- to 11-inch fluted tart pan, with a removable base, with olive or vegetable oil. Place the cereal in a heavy saucepan, and toast over moderate heat until it darkens slightly, about 4 minutes. Stirring continuously, add the cumin, chili powder, 1 teaspoon oil, ½ teaspoon salt, and the water. Cook until the liquid has been absorbed and the cereal is stiff enough to hold the shape of the stirring spoon, about 4 minutes. Spoon the mixture into the tart pan, and when cool enough to handle, spread out with moistened hands to cover the base and sides of the pan. Use your fingers to press the mixture into the fluted edges and level off any excess with a rolling pin.

Heat the oven to 375°F. Heat the remaining 1 teaspoon oil in a nonstick frying pan over moderately high heat. When hot, add the zucchini and crookneck squash and sauté for 2 minutes. Stir in the bell peppers and curry powder and sauté for another 1 or 2 minutes. Remove the pan from the heat and fold in the ricotta, half of the cilantro, the remaining salt, and ¼ cup of shredded cheese. Spread the vegetables over the crust, sprinkle with the remaining cheese, and scatter ½-teaspoon dollops of salsa over the surface.

Bake until heated through and golden on the top, about 25 minutes. Let stand at least 15 minutes before cutting, and garnish with the remaining cilantro.

Zucchini Boats with Apple-Cilantro Chutney

Late-summer vegetables — summer squash, bell peppers, corn, and tomatoes — are the basis of this room-temperature entree. The stuffed zucchini are good for lunch boxes, picnics, and backyard dinners. Try them with Quinoa Macaroni and Cheese (page 122) or a grain salad.   6 SERVINGS

Chutney

3	cups lightly packed cilantro leaves
⅓	cup sliced almonds, pan-toasted until golden
2	sweet apples, peeled, cored, and diced
	Juice of 1 orange
	Juice of 1 lemon
1 to 2	teaspoons chopped fresh ginger
	Salt
	Freshly ground pepper
	Almond-oil or extra-virgin olive-oil spray (see Note)
6	zucchini (each about 12 ounces)
2	large, square orange bell peppers
	Vegetable stock or water
3	cups fresh corn kernels (3 to 4 ears)
3	tomatoes, peeled, seeded, and diced

Combine all of the chutney ingredients (except the salt and pepper), in a food processor and blend until reduced to a smooth pouring consistency, 3 to 4 minutes. Season with salt and pepper. (Chutney can be made 2 days in advance, covered, and refrigerated. If necessary, thin with juice before using.) Just before serving, spray the chutney with oil and transfer to a mustard-type squeeze bottle. Cut the nozzle tip to allow the chutney to flow easily.

Trim the stem end of each zucchini, halve lengthwise, and with a melon-baller, scoop out the insides, leaving a ¼-inch shell. (Reserve the pulp for a

salad, pilaf, or soup.) Steam the shells, cut sides up, over simmering water until bright green and just tender, 3 to 5 minutes. Transfer the shells, cut side down, to paper towels to cool and drain.

Using a vegetable peeler, remove the thin skin from the bell peppers, quarter, derib, seed, and dice. Place a large nonstick skillet over moderately high heat. Add the corn and a few tablespoons of stock. Cover and water-sauté for 2 to 3 minutes. Add the bell pepper and tomato and sauté, uncovered, for 1 to 2 minutes. Remove from the heat, season with salt and pepper, and spray with oil.

Squeeze a little chutney in the bottom of each shell, and fill with the mixed vegetables. Squeeze a zigzag strip of chutney on top of the vegetables. Spray with oil and serve at room temperature.

Note: As of this writing, almond-oil spray is not commercially available. If you want to try it in this recipe, simply pour almond oil into a spray bottle with an adjustable nozzle, and spray as necessary. Keep refrigerated for the longest shelf life.

Side-Dish Vegetables

I have been a vegetarian for twenty-six years now. Vegetable cookery is one of my passions, and my approach to it is constantly evolving. Sometimes I am drawn to study technique. At other times I'm fascinated with the tastes of our ancient past. Or I might become immersed in ethnic cuisines or regional traditions.

Vegetables play a larger role in my kitchen today than ever before. They are the core of lunch and dinner, featured variously in all types of salads and entrees. There are more than two hundred varieties of vegetables cultivated worldwide, and nearly one-third of them are cultivated in America. I cannot think of any other foods with more exciting colors, textures, and shapes.

I believe that the popularity of vegetables will steadily increase in the nineties. They are genuine health foods, loaded with fiber, vitamins, minerals, and carbohydrates. Vegetables are high-water-content foods — most are 70 to 95 percent water — with almost no fat. They are energizing, easy to digest, and cholesterol free. This means that when vegetables are properly prepared, you can eat them to your full satisfaction without worrying about weight gain.

In this chapter, the recipes fall into two broad categories — stovetop or water-cooked vegetables; and dry-heat (broiled, baked, and grilled) vegetables.

STOVETOP VEGETABLES

These dishes are prepared on top of the stove; the methods involved include steaming, blanching, water-sautéing, and stir-frying. They are simply prepared, usually consisting of just one or two varieties, and the seasonings are kept light. I keep a half dozen or so varieties of plain expeller-pressed oil, and a similar quantity of flavor-infused oils in my kitchen. Most of them are stored in spray bottles, so instead of pouring oil into the pan, I spray it on foods to moisturize and flavor them as they cook in their own juices.

The barest trace of a good unrefined oil gives a vegetable dish a distinctive, aromatic flavor. Besides extra-virgin olive oil, fragrant walnut, sesame, almond, avocado, mustard, and corn oil are used frequently.

BROILED, BAKED, AND GRILLED VEGETABLES

This collection comprises foods cooked in a dry-heat environment—surrounded by hot air, or browned near direct heat. Depending on the other elements in the meal, these dishes can serve as entrees, composed dinner salads, or side dishes.

About five years ago, I removed my pot of frying oil from the back burner and began exploring other dry-heat methods. Now even properly fried foods seem greasy to me, leaving a film of oil on the palate. I find grilled and baked foods much more appealing.

Allow these recipes to inspire and excite you. Cook through them, using good oils—perhaps a few flavor-infused varieties—and see how heat, cutting technique, and seasonings influence vegetables. Their simplicity is their wealth.

STOVETOP VEGETABLES

Gingered Butternut Squash Puree

Tan butternut squash, like other winter varieties, such as acorn, turban, and hubbard, has a silky texture and sweet flesh. Offset with ginger and tangerine juice, this whipped squash tastes remarkably rich, though it is made with only a trace of butter. To dress it up for entertaining, transfer the puree to a pastry bag fitted with a large star tip. Pipe the puree into a warm serving dish or swirl it into mounds directly onto dinner plates.   8 SERVINGS

2 large butternut squash (about 5 pounds)
2 tablespoons minced candied ginger or 1½ tablespoons grated fresh ginger
⅔ cup fresh tangerine juice
1 tablespoon maple syrup
½ teaspoon salt
¼ teaspoon cayenne
1 tablespoon butter

Preheat the oven to 375°F. Pierce the squash with a knife in several places and bake them on a tray until the skins easily yield to the touch, 1 to 1¼ hours. (Can be made 1 day ahead, cooled, and refrigerated.)

Halve the squash and remove the seeds. Scoop out the flesh and place it in a large nonstick skillet along with the remaining ingredients. Cook over moderate heat, stirring frequently, until the juice has evaporated and the texture is dry. Transfer to a food processor and blend until creamy. Serve immediately or keep warm in a double boiler.

Duo of Beet Purees

Brilliant color and clean flavor shine through both of these purees. Serve them as side-dish vegetables or as light sauces for cheese or legume entrees. Frozen, they make refreshing granités to serve before a meal or in between courses.
8 SERVINGS

1½ **pounds yellow beets, trimmed**
1½ **pounds red beets, trimmed**
1 **large tart green apple (about ½ pound), peeled, cored, and sliced**
1 to 2 **Bosc pears (about ½ pound), peeled, cored, and sliced**
2 **teaspoons fresh ginger puree (grated on an Oriental ginger grater) or finely minced ginger**
¼ **teaspoon ground coriander**
¼ **teaspoon ground cinnamon**
¼ **cup fresh orange juice**
Salt
Freshly ground pepper

Preheat the oven to 400°F. On two sheets of heavy-duty aluminum foil, wrap the two colored beets in individual parcels. Wrap the apple and pear in separate sheets of foil. Bake the beets until tender, about 1 hour. Bake the apple and pear until tender, about 45 minutes. When the beets are cool enough to handle, trim, peel, and chop.

In one batch, combine the yellow beets, pear, half of the ground spices, and half of the orange juice in a food processor and puree. Transfer to a double boiler and season with salt and pepper. Puree the red beets, apple, and remaining ingredients. Transfer to a second pan, season with salt and pepper, and serve hot.

Smoky Eggplant Caviar

This is a dish known as *baigan bharta* in India. Traditionally, the smoky flavors are captured by ash-baking whole eggplants on dying neem tree embers.

Try this spread chilled at breakfast or brunch, spread on toasted chapatis, sourdough wheat toast, or baked puff-pastry squares. For a lunch or light dinner, spoon the spread into halved pitas and fill them up with sandwich makings.   6 SERVINGS (ABOUT 2½ CUPS)

2 red bell peppers (1 pound)
6 Japanese eggplants (1¼ pounds) or 1 medium eggplant
   Olive-oil spray
⅓ cup plain nonfat yogurt
1 tablespoon chopped cilantro, fresh parsley, or fresh basil
   One quarter-size slice peeled fresh ginger
1 jalapeño chili, seeded
1 teaspoon cumin seeds, pan-toasted until golden
   Salt
   Freshly ground pepper
2 teaspoons virgin olive oil

Preheat a grill over moderately high heat. Quarter, seed, and derib the peppers. Grill them until the skins are blackened and blistered. Transfer to a sealed container to steam for 15 minutes. Peel off the blackened skins and cut into 1-inch pieces.

Reduce the heat to moderate. Peel and cut the eggplants lengthwise into ⅓-inch slices. Spray the grill and both sides of the eggplant with olive oil. Grill the eggplants until the flesh turns dark brown (do not allow it to blacken), 3 to 4 minutes per side. When cool, cut into 1-inch pieces.

Combine the yogurt and cilantro in a serving bowl and stir until creamy. Mince the ginger and chili in a food processor. Add the peppers, eggplant, and cumin seeds to the work bowl and process to a chunky puree or smooth paste. Fold this mixture into the herb-yogurt mixture and season with salt and pepper. Just before serving, drizzle with olive oil. (This keeps well, for 2 to 3 days; the flavors will intensify as they sit.)

Spaghetti Squash with Lime-Cashew Sauce

Spaghetti squash, when baked, yields pasta-like golden-yellow strands with the texture of extra-fine angel hair noodles. It is effortless to prepare — simply scoop the flesh out of a baked whole squash and unravel it. Its delicate flavor is overpowered by a strong sauce; hence this light lime-infused nut sauce. To vary the flavor, try almond, peanut, sesame, or hazelnut butter instead of cashew butter — all are available in natural-food stores.   8 SERVINGS

One **4-pound spaghetti squash**
   3 **tablespoons cashew butter**
1½ **tablespoons fresh lime juice**
   ¼ **teaspoon paprika**
   ¼ **teaspoon coarse-grind pepper, preferably Malabar**
   ⅓ **cup vegetable stock or water**
   2 **tablespoons chopped cilantro or fresh dill**
   2 **tablespoons chopped cashews, pan-toasted until golden**

Preheat the oven to 350°F. Pierce the squash with a knife several times. Bake it in an ovenproof dish until the skin yields to pressure, 1 to 1½ hours. When cool enough to handle, cut in half lengthwise and remove the seeds. Using a fork, scrape out the spaghetti-like strands from the shell and transfer to a serving platter.

While the squash is baking, make the sauce. Combine the cashew butter, lime juice, paprika, pepper, and stock in a small bowl and whisk until smooth. Pour the sauce over the squash and toss to mix. Garnish with cilantro and cashews.

Green Beans with Roasted Peppers in Mustard Butter

This vegetable combination makes a fine dish that is rich with aroma and flavor. The smoky red peppers and thin green beans could easily be replaced by orange peppers and yellow Kentucky wonder beans—use any color and variety in season. It is equally delicious as a summer salad, at room temperature or chilled, with a splash of lime juice and tiny bits of oil-cured black olives. Or you might top it with a dressing of marjoram-laced yogurt.   6 SERVINGS

> 2 large red bell peppers
> 1½ pounds green beans, trimmed
> 1 teaspoon mustard seeds
> 2 teaspoons unsalted butter or corn oil
> Salt
> Freshly ground pepper
> 1 teaspoon chopped fresh dill

Quarter, seed, and derib the peppers. Grill or broil them, skin toward the heat, until charred. Place in a closed container for 15 minutes. Rub off the blackened skin and cut the flesh into long strips.

Steam or blanch the beans until tender-crisp and bright green. Plunge them into ice water to prevent overcooking, then drain.

Heat a wok or skillet over moderate heat. Add the mustard seeds; cover and toast until the seeds sputter and pop. Remove the pan from the heat, add the butter, and cook until it froths and turns to hazelnut brown (or until oil is hot).

Stir the beans and peppers into the seasoned butter and stir-fry until heated through, about 1 minute. Season with salt and pepper. Serve immediately, sprinkled with dill.

Zucchini with Toasted Almonds

This dish was inspired by one sampled at the Scalini restaurant in Rome—square-shaped pieces of zucchini sautéed in garlic-olive oil, topped with almond slivers and grated pecorino cheese.

In this version, the zucchini is stir-fried in ginger-oil and sprinkled with lemon juice instead of cheese. The flavors are uncomplicated and simple, heightened with a garnish of toasted sliced almonds.   6 SERVINGS

> 4 medium zucchini (1½ pounds), trimmed
> 1 tablespoon extra-virgin olive oil
> ½ tablespoon grated fresh ginger
>   Salt
>   Cayenne
> ½ tablespoon fresh lemon juice
> 3 tablespoons sliced almonds, pan-toasted until golden

Cut the zucchini lengthwise into ¼-inch-thick slices. Cut through the stacked slices to yield 1-inch square pieces. Steam the zucchini until tender-crisp, 2 to 3 minutes.

In a nonstick wok or skillet, heat the oil over moderately high heat. Add the zucchini and ginger and stir-fry until heated, about 30 seconds. Season with salt and cayenne.

Transfer to a serving dish and sprinkle with lemon juice and almonds. Serve immediately.

Stir-Fried Savoy Cabbage with Carrots

Throughout India, sliced compact-head cabbage and carrots is a beloved stir-fry combination. In the east and south, plantain wafers might be substituted for the carrots. In the west, cabbage and diced new potatoes might be favored. Give all of them a try.

Though I suggest savoy cabbage for flavor, texture, and color, Chinese cabbage or celery cabbage are equally delicious.   8 SERVINGS

½ tablespoon extra-virgin olive oil
½ tablespoon butter
¼ teaspoon crushed red-pepper flakes
2 large carrots, thin sliced on the diagonal
1 medium savoy cabbage (about 2 pounds), cored and finely sliced
   Salt
   Freshly ground pepper
1 teaspoon chopped fresh dill or 2 tablespoons chopped cilantro

Heat the olive oil and butter in a nonstick wok or casserole over moderately high heat. Add the pepper flakes and carrot and stir-fry for 1 minute. Add the cabbage, and stirring constantly, cook until just tender and bright green, about 5 minutes. Season with salt and pepper and fold in the dill. Transfer to a serving dish and serve immediately.

Orange-Mustard Brussels Sprouts

You can also make this dish with lemons or limes.   6 SERVINGS

    1 **teaspoon mustard seeds**
 1½ **tablespoons unsalted butter**
    2 **tablespoons fresh orange juice**
  ¼ **teaspoon grated orange zest**
  ½ **teaspoon jalapeño puree (optional; see Note)**
    4 **cups steamed Brussels sprouts, trimmed and quartered**
       Salt
       Freshly ground pepper

Place the mustard seeds in a covered large nonstick skillet over moderate heat. When the seeds sputter and turn gray, add the butter, juice, zest, and jalapeño puree. After about 15 seconds, stir in the sprouts and heat through, 2 to 3 minutes. Season with salt and pepper.

Note: To make jalapeño puree, rub the fleshy portion of the chili across the teeth of a Japanese ginger grater. In this quantity, the chili will bring more flavor than heat to the dish.

Bell Pepper Sauté

This colorful sauté combines, red, yellow, orange, green, and purple peppers, which range in flavor from sweet to warm and stimulating. The peppers are sautéed in a flavor-infused oil featuring fresh ginger, black onion seeds, and bay leaves. Onion seed, also called black cumin in Indian and natural-food stores, has a delicate lemon-eucalyptus flavor. If you don't have access to it, use mustard seed. Serve with buttered rice, pasta, or wheat flat breads. Leftovers are great tossed with a green salad.   8 SERVINGS

> 2 **pounds mixed sweet bell peppers: yellow, red, orange, green, and purple**
> 1 **tablespoon peanut oil**
> ½ **tablespoon grated fresh ginger**
> 2 **small bay leaves**
> ½ **tablespoon onion or mustard seeds**
> 1 **tablespoon maple syrup**
> 2 **tablespoons chopped cilantro**
> **Salt**
> **Cayenne**

Seed and derib the peppers; cut them lengthwise into fine julienne. Warm the oil in a nonstick wok over moderately high heat. Add the ginger, bay leaves, and onion seeds and fry for about 15 seconds. Add the peppers and sauté until wilted, stirring frequently, 8 to 10 minutes. Remove from the heat; stir in the maple syrup and cilantro and season with salt and cayenne.

Yellow Squash in Fennel Butter with Pistachios

You want young, immature squash for this dish — from finger-size to five inches long. The skins should be shiny and paper-thin — easily removed when scraped by a fingernail.   4 SERVINGS

6 thin-skinned yellow squash (1½ pounds), trimmed and sliced ⅛ inch thick
1 teaspoon fennel seeds or crushed coriander seeds
2 teaspoons melted butter or herb oil
   Salt
   Freshly ground pepper
2 tablespoons chopped pistachio nuts

Steam the yellow squash until tender-crisp, 2 to 3 minutes. Heat a nonstick wok or skillet over moderate heat. Stir in the fennel seeds and fry until they darken a few shades. Add half of the butter or oil and the squash. Toss to mix and sauté for 1 to 2 minutes. Season with salt and pepper. Serve hot, sprinkled with pistachios and drizzled with the remaining butter or oil.

Swiss Chard with Toasted Sesame Seeds

In India, leafy green dishes — usually spinach based — are known as *saak*. When chard is treated as a *saak* ingredient, the results are outstanding. In this instance, blanched red or green chard is brought to life with a sesame-infused oil, cayenne, and fresh tangerine juice. When chard is out of season, try the dish with a mixture of spinach and collard greens.   6 SERVINGS

5 pounds Swiss chard (5 large bunches)
2 teaspoons extra-virgin olive oil
1 teaspoon sesame seeds
   Salt

Cayenne
2 **tablespoons fresh tangerine or orange juice**
Olive-oil spray (optional)

Cut off the chard stems and reserve them for another use. Wash the leaves under running water to dislodge any sand or grit. In batches, blanch them in a large pot of boiling water for 1 minute. Drain and refresh them in a large bowl of ice water. When cool, squeeze the leaves between your palms to extract as much water as possible; finely chop.

Heat the olive oil in a large nonstick wok or skillet over moderate heat. Add the sesame seeds and fry until golden. Stir in the chard, toss well, and sauté until heated through, 1 to 2 minutes. Season with salt and cayenne.

Serve hot, sprinkled with citrus juice and, if desired, a misting of olive oil.

Sautéed Sugar Snap Peas with Radishes

A refreshing spring vegetable combination, really delicious with organic produce. You can also make this dish with snow peas.   6 SERVINGS

1 **pound sugar snap peas, strings and stems removed**
1 **teaspoon mustard seeds**
1 **tablespoon walnut or almond oil**
1 **teaspoon grated fresh ginger**
1 **cup thinly sliced radishes**
  Salt
  Freshly ground black pepper
1 **tablespoon fresh orange juice**
2 **tablespoons chopped walnuts, pan-toasted**

Blanch the peas in boiling water for 2 minutes. Drain and refresh under cold running water to set the color. Drain and set aside.

Place the mustard seeds in a large nonstick skillet over moderate heat; toast until they pop and turn gray. Add the oil, ginger, and radishes and sauté for 2 to 3 minutes. Add the peas and cook for 3 more minutes. Season with salt and pepper. Sprinkle with juice and nuts and serve immediately.

Parsnips and Carrots with Currants

This brilliant orange-and-white side dish is also terrific as a salad. The sweet root vegetables are offset with splashes of three citrus juices, toasted coriander seeds, and fresh mint. You could also use all carrots or parsnips.   6 SERVINGS

1½ **pounds carrots, peeled and sliced on the diagonal ¼ inch thick**
1 **pound parsnips, peeled and sliced on the diagonal ¼ inch thick**
1 **teaspoon coriander seeds, crushed**
½ **tablespoon unsalted butter**
½ **jalapeño chili, seeded and cut into paper-thin jullienne**
   Juice from 1 lime, 1 lemon, and 1 tangerine
1½ **tablespoons maple syrup**
3 **tablespoons dried currants**
   Salt
   Freshly ground pepper
4 **teaspoons chopped fresh mint**

Steam the carrots and parsnips until tender-crisp. Place the coriander seeds in a large nonstick skillet over moderately high heat. When they darken a few shades, add the butter and jalapeño and sizzle for 15 seconds. Add the citrus juices, maple syrup, and currants. Bring to a boil and cook until the liquid is reduced to half its volume, about 5 minutes. Stir in the vegetables and cook until they are tender and the liquid has been absorbed. Season with salt and pepper. Serve hot or warm, sprinkled with mint.

Cauliflower in Curried Tomato Glaze

Some variation of this cauliflower dish is served frequently in hundreds of thousands of Indian homes. For a late dinner, it might be accompanied with steamed basmati rice or toasted flat breads and a light salad.

If you have access to fresh curry leaves from an Indian or Asian grocer, add a sprig to the sauce for classic North Indian flavor.   6 SERVINGS

  1 **large cauliflower (about 3 pounds), trimmed and cut into 1-inch florets**
  ½ **tablespoon ground coriander**
  ½ **teaspoon curry powder**
  3 **tablespoons water**
  ½ **tablespoon mustard seeds**
  2 **tablespoons melted butter**
 1½ **cups chopped tomato**
     Salt
     Freshly ground pepper
  3 **tablespoons chopped cilantro or fresh parsley**

Steam the cauliflower until half cooked, 4 to 5 minutes; set aside. Combine the coriander and curry powder in a cup and blend with the water.

Heat a large nonstick wok or casserole over moderate heat. Drop in the mustard seeds; cover and fry until they pop and sputter. Add 1 tablespoon of butter and the liquid spice blend. Cook until the water has nearly evaporated; then stir in the tomato and cook until the mixture is reduced to a chunky sauce, 10 to 12 minutes.

Fold the cauliflower into the sauce and season with salt and pepper. Reduce the heat slightly, partially cover, and cook until the cauliflower is fork-tender and the tomato liquid has been absorbed, about 10 minutes, stirring once or twice. Just before serving, fold in the remaining butter and garnish with cilantro.

Belgian Endive with Cilantro Cream Sauce

If you are unfamiliar with Belgian endive, this rendition — tender ivory spears enveloped in a creamy herb sauce — will win you over. The bitterness of green Belgian endive is routinely tempered by a gardening process known as *blanching*. You should therefore look for compact yellowish-white heads without a trace of green.

To turn this dish into a make-ahead gratin, place it in a shallow baking dish, sprinkle with a few tablespoons of buttered bread crumbs and shredded Swiss cheese, and broil until the topping crisps and browns.   6 SERVINGS

12 small heads Belgian endive (1½ pounds)
 2 cups Summer Vegetable Stock (page 77)
 2 sprigs fresh curry leaves or 1 bay leaf and 6 parsley sprigs
 2 tablespoons fresh lime juice
¼ cup chopped cilantro
⅓ cup half-and-half
    Salt
    Freshly ground pepper
 1 tablespoon chopped pistachio nuts

With the tip of a small paring knife, remove the bitter conical cores from the base of the Belgian endives, cutting in a circular motion about ¾ inch into the base.

Combine the stock, curry leaves, and lime juice in a nonreactive skillet and bring to a boil. Reduce the heat, cover, and simmer for 10 minutes. Add the endive, cover, and simmer until the base ends are knife-tender, 20 to 25 minutes. With a slotted spoon, transfer the endive to a dish and set aside.

Remove the curry leaves with a small strainer and boil until the liquid is reduced to about ½ cup, about 20 minutes.

Over low heat, stir in the cilantro and half-and-half, and gently warm. Season with salt and pepper. Place the Belgian endive in the pan, and shake to coat the vegetables with sauce. Serve warm, sprinkled with nuts.

Sautéed Spinach and Spiced Sweet Potatoes

Known as *aloo-saak*, this is a favorite dish in many Indian regional cuisines. In the north and in most restaurants, it is served in the form of a buttery puree that envelops deep-fried white cheese or potato cubes. In this light Bengali-style version, the spinach is sautéed with steamed sweet potatoes and given a peppery kick by mustard oil and jalapeño chilies.   4 SERVINGS

1½ pounds spinach, washed, stems removed
1 large sweet potato (½ pound), peeled and cut into ¼-inch dice
1 teaspoon sweet paprika
1 teaspoon cumin seeds, pan-toasted until a darker shade and crushed
¼ teaspoon freshly ground nutmeg
Salt
Freshly ground pepper, preferably Malabar
2 teaspoons mustard oil or safflower oil
1 jalapeño chili, seeded and minced
1 teaspoon fresh lemon juice

Place the spinach in a large pot with the water clinging to the leaves. Cover and steam over moderate heat until wilted, 2 to 3 minutes. Coarsely chop the spinach and set aside.

Steam the sweet potato until nearly tender, 5 to 7 minutes. Transfer to a bowl; add the paprika, crushed cumin, and nutmeg and toss to mix. Season with salt and pepper.

Heat the oil in a large nonstick skillet over moderately high heat. Add the chili and sizzle for 10 seconds. Stir in the potato and sauté for 3 to 4 minutes. Add the spinach and cook for an additional 1 to 2 minutes, or until heated through. Sprinkle with lemon juice and serve immediately.

BROILED, BAKED, AND GRILLED VEGETABLES

Slow-Baked Tomatoes

These tomatoes, one of my late-summer favorites when the fruit is at its peak, are outrageously good. Because they are baked for a long time at low temperature, they are sweet and almost caramelized. When I have access to a variety of tomatoes, I make a couple of trays, combining Italian plum, red, green, orange, and low-acid yellow tomatoes. Leftovers are terrific in salads and stir-fries.   4 SERVINGS

> 5 to 6 large, vine-ripened tomatoes
> Extra-virgin olive-oil spray
> 1 tablespoon grated fresh ginger
> Salt
> Freshly ground pepper
> 3 tablespoons chopped cilantro or fresh basil

Preheat the oven to 325°F. Halve the tomatoes horizontally and place on baking trays, cut sides up. Spray with oil and dot with the ginger. Bake for 2½ hours, until collapsed and slightly caramelized. Spray with oil once or twice during baking.

Before serving, season with salt and pepper and sprinkle with cilantro. Serve hot or at room temperature.

Note: Vary the flavor nuances with different oil and herb selections. Pair walnut oil with purple basil, almond oil with fresh dill, or Infused Curry Oil (page 293) with summer savory. To make an oil spray, pour a good cold-pressed oil into a spray bottle with an adjustable nozzle and set it on "mist." Keep refrigerated.

Red Pepper and Kohlrabi Gratin

This is one of kohlrabi's ultimate renderings, an ideal dish for a newcomer to the vegetable. It is similar to potato au gratin but lower in fat and more flavorful. This dish combines kohlrabi slices and sweet red-pepper rings, enveloping them in a creamy Indian chickpea-flour sauce called *karhi*. Leftovers are great for breakfast or a brown-bag lunch.   6 SERVINGS

    1 **tablespoon extra-virgin olive oil**
    1 **teaspoon cumin seeds**
    2 **tablespoons chickpea flour or whole-wheat pastry flour**
    2 **cups skim milk**
    ¼ **teaspoon salt**
    3 **thin slices whole-wheat bread**
    3 **tablespoons chopped cilantro or fresh dill**
       Olive-oil spray
    1 **pound thinly sliced pared kohlrabi (7 small bulbs)**
    2 **red bell peppers, seeded, deribbed, and sliced into ¼-inch rings**
    3 **ounces shredded low-fat sharp cheddar cheese**

Heat the oil in a nonstick saucepan over moderate heat. Add the cumin seeds and fry until they darken a few shades. With a whisk, stir in the flour until smooth; cook for 30 seconds. Remove the pan from the heat, and gradually whisk in the milk. Place the pan over the heat, and while whisking, bring the mixture to a boil. Gently boil until thickened, whisking frequently, about 5 minutes. Remove from the heat and stir in the salt.

Preheat the oven to 350°F. Break the bread into pieces; place it in the work bowl of a food processor along with the cilantro, and process into fine crumbs. Bake the crumbs until golden, stirring to ensure even browning.

Spray a 12 × 12-inch gratin or nonstick baking pan with olive oil. Layer one-third of the kohlrabi, pepper rings, and sauce, and repeat three times, ending with the crumbs. Sprinkle with cheese and spray with olive oil.

Bake for 40 to 45 minutes, or until the cheese is bubbly and browned and the vegetables are tender. Let stand for 5 minutes before serving.

Crispy Baked Green Bananas with Lime

You can make this dish with green bananas or plantains, two fruits that are treated as starchy vegetables in Indian, Asian, and South American cuisines. In this side dish, finger-size banana sticks are dipped in buttered lime juice, coated with cilantro-flavored bread crumbs, and baked until crispy. If you have a weakness for fried foods, this will provide guilt-free satisfaction. I've experimented with several types of bread for the crumbs—sourdough, sprouted rye, multigrain, and corn bread—all with delicious results.

4 SMALL SERVINGS

3	slices fresh bread
¼	cup cilantro leaves
¼	cup grated Parmesan
1½	tablespoons melted butter
¼	cup fresh lime juice
¼	teaspoon salt
¼	teaspoon cayenne
Four	9-inch green bananas or plantains
	Olive-oil spray

Preheat the oven to 375°F. Break the bread into pieces; add to the work bowl of a food procesor along with the cilantro and process into fine crumbs. Spread the crumbs out on a baking tray and toast for 5 minutes. Remove from the oven and mix in the Parmesan.

In a shallow dish, whisk the butter and lime juice along with a hint of salt and cayenne. Peel the bananas; cut them in half crosswise and then lengthwise, ending up with sixteen pieces. Coat the bananas in the butter mixture, and individually dredge in the herbed bread crumbs to coat on all sides. Arrange in a single layer on a nonstick baking tray. Spray with olive oil and bake until golden and tender, turning once, 25 to 30 minutes. Drizzle with the remaining butter mixture and serve hot or warm.

Grilled Chili Rellenos

This takeoff on Mexican *rellenos* is light—grilled instead of deep-fried—but tastes rich and delicious. It gets its distinctive, irresistible flavor from a classic quartet: smoky roasted chilies, mellow cheese, assertive cilantro, and nutty toasted cumin seeds.

For a light entree, serve the *rellenos* on a bed of thinly sliced tomatoes or ½ cup sautéed julienned zucchini, and pair with Sweet White Runner Bean Salad with Peanuts (page 68). For heartier fare, serve on ½ cup cooked white or brown rice, with Vegetable Salsa (page 103) or tomato salsa.
6 SERVINGS

12 Italian yellow banana peppers, red or green Anaheim chilies, or two 4-ounce cans whole green chilies
 8 ounces part-skim jalapeño Jack cheese or Monterey Jack cheese
½ tablespoon cumin seeds, pan-toasted until a darker shade
½ cup finely chopped red bell pepper or corn kernels
36 cilantro leaves

Roast the fresh chilies or peppers on a rack over direct heat or flame. Turn to blacken and blister all sides of the chilies. Remove from the heat; immediately place in a paper bag and seal. After about 20 minutes, slip off the blackened skins under running water. (If using canned whole green chilies, omit this step.)

Cut the cheese into twelve sticks about 2 inches long. In a small bowl, mix the cumin seeds and bell peppers. Pat the chilies dry. Make a small slit in the side of each chili. Carefully remove the seeds and ease about 1 tablespoon of the bell-pepper mixture into the bottom of the chili. Slip in a piece of cheese and top with three cilantro leaves. (Can be assembled several hours before use; chill until ready to use.)

Place the stuffed chilies, slit sides up, on a moderately hot nonstick grill for about 5 minutes, or until the cheese has melted. Alternately, bake in a preheated 400°F oven for about 5 minutes. Allow two chilies per serving.

Oven-Roasted Okra

This is my current favorite okra recipe. It has a terrific rich flavor, is low in fat, and is very easy to prepare. Look for smallish okra that are unblemished and as fresh as possible. Though coriander and cumin go well with okra, for a change try crumbled dried marjoram and oregano.   6 SERVINGS

> 2 tablespoons extra-virgin olive oil
> ½ tablespoon ground coriander
> 1 teaspoon ground cumin
> ¼ teaspoon herb salt
> ¼ teaspoon cayenne
> 1½ pounds small okra, rinsed and patted dry
> Olive-oil spray
> 6 lemon or lime wedges

Preheat the oven to 500°F. In a bowl, combine the oil, coriander, cumin, salt, and cayenne; whisk to mix. Toss the okra in the seasoned oil. Spread out in a single layer on one or more baking pan(s). Spray the okra with oil and roast for 10 to 12 minutes, shaking the pan occasionally, until it is tender and golden-brown. Serve hot with a lemon wedge.

Vrindavan Baked Potatoes

I first had long-cooked, literally overbaked, potatoes in the 1970s. They were prepared by Annand Maharaj, senior temple chef of Vrindavan's Sree Krishna Balaram Temple. When I requested simple "oil-free, plain potatoes," this is what he came up with.

The potatoes were ash-baked for nearly two hours, until the charred skins formed a brittle shell. The inside creamy flesh was scooped out, mashed, and seasoned with only a trace of freshly cracked pepper. I now make them often, especially when organic potatoes are just out of the ground.

It was nearly a decade later that I found out about James Beard's fondness for almost the same potato. Good taste eliminates all boundaries.
4 SERVINGS

4 large baking potatoes
  Freshly ground pepper or grated fresh ginger
  Salt

Preheat the oven to 425°F. Wash and dry the potatoes. Pierce them with a fork several times. Bake in the center of the oven for 1¾ to 2 hours. Remove from the oven and slice off an oval of skin from the top. Scoop out the flesh, mash until smooth, and season with pepper and salt. Serve as is or spoon back into the shell.

Summer Vegetable Brochettes

You can turn this into an entree by threading marinated cubes of White Cheese (page 188) or tofu onto the skewers. Using olive-oil spray keeps the vegetables moist, keeps fat and calories to a minimum, and lessens sticking on the grill. For a simple meal, accompany with Pine Nut and Orange Wild Rice (page 113).   4 SERVINGS

1 red bell pepper
1 yellow bell pepper
2 small ears fresh corn
2 green or yellow zucchini
  Olive-oil spray, preferably extra-virgin
½ tablespoon cumin seeds, pan-toasted until a darker shade and crushed
¼ teaspoon ground cayenne or mild paprika
  Salt
  Freshly ground pepper
3 tablespoons chopped cilantro
1 tablespoon fresh lemon or lime juice

Seed and derib the bell peppers and cut them into 1½-inch squares. Husk the corn and cut into rounds 1 inch thick. Slice the zucchini into rounds ½ inch thick.

Prepare a barbecue grill for medium heat or preheat a stovetop grill over moderate heat. Spear the vegetables on bamboo or metal skewers, alternating them (red pepper, yellow pepper, corn, zucchini), and spray well with olive oil. Arrange the skewers on a barbecue rack. Grill the vegetables until tender-crisp and nicely browned, turning and spraying with olive oil occasionally, for up to 15 minutes.

Remove from the grill and sprinkle with cumin, cayenne, paprika, salt, pepper, cilantro, and lemon juice. Serve hot or at room temperature.

Peppery Turnip "Fries"

Though it took me forty-some years to try a turnip, I become an aficionado with this rendering. In the fall and winter I like to serve them to unsuspecting guests, who rarely detect what they are eating while they gobble them up. I have tried numerous seasonings on these "fries," but it's hard to beat the simple duo of nutmeg and pepper.   8 SERVINGS

         8 medium turnips (about 2½ pounds)
         1 teaspoon freshly ground nutmeg
      1½ teaspoons freshly ground pepper, preferably Malabar
       ¼ cup Parmesan or grated fresh coconut
            Olive-oil spray
         2 tablespoons fresh lime juice (optional)

Preheat the oven to 425°F. Spray a nonstick baking pan or a large cookie sheet with olive oil.

Pare the turnips and cut them into 2½ × ½-inch sticks. Combine the spices, Parmesan, and turnips in a large plastic bag. Seal and shake to coat.

Spread the sticks in a single layer on the prepared pan and spray with olive oil. Bake for 30 to 35 minutes, or until the turnip spears are tender and golden, turning once. Serve piping hot, with or without a sprinkle of lime juice.

New Potatoes with Lemon and Bay Leaves

Baked in clay pots, these Bengali-style potatoes are heavenly (see Note). Any freshly dug waxy-fleshed new potato—red, White Rose, Yellow Finnish, or Rose Firs—will yield excellent results. While cassia leaves would be used in India, bay leaves marry equally well with lemon and olive oil. Good 24 hours a day, 365 days a year.   6 SERVINGS

> 2 **pounds small new potatoes, cut into even-sized wedges**
> 1 **tablespoon virgin olive oil**
> 2 **tablespoons fresh lemon juice**
> 1 **bay or cassia leaf, broken**
>   **Paprika or cayenne**
>   **Salt**
>   **Freshly ground pepper**

Preheat the oven to 375°F. If using a clay pot (see Note) soak both halves in water for 15 minutes; drain. Combine the potatoes, oil, lemon juice, and bay leaf in the clay pot or large baking dish and toss to mix. Sprinkle with paprika and season generously with salt and pepper. Cover with the clay lid, or bake, covered, until the potatoes are tender and crusty, stirring occasionally, 45 to 60 minutes. You may want to sprinkle with additional lemon juice just before serving.

Note: Unglazed clay cooking pots are available in better cookware stores and through mail-order sources such as Williams-Sonoma and "The Chef's Catalog," under the La Cloche™ and Rümertopf™ labels.

Baked Vegetable Packets

You can use almost any vegetables, in any combination, for these treasure bundles. I prefer organic, just-harvested vegetables for their intense flavor, aroma, and color. You need only a trace of flavor-infused oil or ghee such as curry, saffron, pineapple, or tomato (see Appendix), to make these vegetables outstanding.

If you cook the packets on a grill, wrap them in a double thickness of heavy-duty foil and place them directly on fading embers for 15 to 20 minutes.

Chilled leftovers make a perfect accompaniment to steamed rice or salad greens.   8 SERVINGS

1   red, 1 yellow, and 1 green bell pepper, seeded, deribbed, and cut
    into long strips
3   medium-size zucchini, sliced ½ inch thick
1   cup fresh corn kernels
1   pound thin green beans, cut into 1-inch pieces
3   tablespoons chopped fresh dill or cilantro
½   teaspoon coriander seeds, crushed
⅔   cup vegetable stock

Preheat the oven to 350°F. Combine all of the ingredients in a large bowl. Divide the vegetables equally between eight 12-inch squares of parchment paper, mounding them in the center. Fold the edges of the squares together at the top and seal the open side seams by folding the ends over twice. Bake on baking trays until the vegetables are tender, about 30 minutes.

Place the packets on dinner plates and allow diners to break them open and inhale the aromas.

Deviled Corn on the Cob

In India, corn is grown primarily for animal feed and flour and is also used in flat breads. Occasionally, some of it is picked before it fully matures on the stalk and is sold by street vendors who specialize in grilled corn. This tough corn gets most of its flavor from the neem wood on which it is grilled. It is served simply, with just a sprinkle of seasoned salt and lime juice. When the same treatment is proffered to succulent white or yellow table corn, the results are mouth-watering.   6 SERVINGS

    1 teaspoon paprika
    ⅛ teaspoon cayenne
    ½ teaspoon cumin seeds, crushed
    ½ teaspoon freshly ground pepper, preferably Tellicherry
    ½ tablespoon maple syrup
    1 tablespoon fresh lemon or lime juice
    1 tablespoon melted butter
    6 ears of corn
       Cold water

Prepare a grill. When the fire has died and the coals are covered in ash, you are ready to grill.

Combine all of the ingredients except the corn and water in a small bowl and mix well. To grill the corn, open up the husks and remove the silk. Brush the corn with the seasoning, sprinkle with cold water, and close up the husks to use as a protective covering. Tie the tops with kitchen twine and spray the husks with water to keep them from catching fire. Grill over moderate heat for about 15 minutes, turning four or five times for even cooking.

Alternately, husk and silk the corn and brush with the seasoning. Wrap in aluminum foil and bake in a preheated 350°F oven for about 20 minutes. Serve the grilled corn piping hot.

Grilled Eggplant Fans
with Cashew Chutney

In the summer, I grill eggplant at least once a week and use it in numerous ways—diced in wild rice or whole-grain salads, cubed in textured tomato sauces, roughly chopped in sandwich spreads, and layered in vegetable casseroles. This is one of the fruits of my experimentation.

For this dish, you need slender Japanese eggplants. They have thin skins and few seeds, do not require salting, and are the ideal size for cutting into fans for individual servings. If you can't find them, use small globe eggplants cut into ⅜-inch-thick slices.

You don't need to grill eggplant over an open fire to bring out its exquisite flavor. Much of the time I use two 12-inch stovetop hot-air grills that fit over large electric or gas stove burners. The grills are available at better cookware stores and through mail-order catalogs (see Appendix).   6 SERVINGS

> 6 Japanese eggplants, 2 to 4 ounces each
>   Flavor-infused oil (pages 291 to 294) or virgin olive-oil spray
>   Herb salt
>   Cayenne

Chutney

> ¼ cup dry-roasted cashews
> 1 jalapeño chili, seeded and chopped
> ¼ cup cilantro leaves
>   Pinch salt
>   Pinch freshly ground pepper
> 1 cup plain nonfat yogurt

Cut off the stems and ¼ inch from the bottoms of the eggplants. Slice them lengthwise, making the cuts ¼ to ⅓ inch apart, leaving the slices securely attached at the stem end. With your palm, gently press on the eggplants to ease

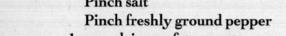

and flatten them into fans. Brush or spray the entire surface of the eggplants with oil.

Spray one or two grills with oil and preheat over moderately low to moderate heat. Grill the fans, adjusting the heat as necessary, until the eggplant is tender and richly browned on both sides, 10 to 15 minutes total time. (Do not allow the flesh to blacken.) Lightly season with herb salt and cayenne.

To make the chutney, place the cashews in a blender and pulse to mince. Add the remaining ingredients and puree until smooth.

Serve the eggplant fans hot, warm, or at room temperature, topped with a spoonful of chutney.

Broiled Tomatoes

In India, I use mustard oil on these tomatoes. Its flavor is hot and pungent, reminiscent of horseradish, and adds zip to the tomatoes. If you have some on hand, give it a try. For a less assertive flavor, use toasted sesame oil or extra-virgin olive oil.   4 SERVINGS

> 1 **teaspoon mustard seeds**
> 2 **large vine-ripened tomatoes**
> 2 **tablespoons plain nonfat yogurt or low-fat, egg-free mayonnaise**
> **Salt**
> **Freshly ground pepper, preferably Tellicherry**
> ½ **tablespoon mustard, sesame, or extra-virgin olive oil**

Preheat the oven to 400°F. Place a small pan over moderate heat. Add the mustard seeds; cover and fry until the seeds sputter and pop. Remove the pan from the heat.

Halve the tomatoes and remove the seeds. Spread ½ tablespoon of yogurt over each half. Sprinkle with salt, pepper, and toasted mustard seeds. Drizzle with oil. Bake on a tray for 15 minutes, then broil until lightly browned. Serve hot, warm, or cold.

Acorn Squash Stuffed with Cranberried Apples

Acorn squash halves are perfect for filling. In this fall dish, they hold a wonderfully aromatic, sweet cranberry and apple chutney. As the squash bakes, the chutney cooks to a chunky perfection. Good served hot or warm.   8 SERVINGS

4   acorn squash, halved and seeded
    Olive-oil spray
2   cups diced green apples, preferably Jonathans
3   tablespoons frozen apple juice concentrate
⅔   cup fresh or frozen cranberries
3   tablespoons fruit-sweetened raspberry jam
¼   cup golden raisins
⅛   teaspoon cayenne
¼   teaspoon ground cinnamon
½   teaspoon ground coriander
    Olive-oil spray
    Salt

Preheat the oven to 350°F. Place the squash in a baking dish and spray with olive oil. Loosely cover with foil and bake for 15 minutes.

Combine the apple, apple juice concentrate, cranberries, jam, raisins, and spices in a bowl and mix well. Spoon the cranberry mixture evenly into the eight squash halves; spray with oil and season with salt. Loosely cover, return to the oven, and bake until the squash are fork-tender, 30 to 45 minutes, depending on their size.

Uncover, spray with oil, and bake for an additional 10 minutes, or until the stuffing is caramelized and lightly browned.

Desserts

The recipes that follow are characterized by ease, simplicity, and lightness—maximum effect with minimum effort. It's not that I don't delight in dessert artistry. It's just that at this time in my life, less dessert extravaganza is appealing to me. The chapter is divided into three sections: frozen desserts, airy mousse creations, and varied fruit conclusions. The quality of any dessert depends on the quality of its ingredients. Most of the ingredients in the following recipes will be familiar; a few may not be. All of the sweeteners and dry ingredients are available at gourmet and natural-food stores. No doubt you have established a few good sources for seasonal fruits and vegetables. If not, seek out a local farmer's market, greengrocer, or market that sells in-season produce.

INGREDIENTS AND EQUIPMENT

Several of the desserts are made with fresh fruit juice. Many supermarkets and natural-food stores sell fresh juices, either through in-house juice bars or directly from the produce department. Most offer freshly squeezed pineapple, carrot, and orange juice on a daily basis. Larger stores also offer a wide variety of high-quality bottled and frozen juices and frozen juice concentrates. But nothing compares with freshly made juice.

For small quantities, you can always use a hand-held reamer to squeeze citrus juice. Some food processors and blender have citrus-juice attachments. You need a special juicer for vegetables, and of the many brands available, I recommend a Champion. (You cannot make juice in a food processor, because it doesn't separate the juice from the pulp.)

These desserts are sweet, but not cloyingly so. Sweeteners are used for flavor, texture, and character, not for their nutritional value. I have tried to limit added sweeteners to less than one tablespoon per serving. All of the sweeteners called for unrefined; they include pure maple syrup, maple sugar granules, date sugar (which is simply pulverized dried dates), and Sucanat raw cane sugar.

If you don't have a local source for organic fruits, you can substitute frozen, organic blueberries, strawberries, raspberries, and peaches, which are available in many natural-food stores.

SORBETS, GRANITÉS, AND OTHER FROZEN DESSERTS

Fruit juices and purees are the basis of frozen granités and sorbets. Because they are frozen differently, their textures are different. Sorbet has a smooth consistency, while a granité ends up with ice crystals, in the form of delicate flakes or chunky grains.

Sorbet has a very creamy texture when made in an ice cream machine by a process known as *churn freezing*. When the ingredients are agitated throughout the freezing process, air is drawn in, keeping the texture smooth.

The food-processer method may be the most convenient way to make sorbet. Just before serving, cubed frozen fruit, purees, or juices are processed with the metal blade until smooth and creamy. The sorbet begins to melt immediately, so as you finish each batch, you must place it in the freezer.

You can also make sorbet in a Champion juicer. Again, frozen fruit and juices are pressed through the juicer, resulting in a fine, light sorbet.

No matter what method you use, sorbets melt quickly. If, for convenience or reasons of presentation, you do opt to refreeze a sorbet, keep it frozen for no longer than a few hours.

MOUSSES

These mousse recipes are light and airy, and highlight the flavors of individual fruit purees. You have the option of making them with Light Mousse Cream (page 264)—whipped skim milk—or whipped heavy cream. To compare calories: 1 tablespoon of heavy cream has 50 calories, while 1 tablespoon of skim milk has barely 6 calories. In these recipes you can save up to 125 calories per serving by using skim milk, and greatly reduce the total fat grams as well.

Mousse made with whipped skim milk, using an industrial immersion blender, became popular in spa kitchens in the eighties. Now household immersion blenders are available through television mail-order sources, and at department and kitchen-supply stores. Before you purchase one, inquire if it whips skim milk.

FRESH FRUIT CONCLUSIONS

Like herbs and edible flowers, quality fruits are an inspiration to the senses. As beautiful to behold as to savor, a goblet of freestone peaches, fraises des bois, Charantais melon, or Alfonso mangoes delights the eye and nose long before the palate. The following fruit desserts are simple pleasures—single fruits barely dressed with supportive flavors or fruit combinations juxtaposing flavors and textures.

Of course the challenge for busy home cooks is finding well-grown fruits where taste considerations precede commercial value. It takes a little time to develop a network of sources that provide high-quality local, seasonal, fresh fruit. You may find them at a local U-pick, farmers market, co-op, or roadside stand. In the cities, look in large natural-food supermarkets or quality greengrocers. If you don't know where to start, contact a restaurant chef who values excellence and ask him to share his sources.

Most of these light fruit desserts pair well with cheese, sorbet, dried fruits, nuts, or cookies. Yet on their own, each one is a perfect end to a meal.

SORBETS, GRANITÉS, AND OTHER FROZEN DESSERTS

Melon Sorbet with Sweet Jalapeño Sauce

Vine pepper, ginger, and hot chilies are warm aromatics used in many tropical cuisines. In this instance they are combined in a sweet sauce to complement melon sorbet. I make the sorbet in a food processor, just before serving.

Try honeydew, cantaloupe, Crenshaw watermelon, Chartentais — or any aromatic melon in season. For an attractive presentation on a buffet table, serve the sorbet and melon balls in a hollowed-out, frozen melon.

8 SERVINGS

Sauce
- 1 jalapeño chili, halved, seeded, and minced
- 1 teaspoon minced crystallized ginger
-    A few turnings of pepper
- ¼ cup honey
- ¼ cup fresh lime juice
- ⅓ cup juice-sweetened marmalade

Sorbet
- 1 ripe Crenshaw melon (about 4 pounds)
- 1 ripe cantaloupe (about 3 pounds)
- ⅓ cup frozen white grape juice concentrate
-    Mint sprigs for garnish

To make the sauce, combine all of the ingredients in a bowl and whisk until blended. Cover and refrigerate.

Halve and seed the Crenshaw melon. Using a melon baller, scoop out 1½ cups of melon balls. Cut the remaining melon into 1-inch cubes. Halve and seed the cantaloupe. Scoop out 1 cup of cantaloupe balls; cut the remaining fruit into 1-inch cubes.

Combine the Crenshaw and cantaloupe balls in a bowl; cover and refrigerate. Combine the cubes on a tray; cover and freeze in a single layer until firm.

Just before serving, add the juice concentrate to the frozen melon cubes. Process the melon cubes, in batches, until they are reduced to a light, smooth sorbet. As you finish, spoon the sorbet into eight large serving goblets. Evenly distribute the melon balls among the goblets and drizzle with sauce. Garnish with mint sprigs and serve immediately.

Grape Sorbet with Frozen Grapes

Wine grapes, with their complex flavors, are well suited to sorbet, but they are rarely available at produce markets. If you live in wine country and can ferret out fresh Muscat or Chardonnay grapes, use them for a full-flavored sorbet. When fresh grapes aren't available, try nonalcoholic Ariel Chardonnay.
6 SERVINGS

   2½ **cups white grape juice, preferably fresh (from about 2½ pounds of grapes)**
   ½ **cup frozen white grape juice concentrate**
   2 **tablespoons fresh lime juice**
   2 **tablespoons honey**
  16 **black seedless grapes, halved and frozen, for garnish**

Pour the grape juice into ice cube trays that make small cubes and freeze.

Combine the grape juice concentrate, lime juice, and honey in a food processor and blend until mixed. Drop the grape juice cubes through the feed tube and process until the mixture has a snowy consistency. Serve in six iced goblets and garnish with frozen grapes.

Tropical Fruit Sorbet

This fresh-juice sorbet will transport you to a palm-lined tropical beach. It can be served like a frozen daiquiri and sipped with a straw as it melts, or served frozen and eaten with a spoon.　8 SERVINGS

½ cup raw cane sugar (Sucanat) or white sugar
½ cup water
½ tablespoon grated fresh ginger
1 pound mango, peeled, seeded, and cubed
1 pound papaya, peeled, seeded and cubed
3 bananas
1 cup guava nectar
1 cup fresh orange juice
¼ cup fresh lime juice
　Mint sprigs for garnish
　Lime wedges for garnish

Combine the sugar, water, and ginger in a saucepan and bring to a boil for 2 minutes. Cool completely.

Combine the mango and papaya in a food processor and puree until smooth. Add to the ginger syrup in the saucepan. Peel the banana and chop. Combine with the guava nectar and orange and lime juices in a food processor and reduce to a puree.

Transfer to the saucepan and blend well. Pour the mixture into small-sized ice cube trays and freeze until solid.

At serving time, process ten to twelve small juice cubes until smooth. Spoon into serving goblets and freeze while making the remaining sorbet. Serve immediately, garnished with mint and lime wedges.

Frozen Peach and Raspberry Terrine

Fragrant, vine-ripened freestone peaches or nectarines are the basis of this frozen dessert. They are paired with fresh berries for vivid color and refreshing taste. Instead of raspberries, try blackberries or loganberries. This beautiful terrine can be assembled the day before serving and is perfect for entertaining.   8 SERVINGS

> 2½ **pounds freestone peaches or nectarines**
> ½ **cup honey or brown-rice syrup**
> 1⅓ **cups fresh tangerine or orange juice**
> ¼ **cup fresh lime juice**
> 2 **cups raspberries**

Reserve one peach for a garnish; peel, quarter, and pit the remaining fruit. Place two-thirds of the peaches in a food processor along with half of the honey, tangerine juice, and lime juice. Puree and transfer to a shallow freezer container. Cover and freeze until firm but not hard. Place the raspberries in the food processor along with the remaining peaches, honey, and juice; puree and freeze.

Line a 6-cup loaf pan with plastic wrap. Place half of the peach sorbet in the lined pan, and level the surface with a rubber spatula. Top with half of the raspberry sorbet and smooth the top the same way. Repeat the layering with the remaining sorbet to make four layers. Tap the pan on a hard surface to collapse any small air bubbles. Cover the pan securely with plastic wrap and freeze overnight.

To serve, remove the plastic wrap, invert the pan on a chilled platter, and remove the remaining plastic wrap. Halve, pit, and slice the remaining peach into thin wedges. Using a knife warmed in hot water, cut the terrine crosswise into generous ½-inch slices, dipping the knife between slices. Serve on dessert plates, garnished with a few fresh peach wedges.

Mandarin Orange and Carrot Granité

If you have ever sampled a glass of fresh organic orange and carrot juice, you have an idea of the sparkling flavor in these chunky frozen flakes. Even nonorganic ingredients will yield a sweet and refreshing treat. The granité doubles as a light dessert or a between-course palate cleanser.   6 SERVINGS

>   ¼ cup maple syrup
>   2 tablespoons water
>   1 teaspoon grated fresh ginger
>   3 cups fresh Mercot tangerine or orange juice
>   1½ cups fresh carrot juice
>   6 mint sprigs for garnish

Combine the maple syrup, water, and ginger in a nonreactive saucepan and bring to a boil. Add the juices and cool. Pour into a 13 × 9-inch baking pan and cover well. Freeze for 6 hours.

Remove from the freezer. Using a fork, scrape the surface of the granité to remove large flaky crystals. Serve in six iced goblets, garnished with mint.

Pomegranate Granité with Almond-Crusted Papaya Nuggets

At Indian juice bars, pomegranate juice is an enduring favorite. At fruit stalls, papaya is second only to mango as the most popular fruit. Here they combine in the form of a ruby-red granité accompanied by nut-crusted baked papaya nuggets.   6 SERVINGS

Granité
3 cups fresh pomegranate juice (about 9 pomegranates)
3 tablespoons maple syrup

Papaya Nuggets
3 tablespoons buttermilk
½ cup unbleached all-purpose flour
½ teaspoon freshly grated nutmeg
2 tablespoons fresh lemon juice
⅔ cup finely chopped almonds
1 ripe papaya (about 1 pound), peeled, seeded, and cut into 18 pieces

Cut the pomegranates in half crosswise. Press and turn the halves on a citrus juicer or reamer to release the juice. Discard the peels, seeds, and pulp. Stir the maple syrup into the pomegranate juice and pour into ice cube trays; freeze overnight.

Preheat the oven to 350°F. Combine the buttermilk, flour, nutmeg, and lemon juice in a small bowl and whisk well. Place the almonds on a plate. One by one, dip the papaya pieces in the buttermilk mixture, and shake off excess. Roll in the almonds, coating on all sides, and transfer to a baking tray. (Can be made 2 hours before baking, covered, and refrigerated.)

Bake until lightly browned, turning once, 10 to 12 minutes. While the nuggets are baking, prepare the granité. Using a food processor, process six to eight frozen juice cubes until smooth. (Do not overprocess or the granité will melt.) Spoon into goblets and freeze while making the remaining servings. Serve immediately, garnished with three warm papaya nuggets.

Frozen Mango Savarin

This dessert rivals the elegance of a ring-shaped yeast savarin cake in flavor. Bananas and ricotta cheese give this light mango sherbet its creamy texture and rich flavor. Fill the center of this showstopper savarin with whole strawberries for a spectactular frozen dessert.   10 SERVINGS

>   3   large ripe mangoes (about 3 pounds), peeled and seeded
>   3   medium bananas (about ¾ pound)
>   2   tablespoons fresh lime juice
>   1   cup part-skim ricotta cheese
>   1   cup skim milk
>   1   tablespoon rose water
>   ⅓   cup sliced almonds, pan-toasted until golden
>   1   pint fresh strawberries, hulled

Cut the mango into ½-inch dice and spread in a single layer on a tray. Peel and slice the bananas; spread on a tray and sprinkle with lime juice. Cover the trays and freeze the fruit until hard. Oil or line with plastic wrap 5- to 6-cup savarin pan or ring mold; freeze it until well chilled.

Place the frozen mango and half of the ricotta, milk, and rose water in food processor. Puree until smooth, stopping as necessary to scrape down the sides. Transfer to a bowl. Puree the frozen banana with the remaining ricotta, milk, and rose water, and blend with the mango puree. Spoon the mixture into the prepared ring mold and smooth the top with a rubber spatula. Cover securely and freeze until firm, 2 to 3 hours.

To serve, run a hot knife around the inner and outer edge of the mango sherbet. Dip the mold in warm water for 5 to 10 seconds; pat the pan dry. Invert the mold onto a platter and place in the freezer for 5 minutes. Remove and smooth the surface with a spatula. Sprinkle the savarin with almonds and fill the center with berries. Serve immediately.

MOUSSES

Gingered Mango Mousse with Pomegranate

Made with fragrant mangoes and cream, this is an exquisite mousse. Though it takes only minutes to make, it consistently receives raves. When pomegranates are out of season, garnish it with raspberries, diced kiwi, or sliced straw-berries.   6 SERVINGS

   2 firm ripe mangoes (about 2 pounds)
   1 lime
   2 tablespoons maple syrup
   1 teaspoon grated fresh ginger (optional)
   1 cup heavy cream or 1 recipe Light Mousse Cream (page 264)
   ⅔ cup pomegranate seeds for garnish

Peel and seed the mangoes and cut six long slivers for garnish. Coarsely chop the remaining fruit. With a zester, remove strips of lime zest. Squeeze 2 tablespoons of lime juice. In a food processor or blender, combine the mango, maple syrup, lime juice, and ginger and process until smooth. (May be prepared to this point several hours ahead.)

Just before serving, whip the cream or prepare the Light Mousse Cream. Gently fold it into the mango puree, leaving marbled swirls of orange and white intact. Spoon into chilled goblets, garnish with lime zest, mango slivers, and pomegranate seeds and serve immediately. (The cream version can be refrigerated for up to 1 hour.)

Light Mousse Cream

Light Mousse Cream is really nothing but whipped skim milk. To make it, an immersion blender is fitted with a whipping nozzle, and as the machine is moved up and down in a tall beaker, the milk is aerated into high, fluffy peaks. If this sounds too good to be true, be forewarned of the down side. The mousse cream must immediately go from the kitchen to the table — within 5 minutes it will return to a liquid state. Not all immersion blenders will whip skim milk. Be sure to check the manufacturer's instructions before you assume it will do the trick.

For best results, both the mixing container and the milk must be chilled in the freezer for about 10 minutes before whipping. If the milk isn't icy cold, it won't whip at all.   SIX ⅓-CUP SERVINGS

   1 **cup icy cold skim milk**
      Freshly ground nutmeg

Insert the blender shaft of an immersion blender, fitted with a whipping nozzle, into the container and turn on the motor. Move the shaft around the container, and in an up-and-down motion, until the milk is whipped into high fluffy peaks, 1 to 2 minutes. Use immediately.

Two-Berry Mousse with Fruit Brochettes

Use any summer or fall berries: red, black, or golden raspberries, loganberries, blackberries, or boysenberries.   6 SERVINGS

   ⅓ **cup fresh or frozen unsweetened raspberries, defrosted**
   ⅓ **cup fresh or frozen unsweetened blackberries, defrosted**
   2 **tablespoons fruit-sweetened raspberry jam**

   2 tablespoons fruit-sweetened blackberry jam
Twelve 1-inch cubes fresh pineapple
  12 large strawberries, hulled
   3 kiwi fruits, peeled and cut into 4 pieces each
Twelve 1-inch cubes fresh papaya
     Juice of 1 lemon
   1 cup heavy cream or 1 recipe Light Mousse Cream (opposite)

In separate batches, puree the raspberries and blackberries, along with their respective jams, in a blender or food processor. Pass each through a fine sieve to remove seeds and set each one aside.

Within 2 or 3 hours of serving, thread six bamboo skewers with two pieces of each fruit selection. Sprinkle with lemon juice; cover and refrigerate until needed.

Just before serving, whip the heavy cream or prepare the Light Mousse Cream; divide in half. Individually fold the berry purees into the whipped cream and divide among chilled dessert plates. Place a skewer of fruit on each plate and serve immediately.

Papaya Mousse with Honeyed Pecans

Too easy to be true. Creamy, light, and luscious.   8 SERVINGS

Honeyed Pecans
    ¼ cup pecan bits
    2 tablespoons honey

Mousse
    2 ripe papayas (about 2 pounds)
    2 tablespoons fresh lemon juice
    1 cup heavy cream or 1 recipe Light Mousse Cream (page 264)
3 to 4 tablespoons date sugar
    ¼ teaspoon ground mace

Place the pecans in a heavy nonstick skillet over moderate heat. Toast them, stirring constantly, until they begin to darken, 3 to 4 minutes. Add the honey, raise the heat slightly, and cook very briefly, until the nuts are coated with carmelized honey (less than 2 minutes). Scrape onto a plate and spread out. When cool, break apart.

Skin and seed the papayas and cut the flesh into 1-inch cubes. In a food processor or blender, combine the papaya and lemon juice; process until smooth. (May be prepared to this point several hours ahead.)

At serving time, whip the cream in a bowl or prepare the Light Mousse Cream. Add the date sugar, mace, and papaya puree and gently fold to mix. Spoon into iced goblets, garnish with pecans, and serve immediately. (The cream version can be refrigerated for up to 1 hour.)

Saffron Yogurt Cheese Mousse

Homemade yogurt cheese, sold commercially as *labna*, is the basis of this light version of a rich Gujarati classic called *shrikand*. Date or maple sugar, available at natural-food stores, most resembles *gur*, the type of unrefined Indian sweetener that has been used on this dish for centuries. If passion fruit is not available, serve the mousse with any seasonal or tropical fresh fruit puree, and sweeten as desired.   6 SERVINGS

	Pinch high-quality saffron threads
4	cups plain nonfat yogurt
½	teaspoon coarsely crushed cardamom seeds
3	tablespoons light cream cheese, at room temperature
⅓	cup granular date or maple sugar
6 to 7	passion fruits or 1 cup raspberries
2	tablespoons chopped almonds, pan-toasted until golden

Place the saffron in a small pan and cook over moderate heat until brittle. Cool and crush with the back of a spoon.

Combine the yogurt, saffron, and cardamom in a bowl and stir to mix. Transfer to a fine-mesh strainer lined with several thicknesses of cheesecloth

or plain paper towels. Place in a larger bowl, in the refrigerator, for 24 hours or until firm curd forms. (You should have about 1¾ cups of yogurt cheese.)

Transfer the yogurt cheese to a bowl, add the cream cheese and sweetener, and beat until light and creamy. (Can be made 1 day ahead, covered, and refrigerated.)

Halve the passion fruits and scoop out the insides into a strainer set over a bowl. Press them with a spatula until you have extracted all of the juice. You should have about ⅓ cup.

Spoon the chilled mousse into iced goblets. Spoon on the fruit puree (or sprinkle with berries). Garnish with almonds.

Pumpkin Mousse with Ginger Cream

Maple or date sugar granules lend a distinctive flavor to this uncomplicated dish; both sweeteners are available in gourmet and natural-food stores. Maple granules are nothing but granulated maple syrup, and date sugar is nothing but pulverized dry dates.   8 SERVINGS

- 2 cups (one 16-ounce can) solid-pack pumpkin (do *not* use pumpkin-pie filling)
- 1¾ cups (one 15-ounce container) part-skim ricotta cheese
- ⅔ cup maple or date sugar granules, or ⅓ cup brown sugar and 1 tablespoon molasses
- ½ teaspoon freshly grated nutmeg
- 1 tablespoon pumpkin-pie spice
- 1 tablespoon grated fresh ginger
- ⅓ cup heavy cream, chilled
- 2 tablespoons fruit-sweetened marmalade
- 1 teaspoon minced candied ginger
  Ground cinnamon

Combine the pumpkin, ricotta, sweetener, and spices in a food processor and process until light and velvety, about 3 minutes. Transfer to a bowl, cover, and chill for several hours or overnight.

Just before serving, whip the cream. Fold in the marmalade and candied ginger. To serve, remove ½-cup portions of mousse with an ice cream scoop and place in chilled sherbet or martini glasses. Garnish with a dollop of cream and a dusting of cinnamon.

Apricot Cheesecake Parfait

A good make-ahead dessert for fall or winter when fresh fruits are sparse.
8 SERVINGS

  10 dried apricots
   8 ounces light cream cheese, softened
  ⅓ cup plain nonfat yogurt
   3 tablespoons fruit-sweetened apricot jam
  ½ teaspoon grated orange zest
   2 tablespoons fresh orange juice
  ¼ teaspoon ground cardamom
  ½ cup graham cracker crumbs
   2 teaspoons almond or walnut oil
  ⅛ teaspoon ground cinnamon
  ⅛ teaspoon freshly ground nutmeg

Soak the apricots in water overnight. Drain and coarsely chop. Place the apricots, soaking juice, cream cheese, yogurt, jam, zest, juice, and cardamon in a food processor or blender and process until silky smooth.

Combine the cracker crumbs, oil, cinnamon, and nutmeg in a small bowl and mix until crumbly.

Using eight 4-ounce stem glasses, assemble the parfaits as follows: 2 tablespoons cheesecake mixture; ½ tablespoon graham cracker mixture; 2 tablespoons cheesecake mixture; ½ teaspoon graham cracker mixture. Cover each glass tightly with plastic wrap and chill at least 3 hours or overnight.

FRESH FRUIT CONCLUSIONS

Summer Fruit Compote

This compote, inspired by the flavor of a fennel-laced Indian fruit chutney, is simple, quick, and refreshing. The fruits are barely poached in fennel-scented white grape juice. If you want a little more "oomph," garnish each serving with shavings of white chocolate or berry frozen yogurt.   8 SERVINGS

  4 **ripe nectarines (about 1¼ pounds)**
  4 **ripe peaches (about 1¼ pounds)**
  4 **ripe apricots (about 1 pound)**
  1 **teaspoon fennel seeds**
 1½ **cups white grape juice**
 One **4-inch-strip orange zest strip**
  1 **cinnamon stick**
  ¼ **teaspoon freshly grated nutmeg**

Blanch the nectarines in boiling water for 10 seconds, then transfer them to a bowl of ice water to cool. Slip off the skins, halve, and pit. Repeat the process for the peaches and apricots.

Place a noncorroding shallow casserole over moderate heat. Add the fennel seeds and stir-fry until they darken slightly. Add the juice, zest, and cinnamon stick and bring to a boil. Reduce the heat and simmer for 10 minutes.

Reduce the heat to very low, add the fruit, and poach until barely softened, 4 to 5 minutes. With a slotted spoon, transfer to a plate.

Raise the heat to medium-high and bring the poaching liquid to a boil. Cook until reduced to about ⅔ cup. Cool and pour over the fruit. Cover and chill for 2 to 6 hours.

Place one half of each fruit with a little chilled sauce into individual stemmed glasses. Sprinkle with nutmeg and serve.

Pineapple with Malabar Pepper, Mint, and Maple Syrup

Throughout India, street fruit vendors entice passersby with mounds of carefully arranged, succulent, peeled pineapples. It's hard to say whether it's the promise of a bargain or the pineapple perfume that lures customers in. Slices of the extraordinarily sweet fruit are sprinkled with lime juice and a touch of the tart salt-pepper spice blend known as *chat masala*. This pineapple dessert is the result of that comforting recollection.   6 SERVINGS

12 peppercorns, preferably Malabar, crushed
 3 tablespoons maple syrup
 1 tablespoon fresh lime juice
 2 tablespoons shredded mint leaves
Six ¾-inch-thick slices peeled, cored fresh pineapple
 2 tablespoons chopped or slivered pistachio nuts
    Herb salt (optional)

Combine the crushed pepper, syrup, juice, and mint leaves in a bowl and stir to mix. Place slices of pineapple on individual dessert plates. Spoon the syrup over the fruit; sprinkle with nuts and a trace of herb salt if desired.

Glazed Papaya Fans with Strawberry Sauce

The taste trio of papaya, lime, and ginger is relished in tropical regions around the world. Here, jalapeño chili is added for a warm heat kick.   6 SERVINGS

Strawberry Sauce
- 1 cup sliced fresh strawberries
- 2 tablespoons honey or fruit-sweetened strawberry jam
- 1 teaspoon rose water or fresh lemon juice

- ⅓ cup fruit-sweetened apricot jam
- 1 tablespoon fresh lime juice
- 2 tablespoons fresh orange juice
- ½ tablespoon grated fresh ginger
- 1 jalapeño chili, seeded and minced
- 3 papayas (about 3 pounds)
  Almond oil
- 2 tablespoons shredded coconut, pan-toasted until golden

Puree the ingredients in a blender or food processor. Cover and chill.

Combine the apricot jam, citrus juices, ginger, and chili in a small bowl. Preheat the oven to 375°F. Brush two nonstick baking trays with almond oil.

To cut the papaya into fans, peel the papayas, halve them lengthwise, and remove the seeds. Place a papaya half, core side down, on a work surface. Holding the knife at a 45-degree angle to the work surface, cut it into five lengthwise slices, leaving the slices attached at the narrow end. Gently transfer the papaya half to the prepared baking tray, and spread the slices out slightly in the shape of a fan. Repeat the process with the remaining papaya halves.

Brush half of the glaze over the papaya fans. Bake until warm, 10 to 12 minutes. Remove from the oven and brush with the remaining glaze.

To serve, spoon some Strawberry Sauce on six individual plates. Using a wide spatula, carefully set a papaya fan on each plate and sprinkle with coconut.

Baked Bananas with Gingered-Marmalade Cream

In India, I use orange-fleshed Mysore or tart Rajapuri bananas for this dish. Whole bananas are baked in ash-covered neem wood embers until barely softened. The warm flesh is thickly sliced, sprinkled with crushed cardamom seeds, and topped with a sweet clotted cream dessert called *rabri* — a sinfully rich legacy from the past.

This version, topped with fruit-sweetened marmalade cream, is lighter. For a special treat, use the organic Mysores grown at Richardson's Seaside Banana Garden in La Conchita, California (see Appendix). They are considered to possess an ideal blend of sugar and acid. Most of the time I use locally purchased organic finger bananas. These 5-inch gems are considerably sweeter than the imports found in grocery stores. No matter what your final choice in bananas, this is a satisfying conclusion to any meal.   8 SERVINGS

    3 tablespoons fresh orange or tangerine juice
    2 tablespoons fresh lemon or lime juice
    3 tablespoons juice-sweetened marmalade
    ¼ cup light cream cheese, softened
    ¼ cup buttermilk
    2 tablespoons minced crystallized ginger
    8 finger bananas or 4 large bananas
    ½ teaspoon cardamom seeds, crushed

Preheat the oven to 400°F. Combine the citrus juices and half of the marmalade in a small bowl and mix well. In another small bowl, thoroughly blend the cream cheese, buttermilk, ginger, and remaining marmalade.

Peel the bananas and cut them in half lengthwise. Lay them in a shallow baking dish and pour the juice mixture over them. Loosely cover the dish with foil and bake until warm and bubbly, 8 to 10 minutes, depending on size.

To serve, place two small bananas in an almond shape on each of eight

warm dessert plates. For large bananas, slash the outside edge in five places, and curve into semicircles. Cover with spoonfuls of citrus sauce and garnish each serving with 1 tablespoon of marmalade cream. Sprinkle with crushed cardamom.

Blood Oranges with Caramel Sauce and Pistachios

Blood oranges, ruby-hued with rich flavor, are sporadically available in green-grocers and supermarkets. If you can't find them or they are out of season, use Valencias, navels, or tangerines. In February, I look forward to organic Mercots or Honeybells from Florida, available from Starr Organic Produce (see Appendix.)   8 SERVINGS

       8 medium seedless blood oranges
    1¾ cups white grape juice
     ⅓ cup raw cane sugar (Sucanat) or white sugar
     ¼ teaspoon cardamom seeds, crushed
       4 fresh or dried dates, pitted and finely chopped
       2 tablespoons chopped pistachio nuts

Using a zester or vegetable peeler, remove the zest from one orange. Place the zest, juice, sugar, and cardamom in a saucepan. Stirring, bring to a boil over moderately high heat. Cook until the liquid is reduced to about ⅔ cup, about 8 minutes. Remove from the heat, stir in the dates, and set aside.

Cut the skins from the oranges, removing all of the white pith, right down to the flesh. Slice into rounds ¼ inch thick and arrange on a platter or individual plates. Spoon sauce over the orange slices. Cover and refrigerate for 2 to 6 hours.

Just before serving, sprinkle with pistachio nuts.

Fresh Figs with Mint Cream

The fig tree belongs to the same family (*Ficus*) as the gigantic sacred banyan and pipal trees. All three, in addition to being beautiful, are auspicious overnight shelters for India's mendicant holy men.

On my first pilgrimage to the famed Lord Nrisinga temple in Orissa, I joined a group of mendicants for a magical meal under a fig tree. It consisted of artfully shaped pieces of *sandesh* (cardamom-laced cheese fudge) from the temple and freshly picked figs, sprinkled with pepper, tangerine juice, and lime juice — elements reflected in this dessert.

There are many varieties of figs, and their flavors, degrees of sweetness, and colors vary enormously. A few good dessert figs are Smyrnas, Calimyrnas, and Missions, all available from midsummer to October.   6 SERVINGS

⅓ **cup fresh mint leaves**
3 **tablespoons fresh tangerine juice**
¼ **teaspoon cardamom seeds**
2 **tablespoons honey**
⅔ **cup White Cheese (page 188) or part-skim ricotta cheese**
12 **fresh figs (about 1½ pounds)**
1 **tablespoon fresh lime juice**
     Freshly ground pepper, preferably Tellicherry
     Fresh mint sprigs

Combine the mint leaves, tangerine juice, and cardamom seeds in a porcelain mortar. Crush the leaves and seeds with a pestle or the back of a wooden spoon, then macerate for at least 15 minutes. Strain through a piece of muslin, pressing all of the juice from the leaves. Combine the mint juice, honey, and cheese in a blender and process until smooth and creamy.

Peel the figs, and using a sharp paring knife, make four cuts from the top to just above the base, about three-quarters of the way down. Carefully force the segments apart, making an eight-petal flower.

Set two figs on a plate. Place 1 tablespoon of mint cream in the center of each flower; sprinkle with lime juice and pepper. Garnish with mint sprigs.

Summer Berry Gratin

In Oregon's Willamette Valley, berry gratin is a summer favorite, from restaurant to home kitchen. The flavor can vary widely, depending on the type of berries used — red or black raspberries, strawberries, marionberries, loganberries, or youngberries. I suggest using any freshly harvested, strongly scented berry. (You need 3 cups, total.) Traditionally made with only berries, sour cream, and brown sugar, it takes just minutes to prepare and tastes elegant. In this light variation, light cream cheese and buttermilk replace sour cream, and rose water brings a subtle floral dimension to an already irresistible combination of flavors.   8 SERVINGS

    1 **cup strawberries, hulled and halved**
    1 **cup fresh blueberries**
    2 **cups red raspberries or boysenberries**
  ½ **cup light cream cheese, softened**
  ¼ **cup buttermilk**
  ⅓ **cup raw cane sugar (Sucanat) or light brown sugar**
    1 **teaspoon rose water**

Preheat the broiler. Divide the berries evenly among eight 4-ounce gratin dishes.

Combine the cream cheese and buttermilk in a small bowl and whisk until creamy. Spread 1½ tablespoons of the mixture over the berries in each dish. Top each gratin with sugar rubbed through a sieve.

Set the gratins on a baking tray and broil until the sugar caramelizes, 2 to 3 minutes. Sprinkle with rose water and serve immediately.

To serve, set two figs on a dessert plate. Place about 1 tablespoon of mint cream in the center of each flower; sprinkle with lime juice and pepper. Garnish with mint sprigs.

Blackberry-Filled Baked Apples with Saffron Pastry Cream

If you don't have a favorite old-time cooking apple in mind, use Gravensteins or McIntosh. Their intriguing balance of tartness and sweetness is showcased by the maple-laced apple–and–blackberry juice syrup. Raspberries or loganberries can be used in place of blackberries.   8 SERVINGS

Saffron Pastry Cream
   12 threads pure saffron
   ½ tablespoon hot skim milk
   1 cup part-skim ricotta cheese
  2½ tablespoons plain nonfat yogurt
   3 tablespoons sugar
   ½ teaspoon rose or orange flower water

   8 baking apples, cored
 1¾ cups apple juice
     Olive-oil spray
   2 cups blackberries
   2 tablespoons maple syrup
   ½ teaspoon freshly grated nutmeg

Toast the saffron threads in a dry pan over warm heat. When brittle, place in a saucer and crush with the back of a spoon. Add the milk and set aside for 10 minutes. Combine all of the pastry cream ingredients in a blender or food processor and process for several minutes until silky smooth and light. (Can be made 1 to 2 days in advance, covered, and refrigerated.)

Preheat the oven to 375°F. Stand the apples in a 2-inch-deep baking dish and pour 1 cup of the juice over them. Spray the apples with olive oil and bake them for 25 minutes.

Remove the apples from the oven and stuff the centers with berries. Pour the remaining juice over the apples, drizzle with maple syrup, and spray with

oil. Bake the apples until they are tender, 20 to 30 minutes more. (If the juice is not thick, transfer the apples to serving dishes. Pour the juice into a saucepan and cook over low heat until reduced to ⅔ cup; reserve.)

To serve, place the apples on individual plates or in stemmed dessert dishes. Spoon some syrup over the apples, and serve with a spoonful of Saffron Pastry Cream. Sprinkle with nutmeg.

Sautéed Tropical Fruits with Passion Fruit Sauce

It's hard to be a tropical-fruit connoisseur in America—much of the fruit is picked immature, in faraway places, and it ripens under less-than-perfect conditions. But come June, I look forward to mail-ordering organic Hayden mangoes from Earl Ebersole Farms (see Appendix), and the rest falls into place.   8 SERVINGS

Passion Fruit Sauce

- 6 passion fruits
- 2 tablespoons maple syrup
- 1 teaspoon grated fresh ginger
- ¼ cup fresh orange juice
- ¼ teaspoon freshly ground nutmeg

- 2 tablespoons unsalted butter
- 2 large mangoes (about 3 pounds), peeled, pitted, and cut lengthwise into long slices
- 2 medium-size papayas (about 2½ pounds), peeled, halved lengthwise, seeded, and cut into chunky triangles
- 1 small pineapple (2 pounds), peeled, cored, sliced crosswise ½ inch thick, and then cut into 1½-inch lengths
- 5 kiwi fruits (¾ pound), peeled and cut lengthwise into ¼-inch-thick slices
- 8 to 10 mint sprigs for garnish

Halve the passion fruits, scoop the insides into a cup, and set aside. Combine the remaining sauce ingredients in a small bowl and set aside.

Place a large, nonstick sauté pan over moderate to moderately high heat. Add ½ tablespoon of butter to the pan and just enough of a single fruit to form a layer on the bottom of the pan. Sauté for 1 to 2 minutes, shaking the pan occasionally, until the fruit is heated through. Transfer to a warm platter and cover while you sauté the remaining batches of fruit.

Pour the maple syrup–orange juice blend into the sauté pan and bring to a boil. When the volume is slightly reduced, stir in the passion fruit. Cook until the mixture comes to a boil again; remove from the heat.

To serve, arrange the fruit pieces on eight individual dessert plates. Top with a spoonful of sauce and garnish with a mint sprig.

Poached Pears with Cranberry-Currant Chutney

Alabaster-white pears contrast with chunky red chutney in this slightly hot and pleasantly sweet dessert. Both pears and chutney can be made the day before serving. Though delicious as is, they are also wonderful served with a small scoop of lemon sorbet or white chocolate frozen yogurt.   6 SERVINGS

    1 bottle sparkling white grape juice
    3 cardamom pods, crushed
   ½ vanilla bean
    1 cinnamon stick
    6 firm but ripe pears (Bosc or Bartlett)
    2 tablespoons fresh lemon juice

Chutney
> 1   tablespoon walnut oil
> ¼   teaspoon crushed red-pepper flakes
> 2   tablespoons chopped walnuts
> 2½ cups fresh or frozen cranberries
> 3   tablespoon currants
> ⅓   cup maple syrup
>   Fresh mint leaves for garnish

Place the grape juice, cardamom, vanilla bean, and cinnamon in a heavy-bottomed casserole and bring to a gentle boil over moderate heat. Meanwhile, peel the pears, leaving the stems intact. Brush the pears with lemon juice as you work to prevent discoloration. Using a melon baller, core them from the bottom, cutting two-thirds through the center toward the stem.

Add the remaining lemon juice to the casserole, and place the pears in the liquid. Reduce the heat to low and poach the pears, very gently turning them to cook evenly, until they are slightly translucent, 20 to 25 minutes. Using a slotted spoon, carefully remove the pears and set them upright on a plate to drain. When cool, cover and refrigerate.

Raise the heat to medium-high and cook the poaching liquid until it is reduced to nearly ⅔ cup of syrup, about 20 minutes. Remove the cardamom pods, vanilla bean, and cinnamon stick and discard.

To make the chutney, place the oil, pepper flakes, and walnuts in a small saucepan over medium-low heat. Stir-fry until the nuts darken a few shades. Add the poaching liquid and remaining chutney ingredients, and raise the heat to medium-high. Cook until the cranberries burst and soften and the chutney is slightly thick, 10 to 12 minutes.

To serve, spoon some of the chutney onto each of six dessert plates. Set a pear in the center and garnish with a mint leaf at the stem end.

Appendix

THE BASICS

With a few of the following "basics" on hand, you are prepared to make all of your favorite foods a little bit livelier, a little bit fresher. Even on the simplest raw or steamed foods, you're in for vibrant new flavors, with the addition of these salt, pepper, and spice blends. You'll find new dimensions of flavor for your old favorite foods. For example, enliven mashed potatoes or hash browns with a few grindings of Sesame-Cumin Salt, Orange Sea Salt, or Herb Salt Blend. Pepper Medley or one of the oil sprays works well on everything from grilled vegetables, salad greens, and sliced tomatoes to grain pilaf or pan-fried cheese. Tex-Mex Garam Masala or Simple Garam Masala adds distinction to all legume and grain dishes. The seasoning blends and flavor-infused oils bring excitement to just about any foods. All store well, in a cool, dark pantry or the freezer. I hope you find many uses for them.

Pepper Medley

This is a simple pepper blend with terrific flavor. Keep it in a pepper grinder near the stove and use it for a week in place of plain black pepper.
MAKES ABOUT ¾ CUP

  ½ **tablespoon date sugar**
  ½ **tablespoon dried lemon peel**
  1 **tablespoon allspice**
  1 **tablespoon coarse sea salt**
  2 **tablespoons white peppercorns, preferably Muntok**
  3 **tablespoons black peppercorns, preferably Tellicherry**
  3 **tablespoons red peppercorns**
  4 **tablespoons freeze-dried green peppercorns**

Mix all of the ingredients. Grind fresh from a pepper mill.

Simple Garam Masala

In Hindi, *garam* means "warm," and *masala* means "blend of spices." Sprinkle some of this mixture into any pot of cooked dried beans, from simmered butter beans to chili. Use it as a flavor garnish for any type of *dal*. If you use this blend infrequently, keep it fresh by storing it in the freezer.   MAKES ABOUT ⅔ CUP

  ¼ **cup cumin seeds**
  ¼ **coriander seeds**
  1 **tablespoon cardamon seeds**
One **3-inch cinnamon stick, crushed into bits with a mortar and pestle**
  1 **tablespoon black peppercorns, preferably Tellicherry**
  ½ **tablespoon whole cloves**

Preheat a heavy skillet over moderate heat. Combine all of the ingredients in the pan, and stirring occasionally, toast until the seeds darken a few shades, about 10 minutes. Cool, then grind to a powder in a spice mill or blender. Store in an airtight container in the refrigerator or freezer.

Tex-Mex Garam Masala

This is my current favorite *garam masala* blend. The nine ingredients provide a wonderful balance of aromatic, sweet, pungent, and hot elements, distinguished by the chocolate-flavored warmth of ancho or New Mexico chilies.

Ancho and New Mexico chilies are available at specialty and Southwestern food stores. Fresh and dried curry leaves are available at Indian grocery stores.   MAKES 1 GENEROUS CUP

        2 dried ancho or New Mexico chili pods
      ¼ cup coriander seeds
        2 tablespoons cumin seeds
        2 tablespoons mustard seeds
      ½ tablespoon fennel seeds
      ½ tablespoon fenugreek seeds
      ½ tablespoon black peppercorns, preferably Tellicherry
25 to 30 fresh curry leaves, if available
        2 tablespoons ground turmeric

Place the chili pods in a frying pan over low heat. Toast, stirring occasionally, until slightly brown and crisp, 8 to 10 minutes. Set aside and cool.

Meanwhile, combine the coriander, cumin, mustard, fennel, fenugreek seeds, peppercorns, and curry leaves in the same pan and toast until aromatic, about 5 minutes. Transfer the mixture to a spice grinder or blender.

Remove the stems and seeds from the toasted dried chilies and discard. Break the chilies into bits and add to the spice grinder. Grind the mixture until it is reduced to a powder, in batches if necessary. Transfer to a bowl.

Dry-roast the fresh curry leaves in a skillet over low heat until they are brittle. Grind the dried leaves and turmeric until the leaves are powdered; mix into the ground spices. When cool, store in an airtight jar.

Sesame-Cumin Salt

Like Oriental *gomasio*, this toasted sesame-seed mixture perks up simple steamed vegetables, green salads, and plain grains and is a good way to cut down on salt. If you like, substitute mustard, fennel, or caraway seeds for the sesame seeds.   MAKES ABOUT 1 CUP

> ⅔ cup sesame seeds
> 2 tablespoons cumin seeds
> 1 tablespoon dried marjoram
> 1 tablespoon dried thyme
> 2 tablespoons coarse sea salt

Place the sesame seeds in a frying pan over low heat. Toast them until they turn golden-brown and release their aroma, stirring occasionally, about 5 minutes. Cool and combine with the remaining ingredients. Transfer the mixture to a pepper mill and grind fresh.

Orange Sea Salt

This mixture has been a staple in my kitchen for more than five years. I keep it in a clear acrylic salt mill, and it is so attractive (and delicious), that dinner guests usually want the recipe. It's also simple to make — perfect for a food gift basket. I use La Baleine coarse sea salt crystals, and dried orange zest, which is available at gourmet and natural-food stores.   MAKES ABOUT ⅔ CUP

> ½ cup coarse sea salt crystals
> 3 tablespoons dried orange zest
> 1 tablespoon dried cilantro

Mix the ingredients and store in a salt mill. Set the mill for a medium grind.

Herb Salt Blend

How much salt to use is a matter of personal preference, based on health concerns or pure taste. There are few specific salt measurements in this book, though I occasionally recommend the use of herb salt. Consisting primarily of dried herbs and salt, commercial blends may also contain dehydrated vegetables and spices. Two good commercial salt blends are Trocomare and Selplante, both available in gourmet and natural food stores.

Here is my favorite homemade herb-infused salt-blend formula, though I rarely make it the same way twice. Use as desired, especially at the end of cooking, for final flavor dimensions.   MAKES ABOUT ⅓ CUP

> 3 **tablespoons dried cilantro**
> 2 **tablespoons dried basil**
> 1 **tablespoon dried dill**
> 2 **teaspoons dried marjoram**
> 1 **teaspoon dried oregano**
> ½ **teaspoon cayenne**
> 4 **tablespoons coarse sea salt**

Combine the ingredients in a blender jar. Cover and blend until the seasonings are finely ground. Store in a spice jar with a shaker top and screw-on lid.

Sour "Real Salt"

Ayurveda, India's ancient science of medicine, self-healing, and well-being, categorizes tastes as sweet, sour, salty, pungent, bitter, or astringent. All foods and tastes fall into these categories. Foods also possess properties and provoke reactions in the body. This seasoning combines two of the basic elements — sour and salty.

Though you can use plain sea salt, this seasoning comes to life when made

with a natural mineral rock salt labeled Real Salt, available at natural-food stores. Mined near the town of Redmond, Utah, the salt is alabaster-hued, flecked with traces of pinkish gray crystallized mineral deposits. This product is the closest American facsimile I've found to an Indian salt called *kala nimak*. The other ingredient, citric acid (also called sour salt and lemon crystals), is available at grocery and natural-food stores.

Try a sprinkle of this mixture over Bengal-Style Oven-Fried Potatoes (page 21), a focaccia-type hearth bread, or a legume dish.   MAKES ¼ CUP

3½ tablespoons Real Salt or fine sea salt
½ tablespoon citric acid crystals

Mix the ingredients and store in a tightly covered jar with a shaker top.

Curry Powder

Indian curry powders vary enormously in character, blending from three to twenty-five ingredients. This is my current favorite. Fresh curry leaves play a central role in its flavor, and unless you have a bush in the backyard, you'll have to purchase them at an Indian grocery store. The subtle heat in the blend comes from dried ancho chilies, more flavorful and milder than dry red chili pods. Alternately, use Williams-Sonoma's ground Chili Blend, a mildly piquant mix of powdered chilies (more than 80 percent Anaheims).

I make curry powder in small batches because I don't use it often. Depending on your needs, double or triple the recipe. Store in a sealed jar, in the refrigerator or a cool place, for 3 to 4 months.   MAKES ABOUT ⅔ CUP

⅓ cup coriander seeds
1½ tablespoons mustard seeds
½ tablespoon cumin seeds
1 teaspoon fenugreek seeds
3 to 4 branches fresh curry leaves
2 dried ancho chilies, seeded and stemmed, or ½ tablespoon
ground red chilies
2 tablespoons ground turmeric

Combine the coriander, mustard, cumin, and fenugreek seeds in a heavy skillet and toast over low heat, stirring occasionally, for 4 to 5 minutes. Add the curry leaves and ancho chilies and toast for another 3 to 4 minutes. Remove from the heat and cool. Break the chilies into bits. Grind the toasted seasonings in a spice grinder or blender until powdered. Add the turmeric, mix well, and store in a container with a screw-top lid.

Salt-Free Seasoning

McCormick's sent me a complete selection of spices and herbs for testing in the recipes in this book, along with several of their salt-free seasoning blends. This inspired me to come up with a few blends of my own, using dried organic herbs from my garden. This dill-based blend is one of my favorites. Yellow asafetida powder is the only unusual ingredient; it is available at Indian grocery stores.   MAKES ABOUT ½ CUP

- 1½ **tablespoons sesame seeds**
- ½ **teaspoon yellow asafetida powder or garlic powder**
- 2 **tablespoons dried dill**
- 1 **tablespoon dried basil**
- 1 **tablespoon dried marjoram**
- 1 **tablespoon dried savory**
- 1 **teaspoon paprika**
- ½ **teaspoon dried lemon zest**

Toast the sesame seeds in a skillet over low heat until golden. (If you use the asafetida, add it to the pan just before removing it from the heat.) Cool the sesame seeds; add the remaining ingredients and mix well. Rub the mixture between your palms to crush the leaves and release their flavor. Store in a well-sealed jar for up to 3 months.

Roasted Bell Peppers

Roasted bell peppers are an essential in my kitchen. They find their way into dips, salads, and salad dressings, sauces, pilafs, cutlets, and coatings. Roasted red peppers are available commercially in small jars — convenient in a pinch. Whenever I find a deal of any variety of organic bell peppers, I spend a couple hours roasting and freezing batches of them. They keep well for up to 2 to 3 months.

To prepare the peppers whole, in quantity, preheat an oven broiler. Set the peppers on the rack of a broiler pan, 2 to 3 inches from the heat. Broil them, turning them every 5 minutes, for 15 to 25 minutes, or until the skins are evenly blistered and charred. Transfer them to a bowl, cover, and steam for 15 minutes. Peel the peppers starting at the blossom ends; cut off the tops and discard the seeds and ribs.

To prepare small quantities, preheat a stovetop grill over moderate heat. Quarter, derib, and seed the peppers. Grill the pieces, skin sides down, until the skins are blistered and charred. Transfer to a plastic bag or bowl; seal and set aside for 15 minutes, then peel.

To freeze, lay the quartered peppers, strips, or cut-out shapes on baking trays in a single layer. Freeze until firm and transfer individual pieces to freezer bags.

Peeled Peppers — An Alternative to Roasted

Red and yellow bell peppers — especially those imported from Europe — frequently have thick, tough skins. According to a study conducted by the Natural Resources Defense Council, 82 percent of the imported peppers contain pesticide residues, as compared with 30 percent of domestic pepper samples. The nonsystemic pesticides are concentrated in the skins, which are best removed. Peeling the peppers also showcases the sweetness of the flesh.

You need smooth, nearly square-shaped peppers to follow this procedure. You'll end up with lengthened, rectangular pieces of pepper. They can be used in place of lasagna noodles in layered casseroles or cut into decorative shapes with cocktail cutters. This is also the fastest way to cut thick and thin julienne slices. If you don't have time to roast peppers, try this.

Using a sharp chef's knife, cut the stem ends and bottoms from the peppers. Make one cut from the top to the bottom of each pepper and open the pepper into a long flat piece. Remove the seeds and ribs. Using a vegetable peeler, cut away the skins.

Use as is, cut into appropriate shapes, or blanch for 30 seconds in boiling water and drain. Place the peppers in single layers on trays and freeze until solid. Store in freezer bags.

Yogurt Cheese

The flavor of yogurt cheese is more intense than that of fresh yogurt. To avoid an overly tangy product, use very fresh, firm yogurt. If you make this type of cheese on a regular basis, you may want to invest in a plastic-mesh cone and a bowl-shaped yogurt-cheese maker, both of which are available in kitchen stores. MAKES ABOUT 1 CUP

2 cups nonfat yogurt

Set a fine-meshed strainer over a bowl; spoon in the yogurt. Cover and refrigerate for 12 to 24 hours, depending on the desired thickness. Use within 4 or 5 days.

Chapatis

For more than fifteen years, I made these flat breads on a daily basis. They are to the Indian diet what tortillas are to the Mexican. If you want to explore the diverse world of chapati cookery, work through the ten recipes in my first book, *Lord Krishna's Cuisine: The Art of Indian Vegetarian Cooking.*

The appearance, flavor, and texture of chapatis depends on the type of flour you use. Ideally, you want to use a very finely milled, soft wheat flour. Alternately, use equal parts of a coarser 100 percent whole-wheat flour and unbleached white flour. If you work a spoon of melted *ghee* (clarified butter), butter, or oil into the flour, the "crumb" will be lighter, and the dough will be easier to roll out. Instead of all water, use a little milk, yogurt, or vegetable or fruit puree to make the dough.

Chapatis, both homemade and commercial, are a staple in my freezer, ready on a moment's notice for burrito-style vegetable sandwiches or pizza crusts. Slow-bake cut wedges into tostada-like wafers for soups or salads. Or sandwich cheese and bell peppers between two chapatis and grill into quesadilla-like sandwiches. Two excellent commercial alternatives, available in natural-food stores, are Garden of Eatin's Organic Whole Wheat Tortillas and Alvarado Street Bakery's Sprouted Wheat Tortillas.

MAKES 12 CHAPATIS

> 2½ cups organic whole-wheat flour or 1½ cups sieved organic whole-wheat flour mixed with ¾ cup unbleached white flour
> ¼ teaspoon salt (optional)
> ⅔ cup warm water or as necessary
>   Sieved whole-wheat flour for dusting

Place the dry ingredients in a large bowl and mix well. Add ⅔ cup of water, pouring fast at first, then in dribbles, until a rough mass of dough forms. Knead until silky smooth, about 5 minutes. (Add flour or water as necessary.) Roll the dough into a smooth ball, cover well, and set aside for ½ hour, or up to 2 hours at room temperature.

Clear some counter space near the stove and gather up your equipment: a

rolling pin, pie dish, cake rack, and kitchen towel–lined basket. Knead the dough briefly, divide it into twelve smooth balls, and cover with a damp cloth.

Warm a heavy griddle over moderately low heat for several minutes. Press a ball of dough into a patty, dip both sides in flour, and roll it into a thin round just over 6 inches in diameter. (Use just enough flour to keep the dough from sticking to the counter.)

Half slap, half slip the disk onto the griddle. If there are wrinkles, don't try to press them out until the bottom firms up. Cook until the top of the bread lightens in color and small bubbles begin to appear, 1 to 2 minutes on the first side. Flip to the second side and cook ½ to 1 minute. Remove the griddle from the heat.

Place the flat bread on a cake rack and hold it 2 inches above a burner set on high. In seconds the bread will swell and fill with steam, hopefully puffing into a balloon. When the surface is flecked with black spots, slip the chapatis into the basket. Set the griddle on moderately low heat and repeat the process for the remaining breads.

Serve hot or warm, with or without a spray of flavor-infused oil or a brush of melted butter. If storing, cool the breads, wrap them tightly, and refrigerate for 3 to 4 days. Freeze for 1 to 2 months.

Flavor-Infused Oils

For twenty years I used *ghee* (Indian clarified butter) in virtually all of my cooking. Hundreds of pots of plain and spice-infused *ghee* have simmered on my back burners, and recipes for them are detailed in my first cookbook. In the last few years, however, I've switched to exploring the flavor of infused oils. Oils are exciting to work with because of their diverse flavors, scents, colors, and nutritional profiles.

The most flavorful and nutritional oils are those that are left unprocessed and unrefined after pressing. If flavor has top priority in your foods, use unrefined oils. Even partially refined oils begin to show a loss of flavor, scent, and hue. Fully refined oils are virtually tasteless, bland, and pale, lending little more than fat to a dish. If you have yet to experience unrefined oils, experiment with unrefined corn oil on baked potatoes or steamed vegetables; try unrefined extra-virgin olive oil on salads and legume dishes or try unrefined peanut,

walnut, or avocado oil on grains or vegetable stir-fries. You'll be amazed at the fragrances and round flavors. When unrefined oils are in turn infused, the colors and flavors bring dramatic appeal to even the simplest foods.

The inspiration behind the technique in preparing these oils came from the gifted New York chef Jean-Georges Vongerichten. When I came across his *Cook's* magazine article on the subject a few years ago, I contacted him and got a quick lesson on the varieties that follow. I keep small quantities of four or five spice and herb oils on hand. I'll make the same amount of vegetable and fruit oils before entertaining or holiday cooking.

Use any of the following oils that strike your fancy: unrefined, expeller-pressed canola, sunflower, safflower, olive, walnut, almond, avocado, or olive oil. These intense flavored oils can work magic on the simplest of foods, from salads to desserts. Mix or match them according to the season in sautéed, steamed, or grilled vegetables, vinaigrettes, sauces, or marinades. As little as a few drops drizzled on plain foods will bring them to life.

Ground Spice–Infused Oil

Curry, *garam masala*, paprika, and saffron oils are all excellent flavor accents to the dishes in the book. Sweet cinnamon, cardamom, and nutmeg oils make wonderful vinaigrettes and are delicious mixed with pomegranate, pineapple, or orange oil.

For more pronounced flavor, pair spice oils with their fresh counterparts —coriander oil with cilantro, fennel oil with fresh fennel, curry oil with fresh curry leaves, and so on.   MAKES 2 CUPS

> ⅓ **cup of any of the following: ground curry powder, *garam masala*, paprika, coriander, fennel, cardamom, cinnamon, ginger, nutmeg, cumin, or mustard**
> 3 **tablespoons water**
> 2 **cups canola, sunflower, or light olive oil**

In a 4-cup container with a lid, mix the selected ground spice and water into a smooth, thick puree. Add the oil, cover, and shake to mix. Set aside in

the kitchen for 3 days, shaking several times the first 2 days to increase the strength of the oil. On the third day, allow the spice puree to settle to the bottom of the container.

Line a funnel with a coffee filter or a triple thickness of fine cheesecloth and place it over a 16-ounce bottle. Carefully ladle the infused oil, *without disturbing the spice puree*, and pour it through the filter into the funnel. *Do not filter or disturb the solids*. The oil should be colored but clear. If it is cloudy, repeat the process and refilter. Discard the solids.

Store the infused oil, tightly covered, in the refrigerator or a cool dark place, for up to 6 months.

Herb-Infused Oil

Curry-infused oil is my favorite fresh herb oil. Unfortunately, fresh curry leaves are only sporadically available at Indian grocers. Aside from the suggested herbs below, there are also scores of mints and basils to choose from, lemon basil, cinnamon basil, licorice basil, chocolate mint, watermint, pineapple mint, and peppermint. These herbs are easy to grow in window boxes. Try this with any dried herbs of your liking.   MAKES ABOUT 2 CUPS

> 1 cup fresh curry leaves, cilantro, basil, rosemary, mint, parsley, or chervil, lightly packed
> 4 cups boiling water
> 2¼ cups cold-pressed almond or avocado oil

Place the herbs in a colander and pour the water over them. Drain well and pat dry. Transfer the herbs to a food processor, add 1 cup of oil, and process to a puree.

Transfer to a 4-cup jar, add the remaining oil, cover, and shake well. Set the oil aside for 3 days, shaking the jar several times to intensify the flavors. Allow the herb puree to settle to the bottom of the jar on the third day.

Filter as in the previous recipe. Store, tightly covered, in the refrigerator for 2 to 3 weeks.

Vegetable- and Fruit-Infused Oil

I bought a Champion juicer to experiment with fresh vegetable- and fruit juice–infused oils. With my first batch of four simple oils — yellow bell pepper, beet, carrot, and pineapple — I became a lifetime aficionado. These vividly colored oils are some of the most exciting ingredients in my kitchen. Used alone, or streaked into another clear infused herb oil, they are simply wonderful.   MAKES ABOUT 1 CUP

> **4 cups fresh or commercially prepared beet, carrot, red or yellow
>   bell pepper, tomato, mango, pineapple, guava, or raspberry juice**
> **½ cup canola, safflower, or light olive oil**

Place the juice in a heavy-bottomed nonstick saucepan and bring to a boil over high heat. Lower the heat slightly, and stirring constantly as it thickens, reduce the juice to about ½ cup of syrup. Do not allow the juice to scorch as it thickens.

Combine the syrup and oil in a jar, and stir to mix. This will result in a marbled or broken oil. If you want a creamy, uniform oil with a homogenized consistency, shake the jar vigorously. Store in a covered container, refrigerated, for up to 2 weeks.

Oil Sprays

I use oil sprays in many of the recipes in this book, both to moisten and flavor foods. Where I once poured oil into a pan, I now spritz foods with a mist of dynamic-flavored oil and use nonstick cookware. The results are divine.

Initially you may want to use commercial oil sprays. Several useful brands are available nationally in gourmet stores and natural-food supermarkets. Extra-virgin and virgin olive-oil spray is distributed by Bertolli, Pam, and Tryson. Also available from Tryson and El Molino are sesame-peanut, canola vegetable, mesquite and flavor-infused oil sprays, all in environmentally friendly containers.

For homemade oil sprays, you need to purchase spray bottles with screw-on lids and manually adjustable nozzles — to regulate the spray from a steady stream to a mist. Without an adjustable nozzle, oil will clog in the spray mechanism. Call department stores, garden-supply stores, and better cookware stores for availability.

I generally spray foods once before they hit the heat, twice during cooking, and once again before they are served. At each stage, the oils work to infuse the foods with compelling, vivid flavors. Nutritionally, not all spray portion sizes are equal, but they are all low in fat and calories. One serving of Pam olive oil spray has 1 gram of fat and 2 calories. One serving of Tryson Peanut and Sesame Oil contains less than 1 gram of fat and fewer than 8 calories. Depending on the amount in each spritz, calories usually stay under 10 per serving, with 1 or 2 grams of fat. This is a very effective way to flavor and moisten foods, raw or cooked.

Pour oils into spray bottles, cover, and store in a cool, dark, dry cupboard. Plain oils can be stored for up to 2 months, herb-infused oils for a week, and spice-infused oils for up to 1 month.

Maple Cream

When you want something rich-tasting without the calories, try this whipped-cream replacement.   MAKES 1 CUP (6 SERVINGS)

- 1 **cup low-fat cottage cheese or silken extra-firm tofu**
- 2 **tablespoons frozen apple juice concentrate**
- 3 **tablespoons maple syrup**
  Freshly ground nutmeg (optional)

Combine the first three ingredients in a food processor and process for several minutes, until velvety smooth and light. Allow 3 tablespoons per serving, garnished with nutmeg if desired.

MENUS

Summer

Yellow Tomato Soup with Fresh Vegetable Salsa
Swiss Chard Rolls Stuffed with Quinoa and Mango
Bengali-Style Oven-Fried Potatoes
Summer Berry Gratin

❊

Green Pea Phyllo Purses
Gujarati-Style Roasted Potato Salad
Adzuki Bean Cakes with Tomato-Cilantro Concasse

Fall

Quick Squash Samosas
Shredded Beets with Fresh Coconut
Split Pea Soup with Cardamom-Saffron Rice Cakes
Pumpkin Mousse with Ginger Cream

❊

Toasted Pecan-Mushroom Pâté
Lime Biscuit Thins
Benaras-Style Wilted Kale with Yams
Millet Pilaf in Peppers

Winter

Vegetable Antipasto in Cilantro Marinade
Lemon Pasta Salad with Peppercorn-Coconut Glaze
Grilled Eggplant Fans with Cashew Chutney
Blood Oranges with Caramel Sauce and Pistachios

❀

Cauliflower in Curried Tomato Glaze
Almond-Crusted Cheese Sticks with Lime Horseradish Mayonnaise
Sautéed Spinach and Spiced Sweet Potatoes

Spring

Spring Lettuce and Papaya
Fresh Pea Soup with Pistachio-Mint Cream
Chickpea Crêpes with Asparagus and Sesame Cream Sauce
Pomegranate Granité with Almond-Crusted Papaya Nuggets

❀

Spring Lettuce and Papaya
Asparagus Tip Soup with Jalapeño Cream
Mixed Grain and Vegetable Stir-Fry with Peanuts
Sautéed Sugar Snap Peas and Radishes

Menus for a Crowd

Carrot Slaw with Cashews
Tamale Pie
Black Bean Chili with Orange-Pepper Sauce and Wheat Chips
Apricot Cheesecake Parfait

❀

Cucumber and Fennel with Orange-Mint Dressing
Baby Potatoes Coated with Almonds
Black Bean Salad with Three Roasted Peppers
Baked Bananas with Gingered-Marmalade Cream

✽

Wilted Cabbage with Dill Yogurt
Mung Bean and Basmati Rice Stew with Vegetables
Slow-Baked Tomatoes
Deviled Corn on the Cob

Soup and Salad Meals

Jícama and Snow Peas with Grapes
Radiatore with Almond-Cream Pesto
Gujarati-Style Corn Soup with Yellow Tomato Chutney

✽

Bibb Salad with Honey-Mustard Vinaigrette
Black Bean Salad with Three Roasted Peppers
Gingered Tomato Broth with Pappadam Noodles

✽

Flame-Toasted Chapatis
Sautéed Spinach and Eggplant Salad
Vegetable Bouillabaisse with Cilantro Pistou

✽

Endive, Apple, and Almond Salad
Appaloosa Bean Salad
Mulligatawny Soup with Toasted Spices and Nuts

✽

Special Meals for Entertaining

Pear Tomatoes with Sarawak Pepper Cheese
Dill-Mung Broth with Wide Zucchini Noodles
Orange-Glazed Winter Vegetable Salad
Cheese Cutlets with Pineapple-Ginger Glaze and Basmati Rice

*

Wheat-Berry Caviar with Oat Bran Wafers
Romaine with Avocado, Radish, and Orange
Yellow Pea Broth with Tomatoes
Cheese Fricadelle with Two Chutneys

*

Avocado Pâté with Pistachio Chutney
Four-Greens Salad with Yellow Tomato Vinaigrette
Indian Ratatouille Soup with Toasted Pumpkin Seeds
Lima Beans with Grilled, Vegetable-Stuffed Vine Leaves

Sunday Brunch Menus

Spicy Mung Bean Pâté with Cilantro-Mint Cream
Oat Bran Wafers
Kale and Corn Strudel with Light Tomato Sauce

*

Roasted Eggplant and Vegetable Pâté
Malabar Pepper–Lemon Crackers
Cheesy Artichoke Croustade

*

Golden Gazpacho with Avocado Cream
Vegetable and Split Pea Crêpes with Yellow Pepper Sauce
Sautéed Tropical Fruits with Passion Fruit Sauce

Fruit and Cheese Breakfast Buffet

Tropical Fruit Brochettes

Dried Fruit Pâté on Fresh Fruit Slices

Glazed Papaya Fans with Strawberry Sauce

Yogurt Cheese Balls

Poppy Seed Wafers

Gingered Chickpeas

Backyard or Tailgate Picnic

Bombay Cashews

Summer Vegetable Brochettes

Scarlet Runner Bean and Potato Salad

Cauliflower and Cheese Croquettes with Horseradish Potatoes

Zucchini Boats with Apple-Cilantro Chutney

A MOSTLY ORGANIC PANTRY

The following is a list of all the ingredients I used during recipe testing. I have included brand names so that you can replicate the flavor nuances of my table. If the list appears intimidating, keep in mind that you may already have many of the items. And you can always substitute an ingredient to suit your own taste preferences and cooking style. For example, if you don't have Kalamata olives on hand for Wheat-Berry Caviar (page 15), use pitted black California olives. If you don't have walnut oil for Yellow Tomato Vinaigrette (page 48), use a good olive oil.

A WORD ABOUT ORGANIC INGREDIENTS

Organic foods, those harvested without the use of chemical fertilizers and pesticides, have increased in sales by more than 20 percent in the last decade. I encourage you to read about the global and national effects of chemical farming on the environment and on animal and human health. You may decide, as I have, to switch to organic ingredients whenever possible.

Organic ingredients are available primarily in gourmet and natural-food stores, and urban and rural farmers' markets. Some supermarket chains sell large quantities of organic produce while others offer none at all. If you have difficulty finding organic ingredients locally, inquire into the mail-order suppliers listed on pages 316 to 322.

Oils and Oil Sprays

Extra-virgin olive-oil spray (El Molino, Tryson)
Extra-virgin and virgin olive oils (Spectrum, Old Monk, Siabica, Westbrae)
Cold-pressed, unrefined (some organic): walnut, almond, hazelnut, corn, peanut, mustard, sesame, canola, safflower (Spectrum, Arrowhead Mills, Norganic, Westbrae Natural, and Eden)
Clarified butter (*ghee*) (Purity Farms)

Pastas

Durum-wheat fettuccine or angel hair pasta, in flavors such as lemon-and-pepper, Cajun, spinach, tomato basil, and vegetable confetti (Eden, Tree of Life, Michelle's Natural)

Asian pasta: Udon noodles, including wheat and/or brown-rice noodles, and buckwheat noodles (Eden)

Whole-wheat pastas: lasagna noodles, spaghetti, macaroni (DeBoles)

Italian-style durum-wheat semolina pasta: ditali, rigatoni, spirals, ziti, shells, and macaroni (Champlain Valley Pasta, Bella Via/Tree of Life)

Brown-rice pasta: Spaghetti and macaroni (Pastariso)

Rice noodles/rice sticks (Not organic)

Legumes — Beans, Split Peas, and Lentils

Dried Appaloosa, China Yellow, Rattlesnake, Calypso, Tongues of Fire, Snowcap, Scarlet Runner, French navy, Swedish brown, Spanish Tolosana, Jacob's Cattle, and Yellow Eye (Dean & DeLuca, Esculent Heirloom Beans — not organic)

Chickpea (garbanzo), mung, black turtle, adzuki, Anazaki, black-eyed pea, split pea, baby lima, kidney, Great Northern, pinto (Arrowhead Mills, Shiloh Farms, Walnut Acres)

Grains

White and brown basmati rice (Ron Hogue Farms)

Sweet wehani, sweet brown, long-grain brown, short-grain brown, royal aromatic wild–brown rice blend (Lundberg Family Farms)

Texmati white, Texmati brown, Texmati lite brand, Texmati royal blend (Texmati — not organic)

Whole pearl barley, bulgar, kasha (buckwheat groats), millet, quinoa, wild rice, semolina, grits, amaranth, triticale, Job's tears, popcorn, rye, oat groats (Arrowhead Mills, Erewhon, Walnut Acres, Shiloh Farms)

Salt, Herb Salts, and Peppercorns

Mineral rock salt (Real Salt)

Sea salt or solar-evaporated salt (De Sousa, Hain, La Baleine)

Herb salt (Herbamare, Trocomare)

Malabar, Tellicherry, Muntok, Sarawak, freeze-dried green, rose, and pepper royale (a blend of five peppers) (Flavorbank, Dean & DeLuca — not organic)

Whole Spices

Whole cardamom pods, cinnamon sticks, cloves, coriander seeds, cumin seeds, yellow mustard seeds, red-pepper flakes, bay leaves, fennel seeds, caraway seeds, celery seeds, saffron threads, poppy seeds (Williams-Sonoma, McCormick, Spice Islands — not organic; Spice Gardens — nonirradiated)

Ground Spices, Seasonings, and Spice Blends

Cumin, coriander, turmeric, cinnamon, allspice, chilli powder, cayenne pepper, curry powder, *garam masala*, dry mustard, paprika, ancho chilies, chili blends, yellow asafetida powder (Williams-Sonoma, McCormick, Spice Islands — not organic; Spice Gardens — nonirradiated)

Salt-free Oriental sesame blend, parsley blend, Italian blend, Mexican blend, and McCormick pepper medley (McCormick — not organic)

Garam masala, *chat masala*, Italian seasonings (Spice Gardens — nonirradiated)

Nuts, Seeds, and Butters

Whole raw almonds, cashews, walnuts, pecans, pine nuts, pistachios, filberts, sesame seeds, sunflower seeds, pumpkin seeds (Arrowhead Mills, Westbrae Natural, Jaffe Brothers, Walnut Acres)

A mixed selection of raw and toasted nut butters including: toasted almond butter, cashew butter, filbert butter, macadamia butter, pecan butter, peanut butter, pistachio butter, sesame butter (tahini) (Once Again Nut Butters, Tree of Life, Westbrae Natural, Maranatha)

Breads and Crackers

Wheat tortillas, yellow and blue corn tortillas, pita breads (Garden of Eatin')

Sprouted wheat tortillas, sprouted grain breads and bagels (Alvarado Street Bakery)

Various sourdough breads (French Meadow Bakery)

Scandinavian-style crisp breads, fiber crisps, rice cakes, rice snaps, whole-wheat matzo (Kavli, AkMak, Wasa Crispbread, Pritikin)

Sweeteners

Organic cane sugar (Sucanat)

Maple syrup and maple sugar granules, maple sprinkles (Vermont Country Maple, Spring Tree)

Honey (Golden Angels Apiary)

Date sugar

Bottled, Canned, and Packaged Goods

Fruit-sweetened jams, jellies, and preserves (Cascadian Farms, Very Berry, Tree of Life, Sorrel Ridge)

Catsup (Tree of Life, Enrico's)

Mayonnaise (Spectrum's Low-Calorie Eggless, Nasoya)

Salsa (Enrico's)

Mustard (Tree of Life)

Tomato puree, crushed tomatoes, peeled and ground, peeled and whole, sauce (Muir Glen, Mokomis Farms, Tree of Life)

Precooked chickpea (garbanzo) beans, pinto beans, Great Northern beans, and adzuki beans in 24-ounce glass jars and 16-ounce cans (Eden)

Candied ginger; raisins, dates, and dried fruits (Jaffe Brothers, Great Date in the Morning)

Olives (Peloponnese Products, Adams Ranch Gourmet Olives)

Dried tomato products (Sonoma, Timber Crest Farms)

Frozen Goods

Unsweetened juice concentrates: natural lemonade, cranberry nectar, cherry cider, red raspberry nectar, orange juice (Knudsen's)

Strawberries, raspberries, blueberries, blackberries, corn, broccoli, green beans, carrots, cauliflower, peas, french fries, hash browns (Cascadian Farms)

Wheat and corn tortillas, puff pastry, phyllo dough/leaves, unsalted butter, won ton dough; homemade vegetable-stock ice cubes, herb-puree ice cubes, roasted bell peppers, cranberries, cherries, pitted peaches and nectarines

Perishables

Organic biodynamic yogurt (Seven Stars, Hawthorne Valley Farm)

Nonfat yogurt, part-skim ricotta, cottage cheese (Nancy's, Brown Cow, Columbo, Continental — not organic)

Ghee (clarified butter) (Purity Farms)

Extra-firm tofu (Nasoya, Mori Nu)

Part-skim or low-fat cheeses: cheddar, aged white cheddar, unpasteurized muenster, unpasteurized Colby, hot-pepper Monterey cheddar, part-skim mozzarella, Swiss, brick (North Farms, Organic Valley, Cabot)

Fresh ginger, jalapeño and serrano chilies, lemons, limes, oranges, cilantro, parsley, and other fresh herbs

Equipment

El Asador's Stovetop Hot-Air Grill — For roasting vegetables and heating flat breads over electric, gas, or wood stoves. No-smoke and no-oil cooking (Williams-Sonoma)

Pyramid's Portable Barbecue-Stove — Stainless-steel unit folds to 1 inch thick and slips into a carrying bag. Available in three sizes. Can be used in a fireplace or on top of the stove. Full meal needs only six to nine briquets. (1-800-824-4288)

GLOSSARY

Almond Butter: Raw or toasted almonds ground to a creamy consistency, like peanut butter. Use in tandem with almond oil for reinforced flavor in baking or to give body to a salad dressing. Available at natural-food stores.

Amaranth: A plant eaten as a vegetable whose grain-like seeds, which are high in protein and low in fat, and contain little gluten, are used as a cereal or ground into flour. Delicious as a pilaf. Available at natural-food stores.

Ancho Chili: Sun-dried pod of a ripe poblano chili. Mild heat and rich flavor; terrific used in place of cayenne or hot paprika. Available at specialty food stores.

Asafetida: The powdered resin of various plants native to India and Italy, with a flavor redolent of garlic and shallot. Always toast the powder in warm, not hot, oil, to release its flavor; you need only about ⅛ teaspoon for four servings. Ground yellow asafetida is available at Indian grocery stores.

Avocado Oil: A bland-flavored, monounsaturated oil good for everything from salad dressings to sautéing. It has a very high smoke point—520°F. Available at specialty food stores.

Bitter Melon: Also known as bitter gourd and balsam pear. This wrinkled green vegetable, 4 to 8 inches long, should be purchased firm to the touch. It

has a pleasant bitter flavor, tempered when fried; good used as a garnish for salads and stews. Available at Chinese and Indian grocery stores.

Black Salt: A reddish-gray salt, colored from the presence of small quantities of trace minerals. Its flavor is a bit like salty mineral water, with sour overtones. Available at Indian grocery stores. A good alternative is Real Salt mined in Utah; available at natural-food stores.

Buckwheat: The seed of a flowering herb (genus *Fagopyrum*). Buckwheat groats (kasha) are the hulled, crushed kernels. When toasted, they have a nutty flavor and make a delicious pilaf.

Bulgur: Wheat kernels that have been steamed, dried, and cracked or crushed into three grades: fine, medium, and coarse.

Cardamom: Dried seed pods or seeds of a plant in the ginger family. A bittersweet, aromatic seasoning used in Indian cuisine.

Cashew Butter: Raw or toasted cashews ground to a creamy consistency. Used in baked goods and salad dressings. Available at natural-food stores.

Chat Masala: A sand-colored spice blend whose principal ingredients are green mango powder, BLACK SALT, and ASAFETIDA. Used in some Indian snacks.

Cilantro: Also known as fresh coriander and Chinese parsley. The leaves of the coriander plant, used in many equatorial and Asian cuisines. It imparts a vibrant lemon-pepper flavor. Available at larger supermarkets, natural-food stores, and specialty grocers.

Citric Acid: Salt-like white crystals with a concentration of the acid present in citrus fruits, predominantly lemon juice. Brush a solution on cut fruits to prevent discoloring. Available at pharmacies and specialty food stores.

Chapati: Also known as *chapatee* and *phulka*. A soft whole-wheat flat bread. A healthy alternative to Mexican flour tortillas for everything from burritos to pan-fried quesadillas. Great instead of toast for breakfast. Available at natural-food stores, and some Indian stores.

Concasse: Peeled, seeded, and diced tomatoes.

Coriander Seed: Earthy-tasting round seed of the herb plant CILANTRO, used extensively in Indian and Latin American cooking. Toasted and ground, it has a sweet, nutty aroma. Available at specialty and natural-food stores.

Corn Oil: A polyunsaturated oil pressed from the germ of maize. Unrefined, cold-pressed corn oil has a buttery flavor and is an excellent substitute for *ghee* (clarified butter) for sautéing foods. Available at natural-food stores.

Coulis: A sieved vegetable or fruit puree.

Crystallized Ginger: Also called candied ginger. Fresh GINGER ROOT preserved with sugar and dried. Can be used interchangeably with stem ginger or ginger root in a sugar syrup. Available at specialty stores.

Cumin Seed: The aromatic yellow-brown seed of an umbelliferous plant similar to caraway. Used extensively in Indian and Latin American cuisine. Toasted and ground, it has a nutty flavor.

Date Sugar: The coarse brown crystals obtained from pulverizing dehydrated dates. Available at natural-food stores.

European Cucumber: Long, thin cucumber with few, small seeds. Available at larger grocery stores and produce markets.

Fennel Bulb: Also called finocchio and Florence fennel. A vegetable with a bulbous stalk and feathery green tops. It has a licorice flavor; delicious raw in salads, or cooked.

Fennel Seed: The aromatic seed from herb fennel, a relative of bulb FENNEL. The seeds are used, whole and ground, in Indian and Italian cooking. When toasted, they are nutty and sweet.

Fenugreek Seed: The brownish-yellow, rectangular seed of a leguminous plant, used as a spice in Indian cooking. The aromatic seeds must be toasted to avoid a strong bitter aftertaste.

Garam Masala: An aromatic mixture of toasted, ground spices used primarily in Indian bean cookery. It usually contains "warm" spices such as peppercorns, cinnamon, coriander, cumin, and cloves.

Ginger Grater: Also called Oriental and Japanese ginger grater. A ceramic or stainless-steel plate covered with tiny teeth. To obtain a creamy ginger puree, simply rub peeled ginger across its surface. Available at Asian and natural-food stores.

Ginger Root, Fresh: The buff-colored rhizome (rootlike stem) of the ginger plant. Used extensively as a seasoning in Indian and Asian cooking.

Hazelnut Oil: A light, monounsaturated or polyunsaturated oil. A delicate, highly aromatic oil, excellent in vinaigrettes, baked goods, and candies. Keep refrigerated after opening.

Herb Salt: A mixture of salt and dehydrated herbs and vegetables. A delicious alternative to sea salt, used before, during, or after cooking. Commercially prepared herb salt usually contain 20 percent ground dried vegetables or herbs; a good way to cut down on salt. Available at natural-food stores.

Jalapeño Chili: A squat, green, medium-hot chili pepper. (The seeds are the hottest part of the chili; eliminate them to reduce intensity.) Do not touch your face or eyes after handling chilies; the volatile oils can cause burning. Available at grocery stores and produce markets.

Jícama: A white-fleshed globular root with brown skin. It is sweet and crunchy, and can be eaten raw or cooked.

Katori: A small metal bowl, which can range in size from 1½ to 3 inches in diameter. Used to hold liquid dishes on a traditional Indian dinner plate.

Maple Sugar Granules: Also called maple sprinkles and granulated maple sugar. A delicately flavored sweetener similar to maple syrup. Though expensive, a little goes a long way. Available at natural-food stores.

Millet: A tiny, buff-colored, nutritious grain about the size of a mustard seed. Millet is generally toasted before cooking and takes on nutty flavor overtones in the process. A good rice-pilaf alternative. Available at natural-food stores.

Muntok Pepper: Also called white pepper. The small, round berries of the pepper vine are allowed to ripen on the vine. They are then dried and the outer skin is removed. Use freshly ground for vibrant flavor. Available at specialty stores.

Mustard Seeds: Tiny, round seeds from various mustard plants. Yellow seeds are pleasantly warm and widely available. Slightly smaller brown seeds, available at Indian grocers, have more flavor and are preferred by Indian cooks, but the two can be used interchangeably in any of the recipes in this book.

Olive Oil: Pressed from numerous types of olives, it is the most frequently used oil in the book. It has a wide range of flavors and aromas, depending on the country of origin and the extraction process. Extra-virgin and virgin oils from the first pressing have the richest flavor. Like wine, olive oil is distingished by words like smooth, full-bodied, round, fruity, sweet, light, and extra bouquet. The best oil is unrefined with low acidity, and has a delicate balance of flavor. Olive oil is monounsaturated and suitable for spraying on foods at medium-heat temperatures (below 320° F).

Passion Fruit: A fragrant, egg-shaped fruit with wrinkled skin, yellow flesh, and many small black seeds. The seeds are edible; the skin is not. Available at specialty stores.

Pappadam: A sun-dried, paper-thin wafer made from wet-ground *moong* or *urad* beans, usually 6 to 10 inches in diameter. In India they are flame-toasted until crispy and eaten before or after dinner. Available at specialty stores and Indian grocers.

Phyllo Leaves: Also called filo. A tissue-thin flour-and-water pastry popular in Greek and Middle Eastern cuisines. Available fresh or frozen at specialty and Middle Eastern grocery stores.

Pine Nuts: Also called pignoli. Seeds from the cone of the stone pine, a tree native to the Mediterranean. Their buttery flavor is intensified when they are lightly toasted.

Pistachio Butter: Raw or toasted pistachio nuts ground to a creamy consistency, like peanut butter. I use it for flavor and body in bell-pepper salad dressings, cake frostings, and quiches. Available at natural-food stores.

Plantain: A starchy variety of banana, cooked before it is eaten. Usually 9 to 12 inches long, with a cream to yellowish flesh. Available at specialty and Latin American grocery stores.

Quinoa: A nutritionally superior grain, one of the finest sources of protein in the vegetable kingdom. This staple of the ancient Incas has a nutlike taste when toasted and simmered into a rice-like pilaf. Available at natural-food stores.

Ramekin: A small, straight-sided glass or porcelain container used for a single portion of food. Similar to a metal Indian *katori*.

Raw Cane Sugar (Sucanat): A delicious, moist brown sugar, with a faint molasses flavor, made by processing the juice from organic sugar cane. Can be used in place of white sugar. Available at natural-food stores.

Sarawak Pepper: Small, brownish-black peppercorns from the northwestern coast of Borneo, Malaysia. A relatively mild pepper, pleasant with bland foods. Available at specialty grocery stores.

Savarin: A smooth, unpatterned, ring-shaped pan (unlike the German bundt pan).

Savoy Cabbage: A variety of head cabbage with crisp, crinkly green leaves and mild flavor.

Sesame Oil: A mild-flavored oil pressed from unroasted sesame seeds. Best used for light sautéing on medium heat.

Silken Tofu: Silky-textured TOFU, ranging in texture from soft to extra-firm, sold in a hermetically sealed package to preserve its mild flavor. If you are on a cholesterol- and/or dairy-free diet, substitute pureed extra-firm silken tofu for cottage cheese in the recipes.

Snow Peas: Also known as *mangetout* and sugar peas. The flat, green pea pods are eaten whole while they are still young and flat.

Sun-Dried Tomatoes: Tomatoes that have been dehydrated in the sun. They have a rich, smoky flavor that is great in pesto sauces, bean dishes, and salad dressings.

Tahini: A creamy paste made from ground sesame seeds. Used to give flavor and body to salad dressings, baked goods, dipping sauces, pesto, and much more.

Tellicherry Pepper: Dried black peppercorns from the northern Malabar coast of India. Prized for its rich, bold flavor and fruity bouquet. Available at specialty stores.

Terrine: A long, loaf-shaped earthenware casserole, or the dish made in it.

Tofu: Also called bean curd. Dense, pressed soybean curd with mild flavor. For best flavor, purchase it vacuum packed. A high-protein, cholesterol-free alternative to homemade WHITE CHEESE in this book. See also SILKEN TOFU.

Tomatillo: A tart, small, tomato-like fruit with a papery husk. Used in salsas, chutneys, and sauces.

Turmeric: A yellow powder from a plant in the ginger family, used extensively in Indian cooking. In Ayruweda, it is regarded as a blood purifier; use it sparingly; too much turmeric leaves a bitter flavor.

Walnut Oil: An aromatic oil pressed from walnuts. Excellent in salads and vegetable dishes; best for medium-heat cooking. Available at specialty and natural-food stores.

Wheat Berries: Whole, unprocessed wheat kernels. When cooked until tender, they are chewy with a nutty taste. Available in natural-food stores.

White Cheese (*Panir*): A homemade, soft, unripened cheese curd made by adding an acid element (lemon juice or soured whey) to boiled milk. Not available commercially. You can use extra-firm tofu instead of white cheese in the book's recipes.

Wild Rice: The seed of a water grass native to the Great Lakes region. Not a true grain, but cooked like one.

Zest: The colored, flavorful, outermost layer of citrus rind. Remove it carefully to avoid the bitter white pith beneath it.

BEANS AND LEGUMES

Adzuki Beans: Also called *aduki* and *feijao*. Small, oblong, reddish-brown beans native to China and Japan. The texture is creamy and the taste is slightly sweet. Available at natural-food stores, dried and bottled; delicious in soups, in stews, or sprouted. Soaking time 1 hour; cooking time 1 to 1½ hours.

Anazaki Beans: Beautiful, mottled purple-and-white beans, cultivated in past centuries by the Anazaki Indians, and grown today in Colorado. Similar to the size of pinto beans, the flavor is rich and smoky. Available dried, at natural-food stores. Soaking time 5 to 6 hours; cooking time 1 to 1½ hours.

Appaloosa Beans: An old-world legume grown in the Palouse area, famed for the speckled horse with the same name. The kidney-shaped beans, mottled white and purple-brown, have a rich flavor. Receptive to seasonings like jalapeños, fresh ginger, turmeric, and cilantro, they are wonderful in equatorial ethnic soups and stews. Dried beans do not require soaking; parboil and cook 45 to 90 minutes. Available at specialty food stores and through Dean & DeLuca Mail Order (page 321).

Black Beans: Also called turtle beans. Small, oblong, ivory beans with black skins. The texture is creamy and the flavor slightly sweet. Popular in West Indian cuisine, they make terrific chili and bean pancakes, and are versatile in salads. Available dried, bottled, and canned. Soaking time 6 hours; cooking time 1 to 1½ hours.

Butter Beans or Lima Beans: Also called Madagascar beans. Creamy white or pale green beans in two sizes, one slightly larger than the other. They have a soft, floury texture and mild flavor. Good in salads, stew, and side dishes.

Available fresh, dried, frozen, and bottled. Soaking time 8 hours; cooking time 1 to 2 hours.

Calypso Beans: An old-world, kidney-shaped bean with a black-and-white pattern and silky texture. Calypsos are terrific in soups and stews and delicious pureed. They are well suited to Indian and Southwestern seasonings, tomatoes, and cilantro. For an exciting soup, cook beans with rosemary, tomatoes, potatoes, and chard, and top off with salt and freshly ground pepper. Dried beans do not require soaking; parboil and cook 45 to 90 minutes. Available at specialty food stores and through Dean & DeLuca Mail Order (page 321).

Chickpeas: Also called garbanzo beans and ceci beans. The hard, dried, round peas are about ⅓ inch in diameter and biscuit to light-brown in color with a wrinkled surface. The flavor is nut-like, and the texture is firm. Available dried, bottled, and canned. Soaking time 8 hours; cooking time 1½ to 3 hours.

China Yellow Beans: An old-world New England bean, small and oval with a mild flavor and silky texture. They are delicious simmered into a smooth puree with ginger, turmeric, and corn oil, excellent as a gravy for grains, pasta, or vegetables. Dried beans do not require soaking; parboil and cook 45 to 90 minutes. Available at specialty food stores and through Dean & DeLuca Mail Order (page 321).

Christmas Lima Beans: A traditional, old-world bean with a buttery, chestnut flavor and batik pattern. The texture is smoother than supermarket limas and cooks without soaking. Delicious in bean side dishes and salads. Dried beans do not require soaking; parboil and cook 45 to 90 minutes. Available at specialty food stores and through Dean & DeLuca Mail Order (page 321).

European Soldier Beans: An old-world white kidney bean named for the splash of color (shaped in the silhouette of a soldier standing at attention) at its eye. Perfect in vegetable soups such as garbure or minestrone. Dried beans do not require soaking; parboil and cook 45 to 90 minutes. Available at specialty food stores and through Dean & DeLuca Mail Order (page 321).

French Lentils: Tiny, plump old-world lentils, darkly mottled in shades of green and slate. These lentils are prized for their subtle flavor, more distinctive than many domestic varieties. They tend to retain their shape after cooking,

though mashed, they are delicious in stuffings or cutlets. Dried beans do not require soaking; cook in about 1 hour. Available at specialty food stores and through Dean & DeLuca Mail Order (page 321).

Jacob's Cattle Beans: Mottled wine-and-white old-world beans named for their resemblance to spotted Jacob's sheep. Excellent in bean salads; pair well with Italian seasonings, olives, and roasted bell peppers. Can be used interchangeably with Anazaki beans or pink pinto beans. Available dried. Dried beans do not require soaking; parboil and cook 45 to 90 minutes. Available at specialty food stores and through Dean & DeLuca Mail Order (page 321).

Maine Yellow Eyes: Old-world, small, oval beans with a pale gold hue and creamy texture. Likely the original ingredient in Boston baked beans; still used today instead of black-eyed peas for Southern Hoppin' John. Delicious in place of mung beans for stewed Indian rice-and-bean *kitcheree*. Dried beans do not require soaking; parboil and cook 45 to 90 minutes. Available at specialty food stores and through Dean & DeLuca Mail Order (page 321).

Mung Beans: Slightly oval, BB-size beans with olive-green skins. Quick to cook without soaking and easy to digest, mung beans are commonly used in Indian soup or stew. They are available in most supermarkets. Soaking time 1 hour; parboil and cook 45 to 90 minutes. Whole beans are available at natural-food stores; split and skinless beans are sold as *moong dal* at Indian grocery stores.

Scarlet Runner Beans: Old-world, purple-and-black kidney-shaped beans. Named after the vividly hued flower that grows on its low-growing runner vine. The texture is creamy and the flavor is bright and vibrant. Excellent in chili and salads. Dried beans do not require soaking; parboil and cook 45 to 90 minutes. Available at specialty food stores and through Dean & DeLuca Mail Order (page 321).

Split Peas: Yellow and green split peas are different types of common dried peas. About ¼ inch in diameter, both have a sweet flavor, though the green variety's is slightly more pronounced. Good in creamy or textured soups and vegetable-pot stews, and can be pureed and seasoned for a sauce. Soak for 2 hours; cook 45 to 90 minutes. Available dried, at natural-food stores and supermarkets.

SPECIALTY AND ORGANIC FOOD MAIL-ORDER SUPPLIERS

I have been on the move for nearly three decades. Home has been everything from a tent by the Ganges to a Manhattan skyscraper to an estate in South Cornwall. Every area has had its fill of good local markets, but I have always relied on mail-order sources for specialty produce and staples. When organic Hayden mangoes or Mercot oranges are in season in Florida, I call the Ebersole Farms and order a case. What I don't use, I freeze. Every now and then, I order several kinds of freshly milled flours from Walnut Acres Organic Farms in Pennsylvania. Or I stock up on a few months' supply of aromatic, freshly dried ground chilies from Los Chileros de Nuevo Mexico in Sante Fe. The same goes for Dean & DeLuca's old-world legumes and Jaffe Brothers' plump, succulent dried fruits.

If ordering foods by mail is new to you, or just seems strange, keep in mind that the quality of these foods is often better than what is available locally. This is especially true for the health-conscious cook who wants seasonal organic produce, low-fat cheeses with real flavor, or maple sugar in bulk for economy.

Many mail-order businesses are family owned, and you get to know the owners on a personal basis. They deliver the kind of service available from a local source and are eager to see goods arrive in perfect order. If goods are damaged, some firms request that you return them and will pay for postage and pickup. The following sources are some of my favorites, offering the best quality and service.

A few of the following companies do not sell through mail-order, but are included because I frequently use their products. If you are unable to find them at your local store, contact the company directly for the retail location nearest you. Some store managers will carry a product when requested by customers. These companies are indicated by *(N)*.

Most of the following growers and distributors ship their products directly to individual consumers. Nonperishable items are generally shipped by UPS Ground, which takes about three to eight working days. Perishables are sent by Federal Express, UPS Next Day Service, and Airborne, and are usually delivered in the morning. Try to be home when your order arrives so you can put perishable items in the refrigerator right away. Write or call for a complete catalog or product listing.

Organic certification methods are indicated for each of the companies. A *(C)* indicates that all of the listed products have been certified organic by an independent agency. Those suppliers that establish their own standards are considered self-certified and are labeled with an *(S)*.

For more information about the production and marketing of organic foods, write to Americans for Safe Food, a project of the Center for Science in the Public Interest. For a list of organic-food sources not listed below, please send $1.00 and a self-addressed envelope ($.45) to Mail-Order Organic, 1501 16th Street, N.W., Washington, DC 20036.

Adams Ranch Gourmet Olives
and Olive Oil
Bob Bente
P. O. Box 821
Meadow Vista, CA 95722
(916) 878-2143

Several varieties of cured olives and California olive oil. Write or call for price list. (S)

Arrowhead Mills, Inc.
P. O. Box 2059
Hereford, TX 79045
(806) 364-0730

Organic grains, flour, hot and cold cereal, brown rice. My favorite corn oil, toasted sesame butter, and peanut butter. (N) (C)

Cascadian Farms
311 Dillard Street
Concrete, WA 98237
(206) 853-8175

I use many of this company's products, including fruit-sweetened huckleberry, marionberry, raspberry-rhubarb, apricot, and loganberry conserves and orange marmalade; pickles: cured and fresh-pack baby dills, genuine (no-vinegar) baby sweet pickles, spicy and low-sodium kosher dills; and a wide variety of organic frozen vegetables and fruits. (C)

Cooks Maple Products
Bashan Hill Road
Worthington, MA 01098
(413) 238-5827

Maple syrup. Write for prices and other products. (S)

Dean & DeLuca Retail and
Mail-Order Department
560 Broadway
New York, NY 10012
(212) 431-1691

Sells the old-world beans mentioned in many recipes. Call to find which retail stores sell them in your area. This firm also sells high-quality oils, specialty foods, equipment, and books. Catalog available.

Earl Ebersol Farms
27828 S.W. 127th Avenue
Homestead, FL 33032
(305) 247-3905

For nearly a decade, my preferred source for seasonal organic grapefruit, Marcots and Honeybell oranges, tangerines, avocados, mangoes, limes, lemons, and persimmons. They have a 20-pound minimum, but will mix varieties in a box. Call or write for availability. (S)

Ecology Sound Farms
42126 Road 168
Orosi, CA 93647
(209) 528-3816

Depending on seasonal availability: oranges, plums, Asian pears, kiwi, persimmons. Minimum: 8–40 pounds. (C)

Eden Foods
701 Tecumseh
Clifton, MI 49236
1-800-248-0301

Organic durum wheat pastas, beans and grains, precooked beans, barley malt, molasses, oils, Oriental noodles. Outstanding pasta. Canned and bottled chickpeas, pinto beans, and adzuki beans. (N) (C)

French Meadow Bakery
2601 Lyndale Avenue, South
Minneapolis, MN 55972
(612) 870-4740

Outstanding old-world, hearth-baked sourdough breads. Unleavened pizza crusts. Minimum: $20. (C)

Garden of Eatin'
5300 Santa Monica Boulevard
Los Angeles, CA 90029
1-800-333-5244

Two wheat flat breads: whole-wheat tortillas and chapatis. My preference is the former. The tortillas are large, thin, and flexible, the type made daily in Indian kitchens. (N) (C)

Great Date in the Morning
P. O. Box 31
Coachella, CA 92236
(619) 398-6171

A good variety of fresh dates, a few of which are mentioned in the recipes. Catalog available. (C)

The Herb Farm
32804 Issaquah–Fall City Road
Fall City, WA 98024
1-800-866-HERB

The Herb Farm will ship beautiful healthy plants anywhere. The apple mint, French lavender, blue heliotrope, and lemon thyme that I ordered arrived healthy and ready to grow. Hundreds of organically grown herbs available. About $3.79 for a 2- or 4-inch pot, shipping not included — a good deal. Free catalog. (S)

J. Francis Co.
Route 3, Box 54
Atlanta, TX 75551
(214) 796-5364

Pecans. Minimum: 5 pounds (S)

Jaffe Brothers
P. O. Box 636
Valley Center, CA 92082-0636
(619) 749-1133

Dried fruits, organically grown and dried without sulfur or fumigants. Each piece of tiny fruit in the 4-pound sampler packs a knockout flavor punch, well worth the $23.95 (shipping not included). Jaffe also offers unsweetened coconut, beans, seeds, grains, and other organic goods. Minimum: 5 pounds. Free catalog. (S)

Lakewood Natural Products
P. O. Box 420708
Miami, FL 33242
(305) 324-5932

More than sixty types of juice, juice blends, and juice concentrates, including red and yellow papaya concentrate. (N)

Los Chileros de Nuevo Mexico
P. O. Box 6215
Sante Fe, NM 87502
(505) 471-6967

As a chili aficionado always in search of freshness and quality, I was very happy to find this source. Los Chileros offers several varieties of richly flavored dried chilies, including ancho, arbol, cascabel, negro, jalapeño, and pasilla. They range in price from $2.70 for a 3-ounce package of ancho chilies to $5.70 for a 3-ounce package of cascabels. Free brochure. (N)

Lundberg Family Farms
P. O. Box 369
Richvale, CA 95974-0369
(916) 822-4551

High-quality brown rice and rice blends. (C)

Malibu Greens
P. O. Box 6286
Malibu, CA 90264
1-800-383-1414

Offers a good assortment of baby vegetables, lettuces, and greens grown at their own farm, without herbicides or pesticides. The gift baskets are centerpiece-quality — bursting with such items as crisp baby turnips and carrots, purple and green kohlrabi, red and golden beets, and tender lettuces. The fruits, which are imported from New Zealand in winter, are also of high quality. A 15-pound super-deluxe assortment with juicy feijoa, Asian pear, kiwi, and pineapples is excellent and runs $89 plus shipping. Free brochure.

M & S Produce
P. O. Box 220
Alcalde, NM 87511

A good source of freshly ground South-western chilies such as medium-hot sandia and española. They also carry New Mexico and other dried chilies. Price list available. (S)

Once Again Nut Butters, Inc.
12 State Street
Nunda, NY 14517
(716) 468-2535

A good variety of nut butters, many organic, including terrific almond, cashew, and pistachio butters. Call or write for availability. (C)

Organic Foods Express
11003 Emack Road
Beltsville, MD 20705
(301) 816-4944

A good selection of seasonal organic fruits and vegetables at reasonable prices. Packed in waxed cardboard and layered with newspapers, the produce arrives in excellent condition. Current prices (average): potatoes about $.65 a pound; tomatoes about $.95 a pound; avocados about $1.50 each; and grapefruit about $.80 each. Price don't include second-day-air shipping. Also offers grains, flour, and other pantry items. Free catalog.

Peloponnese Products
Aegean Trader
P. O. Box 1015
Point Reyes Station, CA 94956

They specialize in good Greek olive oil and Greek olives, including cracked green and Kalamata. (N)

Purity Farms, Inc.
Box 496
Lancaster, MA 01523
(508) 840-1514

As of this writing, the only source of organic clarified butter (*ghee*). An outstanding product, very sweet and aromatic. Call or write for price list and retail availability. (S)

Richardson's Seaside Banana Garden
6823 Santa Barbara Avenue
La Conchita, CA 93001
(805) 643-4061

The variety and quality of these bananas are outstanding. Seaside has numerous exotic offerings, all organic, that range from dry and mealy to custardy, with spectacular flavor. A 5½-pound sampler box includes some of the fattest, prettiest, and smallest bananas I've seen, in hues of pale peach, salmon, and creamy ivory. With names like Ice Cream, Mysore, Lady Fingers, Enanogigantes, Manzano, and Cardaba, these sweet treats are sure to delight. The sampler runs about $40 ($35 in California), including shipping. Catalog: $2.(C)

Rogue River Valley Creamery
P. O. Box 3606
Central Point, OR 97502
(503) 644-2233

This creamery was a regular stop when I lived in the Rogue Valley. Their vegetable-enzyme, low-fat cheeses have real flavor and are just 14 percent fat. The cheddar is rich and sharp. The jalapeño brick Jack is smooth and nippy. Plain Jack is mild and creamy, but not bland. Prices range from $11 to $14 for 2 pounds. Free brochure.

Ron Hogue Farms
P. O. Box 185
Weiner, AR 72479
(501) 684-2354

Several strains of organic white and brown basmati rice. Call or write for price list. (S)

Shepherd's Garden Seeds
Shipping Office
30 Irene Street
Torrington, CT 06790
(203) 482-3638

A unique selection of the finest-quality seeds for American home gardeners: vegetables, herbs, and flowers. Individual packets and collections include the baby vegetable collection, harvest ornamental collection, mesclun salad mix, beginner's garden collection, a garden especially for children, a collection of basils, and a collection for container gardens.

Starr Organic Produce, Inc.
P. O. Box 561502
Miami, FL 33256
(305) 262-1242

A wide variety of fruits. Slightly expensive. Minimum: 20 pounds. Call or write for availability. (S)

Timber Crest Farms
4791 Dry Creek Road
Healdsburg, CA 95448
(707) 433-8251

Organic dried fruits: apples, apricots, dates, and cherries; fruit butters; tropical fruits: pineapple rings, star fruit, mango, papaya, figs, and prunes; dried tomato products: minced dried tomatoes, tomato halves, marinated dried tomatoes, dried tomato pasta sauce. (S)

Tryson Olive Mist ™
750 West 17th Street
Costa Mesa, CA 92627
1-800-472-7929

Oil sprays, including 100 percent extra-virgin olive oil; Vegalene pan coating (made with canola, safflower, sunflower, and corn oils); Oriental mist (made with peanut and sesame oils); mesquite mist (soybean oil with natural mesquite flavor). Write or call for price list.

Vermont Country Maple, Inc.
Industrial Products Division
Jericho Center, VT 05465
(802) 864-7519

Organic maple sugar granules (also
called powdered maple sugar and granulated maple sugar). Can be used in place
of white sugar. Very good flavor. Call or
write for price list. (S)

Walnut Acres Organic Farms
Penns Creek, PA 17862
1-800-433-3998

They carry freshly milled flours and a
wide variety of whole foods, including
oils, grains, seeds, beans, cereals, flours,
rice, nut and seed butters, baked goods,
and mixes. Fresh organic fruits catalog
also available. (S)

Wax Orchards
22744 Wax Orchards Road SW
Vashon Island, WA 98070
1-800-634-6132

I found this source last year on a trip to
Washington. Locals recommended it for

"Northwest" conserves and low-calorie,
fruit-sweetened chocolate sauces. And
they do deliver, having little trouble sell-
ing what they make. The jams, called
Fruit Fancifuls, are bold and sweet, like
freshly harvested fruit. The chocolate
sauces — orange passion, amaretto, peanut butter, and peppermint — are dark
and silken, good over ice cream or fresh
fruit. Free catalog.

Williams-Sonoma
P. O. Box 7456
San Francisco, CA 94120
(415) 421-4242

Specialty food items and kitchen equipment. (I use their organic herbs, chili
blend, and a stovetop grill.) More than
sixty retail stores nationwide. Catalog
available.

Index